John George Bourinot

Canada

John George Bourinot

Canada

ISBN/EAN: 9783337207670

Printed in Europe, USA, Canada, Australia, Japan

Cover: Foto ©Andreas Hilbeck / pixelio.de

More available books at **www.hansebooks.com**

CHÂTEAU ST. LOUIS (1694–1834), DESTROYED BY FIRE IN 1834. (*See note on page* xiii)

Frontispiece.

BY

J. G. BOURINOT, C.M.G., LL.D., D.C.L.

CLERK OF THE CANADIAN HOUSE OF COMMONS; HONORARY SECRETARY OF THE
ROYAL SOCIETY OF CANADA; DOCTEUR-ÈS-LETTRES OF LAVAL UNIVERSITY
HONORARY MEMBER OF THE AMERICAN ANTIQUARIAN SOCIETY

London

T. FISHER UNWIN

PATERNOSTER SQUARE

NEW YORK: G. P. PUTNAM'S SONS

MDCCCXCVII

PREFATORY NOTE.

IN writing this story of Canada I have not been
able to do more, within the limited space at my
command, than briefly review those events which
have exercised the most influence on the national
development of the Dominion of Canada from the
memorable days bold French adventurers made their
first attempts at settlement on the banks of the
beautiful basin of the Annapolis, and on the picturesque heights of Quebec, down to the establishment of a Confederation which extends from the
Atlantic to the Pacific Ocean. Whilst the narrative
of the French régime, with its many dramatic episodes, necessarily occupies a large part of this story,
I have not allowed myself to forget the importance
that must be attached to the development of institutions of government and their effect on the
social, intellectual, and material conditions of the
people since the beginning of the English régime.
Though this story, strictly speaking, ends with the
successful accomplishment of the federal union of
all the provinces in 1873, when Prince Edward Island
became one of its members, I have deemed it necessary to refer briefly to those events which have

happened since that time—the second half-breed rebellion of 1885, for instance—and have had much effect on the national spirit of the people. I endeavour
to interest my reader in the public acts of those eminent men whose names stand out most prominently
on the pages of history, and have made the deepest
impress on the fortunes and institutions of the
Dominion. In the performance of this task I have
always consulted original authorities, but have not
attempted to go into any historical details except
those which are absolutely necessary to the intelligent understanding of the great events and men
of Canadian annals. I have not entered into the
intrigues and conflicts which have been so bitter
and frequent during the operation of parliamentary
government in a country where politicians are so
numerous, and statesmanship is so often hampered
and government injuriously affected by the selfish
interests of party, but have simply given the conspicuous and dominant results of political action
since the concession of representative institutions to
the provinces of British North America. A chapter
is devoted, at the close of the historical narrative,
to a very brief review of the intellectual and material
development of the country, and of the nature of its
institutions of government. A survey is also given
of the customs and conditions of the French Canadian people, so that the reader outside of the Dominion may have some conception of their institutions
and of their influence on the political, social, and
intellectual life of a Dominion, of whose population
they form so important and influential an element.

The illustrations are numerous, and have been carefully selected from various sources, not accessible to
the majority of students, with the object, not simply
of pleasing the general reader, but rather of eluci-
dating the historical narrative. A bibliographical
note has also been added of those authorities which
the author has consulted in writing this story, and to
which the reader, who wishes to pursue the subject
further, may most advantageously refer.

HOUSE OF COMMONS, OTTAWA,
  Dominion Day, 1896.

CONTENTS.

VIII.

XXVI.

XXVII.

XXVIII.

XXIX.

LIST OF ILLUSTRATIONS.

   * To explain these dates it is necessary to note that Champlain
lived for years in one of the buildings of the Fort of Saint Louis
which he first erected, and the name château is often applied to that
structure ; but the château, properly so-called, was not commenced
until 1647, and it as well as its successors was within the limits of the
fort. It was demolished in 1694 by Governor Frontenac, who rebuilt it on the original foundations, and it was this castle which, in
a remodelled and enlarged form, under the English régime, lasted
until 1834.

BIBLIOGRAPHICAL NOTE.

Jacques Cartier's *Voyages*, in English, by Joseph Pope (Ottawa, 1889), and H. B. Stephens (Montreal, 1891); in French, by N. E. Dionne (Quebec, 1891); Toüon de Longrais (Rennes, France), H. Michelant and E. Ramé (Paris, 1867). L'Escarbot's *New France*, in French, Tross's ed. (Paris, 1866), which contains an account also of Cartier's first voyage. Sagard's *History of Canada*, in French, Tross's ed. (Paris, 1866). Champlain's works, in French, Laverdière's ed. (Quebec, 1870); Prince Society's English ed. (Boston, 1878-80). Lafitau's *Customs of the Savages*, in French (Paris, 1724). Charlevoix's *History of New France*, in French (Paris, 1744); Shea's English version (New York, 1866). *Jesuit Relations*, in French (Quebec ed., 1858). Ferland's *Course of Canadian History*, in French (Quebec, 1861-1865). Garneau's *History of Canada*, in French (Montreal, 1882). Sulte's *French Canadians*, in French (Montreal, 1882-84). F. Parkman's series of histories of French Régime, viz. : *Pioneers of France in the New World ; The Jesuits in North America ; The old Régime ; Frontenac ; The Discovery of the Great West ; A Half Century of Conflict ; Montcalm and Wolfe ; Conspiracy of Pontiac* (Boston, 1865-1884). Justin Winsor's *From Cartier to Frontenac* (Boston, 1894). Hannay's *Acadia* (St. John, N. B., 1879). W. Kingsford's *History of Canada*, 8 vols. so far (Toronto and London, 1887-1896), the eighth volume on the war of 1812 being especially valuable. Bourinot's "Cape Breton and its Memorials of the French Régime," *Trans. Roy. Soc. Can.*, vol. ix, and separate ed. (Montreal, 1891). Casgrain's *Montcalm and Lévis*, in French (Quebec, 1891). Haliburton's *Nova Scotia* (Halifax, 1829). Murdoch's *Nova Scotia* (Halifax, 1865-67). Campbell's *Nova Scotia* (Halifax, 1873). Campbell's *Prince Edward Island* (Charlottetown,

1875). Lord Durham's *Report*, 1839. Christie's *History of Lower Canada* (Quebec, 1848–1855). Dent's *Story of the Upper Canadian Rebellion* ('Toronto, 1855). Lindsey's *W. Lyon Mackenzie* (Toronto, 1873). Dent's *Canada since the Union of 1841* (Toronto, 1880–81). Turcotte's *Canada under the Union*, in French (Quebec, 1871). Bourinot's *Manual of Constitutional History* (Montreal, 1888), "Federal Government in Canada" (*Johns Hopkins University Studies*, Baltimore, 1889), and *How Canada is Governed* (Toronto, 1895). Withrow's *Popular History of Canada* ('Toronto, 1888). MacMullen's *History of Canada* (Brockville, 1892). Begg's *History of the Northwest* ('Toronto, 1894). Canniff's *History of Ontario* ('Toronto, 1872). Egerton Ryerson's *Loyalists of America* ('Toronto, 1880). Mrs. Edgar's *Ten Years of Upper Canada in Peace and War* (Toronto, 1890).

For a full bibliography of archives, maps, essays, and books relating to the periods covered by the Story of Canada, and used by the writer, see appendix to his "Cape Breton and its Memorials," in which all authorities bearing on the Norse, Cabot, and other early voyages are cited. Also, appendix to same author's "Parliamentary Government in Canada" (*Trans. Roy. Soc. Can.*, vol. xi., and American Hist. Ass. Report, Washington, 1891). Also his "Canada's Intellectual Strength and Weakness" (*Trans. Roy. Soc. Can.*, vol. xi, and separate volume, Montreal, 1891). Also, Winsor's *Narrative and Critical History of America* (Boston, 1886–89).

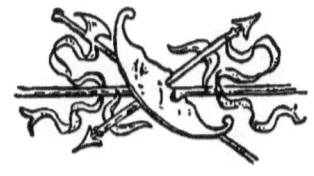

THE STORY OF CANADA.

I.

INTRODUCTION.

THE CANADIAN DOMINION FROM OCEAN TO OCEAN.

THE view from the spacious terrace on the verge
of the cliffs of Quebec, the ancient capital of Canada,
cannot fail to impress the imagination of the statesman or student versed in the history of the American continent, as well as delight the eye of the lover
of the picturesque. Below the heights, to whose
rocks and buildings cling so many memories of the
past, flows the St. Lawrence, the great river of
Canada, bearing to the Atlantic the waters of the
numerous lakes and streams of the valley which was
first discovered and explored by France, and in
which her statesmen saw the elements of empire.
We see the tinned roofs, spires and crosses of quaint
churches, hospitals and convents, narrow streets
winding among the rocks, black-robed priests and

sombre nuns, *habitans* in homespun from the neighbouring villages, modest gambrel-roofed houses of
the past crowded almost out of sight by obtrusive
lofty structures of the present, the massive buildings
of the famous seminary and university which bear
the name of Laval, the first great bishop of that
Church which has always dominated French Canada.
Not far from the edge of the terrace stands a monument on which are inscribed the names of Montcalm
and Wolfe, enemies in life but united in death and
fame. Directly below is the market which recalls
the name of Champlain, the founder of Quebec, and
his first Canadian home at the margin of the river.
On the same historic ground we see the high-peaked
roof and antique spire of the curious old church,
Notre-Dame des Victoires, which was first built to
commemorate the repulse of an English fleet two
centuries ago. Away beyond, to the left, we catch
a glimpse of the meadows and cottages of the beautiful Isle of Orleans, and directly across the river are
the rocky hills covered with the buildings of the
town, which recalls the services of Lévis, whose fame
as a soldier is hardly overshadowed by that of Montcalm. The Union-jack floats on the tall staff of the
citadel which crowns the summit of Cape Diamond,
but English voices are lost amid those of a people
who still speak the language of France.

As we recall the story of these heights, we can see
passing before us a picturesque procession : Sailors
from the home of maritime enterprise on the Breton
and Biscayan coasts, Indian warriors in their paint and
savage finery, gentlemen-adventurers and pioneers,

rovers of the forest and river, statesmen and soldiers
of high ambition, gentle and cultured women who
gave up their lives to alleviate suffering and teach
the young, missionaries devoted to a faith for which
many have died. In the famous old castle of Saint
Louis,* long since levelled to the ground—whose
foundations are beneath a part of this very terrace—
statesmen feasted and dreamt of a French Empire
in North America. Then the French dominion
passed away with the fall of Quebec, and the old
English colonies were at last relieved from that
pressure which had confined them so long to the
Atlantic coast, and enabled to become free commonwealths with great possibilities of development before them. Yet, while England lost so much in
America by the War of Independence, there still
remained to her a vast northern territory, stretching
far to the east and west from Quebec, and containing
all the rudiments of national life—

> " The raw materials of a State,
> Its muscle and its mind."

A century later than that Treaty of Paris which
was signed in the palace of Versailles, and ceded
Canada finally to England, the statesmen of the
provinces of this northern territory, which was still
a British possession,—statesmen of French as well as
English Canada—assembled in an old building of
this same city, so rich in memories of old France,

*See frontispiece. The first terrace, named after Lord Durham,
was built on the foundations of the castle. In recent years the platform has been extended and renamed Dufferin, in honour of a popular governor-general.

and took the first steps towards the establishment
of that Dominion, which, since then, has reached the
Pacific shores.

It is the story of this Canadian Dominion, of its
founders, explorers, missionaries, soldiers, and statesmen, that I shall attempt to relate briefly in the following pages, from the day the Breton sailor ascended the St. Lawrence to Hochelaga until the formation of the confederation, which united the people
of two distinct nationalities and extends over so
wide a region—so far beyond the Acadia and Canada
which France once called her own. But that the
story may be more intelligible from the beginning,
it is necessary to give a bird's-eye view of the country, whose history is contemporaneous with that of
the United States, and whose territorial area from
Cape Breton to Vancouver—the sentinel islands of
the Atlantic and Pacific approaches—is hardly inferior to that of the federal republic.

Although the population of Canada at present
does not exceed five millions of souls, the country
has, within a few years, made great strides in the
path of national development, and fairly takes a
place of considerable importance among those nations whose stories have been already told; whose
history goes back to centuries when the Laurentian
Hills, those rocks of primeval times, looked down on
an unbroken wilderness of forest and stretches of
silent river. If we treat the subject from a strictly
historical point of view, the confederation of provinces and territories comprised within the Dominion may be most conveniently grouped into

several distinct divisions. Geographers divide the
whole country lying between the two oceans into
three well-defined regions: 1. The Eastern, extending from the Atlantic to the head of Lake Superior.
2. The Central, stretching across the prairies and
plains to the base of the Rocky Mountains. 3. The
Western, comprising that sea of mountains which
at last unites with the waters of the Pacific. For
the purposes of this narrative, however, the Eastern
and largest division—also the oldest historically—
must be separated into two distinct divisions,
known as Acadia and Canada in the early annals
of America.

The first division of the Eastern region now comprises the provinces of Nova Scotia, New Brunswick, and Prince Edward Island, which, formerly,
with a large portion of the State of Maine, were best
known as Acadie,* a memorial of the Indian occupation before the French régime. These provinces are
indented by noble harbours and bays, and many
deep rivers connect the sea-board with the interior.
They form the western and southern boundaries of
that great gulf or eastern portal of Canada, which
maritime adventurers explored from the earliest
period of which we have any record. Ridges of the
Appalachian range stretch from New England to

* *Akäde* means a place or district in the language of the Micmacs
or Souriquois, the most important Indian tribe in the Eastern provinces, and is always united with another word, signifying some natural characteristic of the locality. For instance, the well-known river
in Nova Scotia, *Shubenacadie* (Sĕgĕbŭn-äkäde), the place where the
ground-nut or Indian potato grows.

the east of these Acadian provinces, giving picturesque features to a generally undulating surface, and
find their boldest expression in the northern region
of the island of Cape Breton. The peninsula of
Nova Scotia is connected with the neighbouring
province of New Brunswick by a narrow isthmus,
on one side of which the great tides of the Bay of
Fundy tumultuously beat, and is separated by a
very romantic strait from the island of Cape Breton.
Both this isthmus and island, we shall see in the
course of this narrative, played important parts in
the struggle between France and England for dominion in America. This Acadian division possesses
large tracts of fertile lands, and valuable mines of
coal and other minerals. In the richest district of
the peninsula of Nova Scotia were the thatch-
roofed villages of those Acadian farmers whose sad
story has been told in matchless verse by a New
England poet, and whose language can still be heard
throughout the land they loved, and to which some
of them returned after years of exile. The inex-
haustible fisheries of the Gulf, whose waters wash
their shores, centuries ago attracted fleets of adventurous sailors from the Atlantic coast of Europe,
and led to the discovery of Canada and the St.
Lawrence. It was with the view of protecting these
fisheries, and guarding the great entrance to New
France, that the French raised on the southeastern
shores of Cape Breton the fortress of Louisbourg, the
ruins of which now alone remain to tell of their ambition and enterprise.

Leaving Acadia, we come to the provinces which

are watered by the St. Lawrence and the Great
Lakes, extending from the Gulf to the head of Lake
Superior, and finding their northern limits in the
waters of Hudson's Bay. The name of Canada appears to be also a memorial of the Indian nations
that once occupied the region between the Ottawa
and Saguenay rivers. This name, meaning a large
village or town in one of the dialects of the Huron-
Iroquois tongue, was applied, in the first half of the
sixteenth century, to a district in the neighbourhood
of the Indian town of Stadacona, which stood on the
site of the present city of Quebec. In the days of
French occupation the name was more generally
used than New France, and sometimes extended to
the country now comprised in the provinces of Ontario and Quebec, or, in other words, to the whole
region from the Gulf to the head of Lake Superior.
Finally, it was adopted as the most appropriate
designation for the new Dominion that made a step
toward national life in 1867.

The most important feature of this historic country is the remarkable natural highway which has
given form and life to the growing nation by its side
—a river famous in the history of exploration and
war—a river which has never-failing reservoirs in
those great lakes which occupy a basin larger than
Great Britain—a river noted for its long stretch of
navigable waters, its many rapids, and its unequalled
Falls of Niagara, around all of which man's enterprise and skill have constructed a system of canals
to give the west a continuous navigation from Lake
Superior to the ocean for over two thousand miles.

The Laurentian Hills—"the nucleus of the North American continent"—reach from inhospitable, rock-bound Labrador to the north of the St. Lawrence, extend up the Ottawa valley, and pass eventually to the northwest of Lakes Huron and Superior, as far as the "Divide" between the St. Lawrence valley and Hudson's Bay, but display their boldest forms on the north shore of the river below Quebec, where the names of Capes Eternity and Trinity have been so aptly given to those noble precipices which tower above the gloomy waters of the Saguenay, and have a history which "dates back to the very dawn of geographical time, and is of hoar antiquity in comparison with that of such youthful ranges as the Andes and the Alps." *

From Gaspé, the southeastern promontory at the entrance of the Gulf, the younger rocks of the Appalachian range, constituting the breast-bone of the continent, and culminating at the north in the White Mountains, describe a great curve southwesterly to the valley of the Hudson; and it is between the ridge-like elevations of this range and the older Laurentian Hills that we find the valley of the St. Lawrence, in which lie the provinces of Quebec and Ontario.

The province of Quebec is famous in the song and story of Canada; indeed, for a hundred and fifty years, it was Canada itself. More than a million and a quarter of people, speaking the language and profess-

* Sir J. W. Dawson, *Salient Points in the Science of the Earth*, p. 99.

VIEW OF CAPE TRINITY ON THE LAURENTIAN RANGE.

ing the religion of their forefathers, continue to occupy the country which extends from the Gulf to
the Ottawa, and have made themselves a power in
the intellectual and political life of Canada. Everywhere do we meet names that recall the ancient
régime—French kings and princes, statesmen, soldiers, sailors, explorers, and adventurers, compete
in the national nomenclature with priests and saints.
This country possesses large tracts of arable land,
especially in the country stretching from the St.
Lawrence to Lake Champlain, and watered by the
Richelieu, that noted highway in Canadian history.
Even yet, at the head-waters of its many rivers, it
has abundance of timber to attract the lumberman.

The province of Ontario was formerly known as
Upper or Western Canada, but at the time of the
union it received its present name because it largely
lies by the side of the lake which the Hurons and
more famous Iroquois called "great." It extends
from the river of the Ottawas—the first route of the
French adventurers to the western lakes as far as
the northwesterly limit of Lake Superior, and is the
most populous and prosperous province of the Dominion on account of its wealth of agricultural land,
and the energy of its population. Its history is
chiefly interesting for the illustrations it affords of
Englishmen's successful enterprise in a new country.
The origin of the province must be sought in the
history of those " United Empire Loyalists," who
left the old colonies during and after the War of
Independence and founded new homes by the St.
Lawrence and great lakes, as well as in Nova Scotia

and New Brunswick, where, as in the West, their descendants have had much influence in moulding institutions and developing enterprise.

In the days when Ontario and Quebec were a wilderness, except on the borders of the St. Lawrence from Montreal to the Quebec district, the fur-trade of the forests that stretched away beyond the Laurentides, was not only a source of gain to the trading companies and merchants of Acadia and Canada, but was the sole occupation of many adventurers whose lives were full of elements which assume a picturesque aspect at this distance of time. It was the fur-trade that mainly led to the discovery of the great West and to the opening up of the Mississippi valley. But always by the side of the fur-trader and explorer we see the Recollet or Jesuit missionary pressing forward with the cross in his hands and offering his life that the savage might learn the lessons of his Faith.

As soon as the Mississippi was discovered, and found navigable to the Gulf of Mexico, French Canadian statesmen recognised the vantage-ground that the command of the St. Lawrence valley gave them in their dreams of conquest. Controlling the Richelieu, Lake Champlain, and the approaches to the Hudson River, as well as the western lakes and rivers which gave easy access to the Mississippi, France planned her bold scheme of confining the old English colonies between the Appalachian range of mountains and the Atlantic Ocean, and finally dominating the whole continent.

So far we have been passing through a country

where the lakes and rivers of a great natural basin or valley carry their tribute of waters to the Eastern Atlantic; but now, when we leave Lake Superior and the country known as Old Canada, we find ourselves on the northwestern height of land and overlooking another region whose great rivers—notably the Saskatchewan, Nelson, Mackenzie, Peace, Athabasca, and Yukon—drain immense areas and find their way after many circuitous wanderings to Arctic seas.

The Central region of Canada, long known as Rupert's Land and the Northwestern Territory, gradually ascends from the Winnipeg system of lakes, lying to the northwest of Lake Superior, as far as the foothills of the Rocky Mountains, and comprises those plains and prairies which have been opened up to civilisation within two decades of years, and offer large possibilities of power and wealth in the future development of the New Dominion. It is a region remarkable for its long rivers, in places shallow and rapid, and extremely erratic in their courses through the plains.

Geologists tell us that at some remote period these great central plains, now so rich in alluvial deposits, composed the bed of a sea which extended from the Arctic region and the ancient Laurentian belt as far as the Gulf of Mexico and made, in reality, of the continent, an Atlantis—that mysterious island of the Greeks. The history of the northwest is the history of Indians hunting the buffalo and fur-bearing animals in a country for many years under the control of companies holding royal charters of exclusive

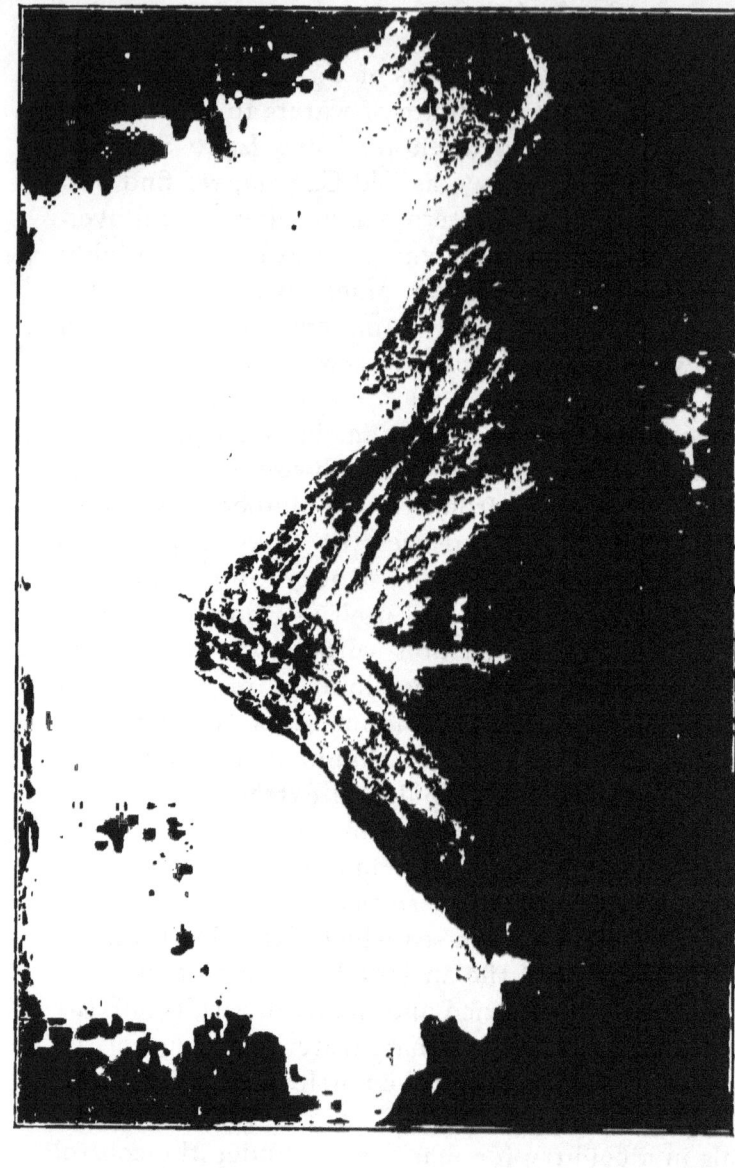

ROCKY MOUNTAINS AT DONALD, B. C.

13

trade and jealously guarding their game preserves
from the encroachments of settlement and attendant
civilisation. French Canadians were the first to
travel over the wide expanse of plain and reach the
foothills of the Rockies a century and a half ago,
and we can still see in this country the Métis or
half-breed descendants of the French Canadian
hunters and trappers who went there in the days
when trading companies were supreme, and married
Indian women. A cordon of villages, towns, and
farms now stretches from the city of Winnipeg,
built on the site of the old headquarters of the
Hudson's Bay Company, as far as the Rocky Mountains. Fields of golden grain brighten the prairies,
where the tracks of herds of buffalo, once so numerous but now extinct, still deeply indent the surface
of the rich soil, and lead to some creek or stream, on
whose banks grows the aspen or willow or poplar
of a relatively treeless land, until we reach the more
picturesque and well-wooded and undulating country
through which the North Saskatchewan flows. As
we travel over the wide expanse of plain, only
bounded by the deep blue of the distant horizon,
we become almost bewildered by the beauty and
variety of the flora, which flourish on the rich soil;
crocuses, roses, bluebells, convolvuli, anemones, as-
ters, sunflowers, and other flowers too numerous
to mention, follow each other in rapid succession
from May till September, and mingle with

" The billowy bays of grass ever rolling in shadow and sunshine."

Ascending the foothills that rise from the plains

UPPER END OF FRASER CAÑON, B. C.

15

to the Rocky Mountains we come to the Western region, known as British Columbia, comprising within a width varying from four to six hundred miles at the widest part, several ranges of great mountains which lie, roughly speaking, parallel to each other, and give sublimity and variety to the most remarkable scenery of North America. These mountains are an extension of the Cordilleran range, which forms the backbone of the Pacific coast, and in Mexico rises to great volcanic ridges, of which the loftiest are Popocatepétl and Iztaccihuatl. Plateaus and valleys of rich, gravelly soil lie within these stately ranges.

Here we find the highest mountains of Canada, some varying from ten to fifteen thousand feet, and assuming a grandeur which we never see in the far more ancient Laurentides, which, in the course of ages, have been ground down by the forces of nature to their relatively diminutive size. Within the recesses of these stupendous ranges there are rich stores of gold and silver, while coal exists most abundantly on Vancouver.

The Fraser, Columbia, and other rivers of this region run with great swiftness among the cañons and gorges of the mountains, and find their way at last to the Pacific. In the Rockies, properly so called, we see stupendous masses of bare, rugged rock, crowned with snow and ice, and assuming all the grand and curious forms which nature loves to take in her most striking upheavals. Never can one forget the picturesque beauty and impressive grandeur of the Selkirk range, and the ride by the side of the broad, rapid Fraser, over trestle-work, around curves, and through tunnels, with the forest-clad mountains ever rising as far as the eye can reach, with glimpses of precipices and cañons, of cataracts and cascades that tumble down from the glaciers or snow-clad peaks, and resemble so many drifts of snow amid the green foliage that grows on the lowest slopes. The Fraser River valley, writes an observer, "is one so singularly formed, that it would seem that some superhuman sword had at a single stroke cut through a labyrinth of mountains for three hundred miles, down deep into the bowels of the land." * Further along the Fraser the Cascade Mountains lift their rugged heads, and the river "flows at the bottom of a vast tangle cut by nature through the heart of the mountains." The glaciers fully equal in magnitude and grandeur those of Switzerland. On the coast and in the rich valleys stand the giant pines and cedars, compared with which the trees of the Eastern division seem mere saplings. The coast is very mountainous and broken into innumerable inlets and islands, all of them heavily timbered to the water's edge. The history of this region offers little of picturesque interest except what may be found in the adventures of daring sailors of various nationalities on the Pacific coast, or in the story of the descent of the Fraser by the Scotch fur-trader who first followed it to the sea, and gave it the name which it still justly bears.

The history of the Western and Central regions of the Dominion is given briefly towards the end of this

* H. H. Bancroft, *British Columbia*, p. 38.

2

narrative, as it forms a national sequence or supplement to that of the Eastern divisions, Acadia and Canada, where France first established her dominion, and the foundations were laid for the present Canadian confederation. It is the story of the great Eastern country that I must now tell in the following pages.

II.

THE DAWN OF DISCOVERY IN CANADA.

(1497—1525.)

ON one of the noble avenues of the modern part
of the city of Boston, so famous in the political and
intellectual life of America, stands a monument of
bronze which some Scandinavian and historical enthusiasts have raised to the memory of Leif, son of
Eric the Red, who, in the first year of the eleventh
century, sailed from Greenland where his father, an
Icelandic jarl or earl, had founded a settlement.
This statue represents the sturdy, well-proportioned
figure of a Norse sailor just discovering the new
lands with which the Sagas or poetic chronicles of
the North connect his name. At the foot of the
pedestal the artist has placed the dragon's head
which always stood on the prow of the Norsemen's
ships, and pictures of which can still be seen on the
famous Norman tapestry at Bayeux.

The Icelandic Sagas possess a basis of historical
truth, and there is reason to believe that Leif Ericson discovered three countries. The first land he
made after leaving Greenland he named Helluland
on account of its slaty rocks. Then he came to a

flat country with white beaches of sand, which he
called Markland because it was so well wooded.
After a sail of some days the Northmen arrived on a
coast where they found vines laden with grapes, and
very appropriately named Vinland. The exact situation of Vinland and the other countries visited by
Leif Ericson and other Norsemen, who followed in
later voyages and are believed to have founded settlements in the land of vines, has been always a subject of perplexity, since we have only the vague Sagas
to guide us. It may be fairly assumed, however,
that the rocky land was the coast of Labrador ; the
low-lying forest-clad shores which Ericson called
Markland was possibly the southeastern part of
Cape Breton or the southern coast of Nova Scotia ;
Vinland was very likely somewhere in New England.
Be that as it may, the world gained nothing from
these misty discoveries—if, indeed, we may so call
the results of the voyages of ten centuries ago. No
such memorials of the Icelandic pioneers have yet
been found in America as they have left behind them
in Greenland. The old ivy-covered round tower at
Newport in Rhode Island is no longer claimed as a
relic of the Norse settlers of Vinland, since it has
been proved beyond doubt to be nothing more than
a very substantial stone windmill of quite recent
times, while the writing on the once equally famous
rock, found last century at Dighton, by the side of
a New England river, is now generally admitted to
be nothing more than a memorial of one of the
Indian tribes who have inhabited the country since
the voyages of the Norsemen.

Leaving this domain of legend, we come to the last years of the fifteenth century, when Columbus landed on the islands now often known as the Antilles—a memorial of that mysterious Antillia, or Isle of the Seven Cities, which was long supposed to exist in the mid-Atlantic, and found a place in all the maps before, and even some time after, the voyages of the illustrious Genoese. A part of the veil was at last lifted from that mysterious western ocean—that Sea of Darkness, which had perplexed philosophers, geographers, and sailors, from the days of Aristotle, Plato, Strabo, and Ptolemy. As in the case of Scandinavia, several countries have endeavoured to establish a claim for the priority of discovery in America. Some sailors of that Biscayan coast, which has given so many bold pilots and mariners to the world of adventure and exploration —that Basque country to which belonged Juan de la Cosa, the pilot who accompanied Columbus in his voyages—may have found their way to the North Atlantic coast in search of cod or whales at a very early time; and it is certainly an argument for such a claim that John Cabot is said in 1497 to have heard the Indians of northeastern America speak of Baccalaos, or Basque for cod—a name afterwards applied for a century and longer to the islands and countries around the Gulf. It is certainly not improbable that the Normans, Bretons, or Basques, whose lives from times immemorial have been passed on the sea, should have been driven by the winds or by some accident to the shores of Newfoundland or Labrador or even Cape Breton, but such theories are not

based upon sufficiently authentic data to bring them
under the consideration of the serious historian.

It is unfortunate that the records of history should
be so wanting in definite and accurate details, when
we come to the voyages of John Cabot, a great navigator, who was probably a Genoese by birth and a
Venetian by citizenship. Five years after the first
discovery by Columbus, John Cabot sailed to unknown seas and lands in the Northwest in the ship
Matthew of Bristol, with full authority from the King
of England, Henry the Seventh, to take possession
in his name of all countries he might discover.
On his return from a successful voyage, during
which he certainly landed on the coast of British
North America, and first discovered the continent of
North America, he became the hero of the hour and
received from Henry, a very economical sovereign,
a largess of ten pounds as a reward to "hym that
founde the new ile." In the following year both he
and his son Sebastian, then a very young man, who
probably also accompanied his father in the voyage
of 1497, sailed again for the new lands which were
believed to be somewhere on the road to Cipango
and the countries of gold and spice and silk. We
have no exact record of this voyage, and do not
even know whether John Cabot himself returned
alive; for, from the day of his sailing in 1498, he disappears from the scene and his son Sebastian not
only becomes henceforth a prominent figure in the
maritime history of the period, but has been given
by his admirers even the place which his father alone
fairly won as the leader in the two voyages on which

England has based her claim of priority of discovery on the Atlantic coast of North America. The weight of authority so far points to a headland of Cape Breton as the *prima tierra vista,* or the landfall which John Cabot probably made on a June day, the four hundredth anniversary of which arrives in 1897, though the claims of a point on the wild Labrador coast and of Bonavista, an eastern headland of Newfoundland, have also some earnest advocates. It is, however, generally admitted that the Cabots, in the second voyage, sailed past the shores of Nova Scotia and of the United States as far south as Spanish Florida. History here, at all events, has tangible, and in some respects irrefutable, evidence on which to dwell, since we have before us a celebrated map, which has come down from the first year of the sixteenth century, and is known beyond doubt to have been drawn with all the authority that is due to so famous a navigator as Juan de la Cosa, the Basque pilot. On this map we see delineated for the first time the coast apparently of a continental region extending from the peninsula of Florida as far as the present Gulf of St. Lawrence, which is described in Spanish as *mar descubierta por los Ingleses* (sea discovered by the English), on one headland of which there is a *Cavo de Ynglaterra,* or English Cape. Whether this sea is the Gulf of St. Lawrence and the headland is Cape Race, the southeastern extremity of Newfoundland, or the equally well-known point which the Bretons named on the southeastern coast of Cape Breton, are among the questions which enter into the domain of speculation and imagination. Juan de la Cosa, however, is conclusive evidence in favour of the English claim to the first discovery of Northern countries, whose greatness and prosperity have already exceeded the conceptions which the Spanish conquerors formed when they won possession of those rich Southern lands which so long acknowledged the dominion of Spain.

But Cabot's voyages led to no immediate practical results. The Bristol ships brought back no rich cargoes of gold or silver or spices, to tell England that she had won a passage to the Indies and Cathay. The idea, however, that a short passage would be discovered to those rich regions was to linger for nearly two centuries in the minds of maritime adventurers and geographers.

If we study the names of the headlands, bays, and other natural features of the islands and countries which inclose the Gulf of St. Lawrence we find many memorials of the early Portuguese and French voyagers. In the beginning of the sixteenth century Gaspar Cortereal made several voyages to the northeastern shores of Newfoundland and Labrador, and brought back with him a number of natives whose sturdy frames gave European spectators the idea that they would make good labourers; and it was this erroneous conception, it is generally thought, gave its present name to the rocky, forbidding region which the Norse voyagers had probably called Helluland five hundred years before. Both Gaspar Cortereal and his brother Miguel disappeared from history somewhere in the waters of Hudson's

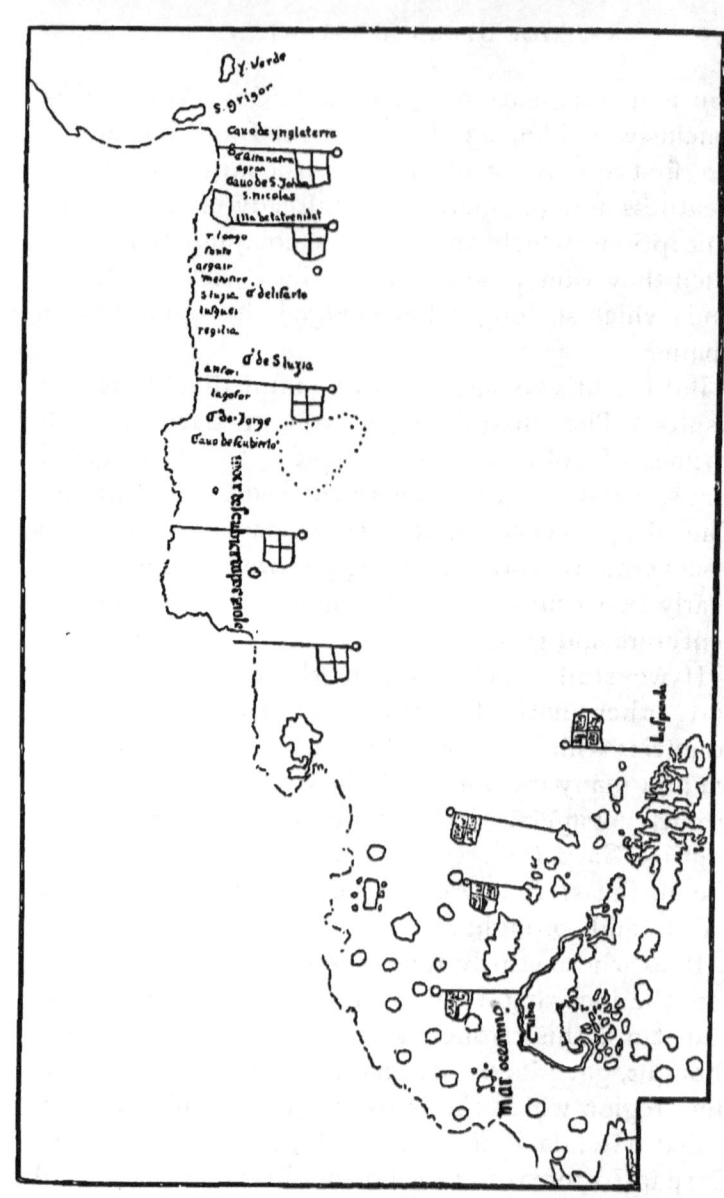

SKETCH OF JUAN DE LA COSA'S MAP, A.D. 1500.

25

Bay or Labrador; but they were followed by other adventurous sailors who have left mementos of their nationality on such places as Cape Raso (Race), Boa Ventura (Bonaventure), Conception, Tangier, Porto Novo, Carbonear (Carboneiro), all of which and other names appear on the earliest maps of the north-eastern waters of North America.

Some enterprising sailors of Brittany first gave a name to that Cape which lies to the northeast of the historic port of Louisbourg. These hardy sailors were certainly on the coast of the island as early as 1504, and Cape Breton is consequently the earliest French name on record in America. Some claim is made for the Basques—that primeval people, whose origin is lost in the mists of tradition—because there is a Cape Breton on the Biscayan coast of France, but the evidence in support of the Bretons' claim is by far the strongest. For very many years the name of Bretons' land was attached on maps to a continental region, which included the present Nova Scotia, and it was well into the middle of the sixteenth century, after the voyages of Jacques Cartier and Jehan Alfonce, before we find the island itself make its appearance in its proper place and form.

It was a native of the beautiful city of Florence, in the days of Francis the First, who gave to France some claim to territory in North America. Giovanni da Verrazano, a well-known corsair, in 1524, received a commission from that brilliant and dissipated king, Francis the First, who had become jealous of the enormous pretensions of Spain and Portugal in the new world, and had on one occasion sent word to

his great rival, Charles the Fifth, that he was not
aware that "our first father Adam had made the
Spanish and Portuguese kings his sole heirs to the
earth." Verrazano's voyage is supposed on good
authority to have embraced the whole North American coast from Cape Fear in North Carolina as far
as the island of Cape Breton. About the same time
Spain sent an expedition to the northeastern coasts
of America under the direction of Estevan Gomez,
a Portuguese pilot, and it is probable that he also
coasted from Florida to Cape Breton. Much disap-
pointment was felt that neither Verrazano nor Gomez
had found a passage through the straits which were
then, and for a long time afterwards, supposed to lie
somewhere in the northern regions of America and
to lead to China and India. Francis was not able to
send Verrazano on another voyage, to take formal
possession of the new lands, as he was engaged in
that conflict with Charles which led to his defeat at
the battle of Pavia and his being made subsequently
a prisoner. Spain appears to have attached no importance to the discovery by Gomez, since it did not
promise mines of gold and silver, and happily for the
cause of civilisation and progress, she continued to
confine herself to the countries of the South, though
her fishermen annually ventured, in common with
those of other nations, to the banks of Newfoundland. However, from the time of Verrazano we find
on the old maps the names of Francisca and Nova
Gallia as a recognition of the claim of France to
important discoveries in North America. It is also
from the Florentine's voyage that we may date the

discovery of that mysterious region called Norumbega, where the fancy of sailors and adventurers
eventually placed a noble city whose houses were
raised on pillars of crystal and silver, and decorated
with precious stones. These travellers' tales and
sailors' yarns probably originated in the current belief that somewhere in those new lands, just discovered, there would be found an El Dorado. The
same brilliant illusion that led Ralegh to the South
made credulous mariners believe in a Norumbega in
the forests of Acadia. The name clung for many
years to a country embraced within the present limits
of New England, and sometimes included Nova
Scotia. Its rich capital was believed to exist somewhere on the beautiful Penobscot River, in the present
State of Maine. A memorial of the same name still
lingers in the little harbours of Norumbec, or Lor-
ambeque, or Loran, on the southeastern coast of
Cape Breton. Enthusiastic advocates of the Norse
discovery and settlement have confidently seen in
Norumbega, the Indian utterance of Norbega, the
ancient form of Norway to which Vinland was subject, and this belief has been even emphasised on a
stone pillar which stands on some ruins unearthed
close to the Charles River in Massachusetts. *Si non
è vero è ben trovato.* All this serves to amuse, though
it cannot convince, the critical student of those
shadowy times. With the progress of discovery
the city of Norumbega was found as baseless as
the fables of the golden city on the banks of the
Orinoco, and of the fountain of youth among the
forests and everglades of Florida.

III.

A BRETON SAILOR DISCOVERS CANADA AND ITS GREAT RIVER.

(1534-36.)

IN the fourth decade of the sixteenth century we find ourselves in the domain of precise history. The narratives of the voyages of Jacques Cartier of St. Malo, that famous port of Brittany which has given so many sailors to the world, are on the whole sufficiently definite, even at this distance of three centuries and a half, to enable us to follow his routes, and recognise the greater number of the places in the gulf and river which he revealed to the old world. The same enterprising king who had sent Verrazano to the west in 1524, commissioned the Breton sailor to find a short passage to Cathay and give a new dominion to France.

At the time of the departure of Cartier in 1534 for the "new-found isle" of Cabot, the world had made considerable advances in geographical knowledge. South America was now ascertained to be a separate continent, and the great Portuguese Magellan had passed through the straits, which ever since have borne his name, and found his way across the Pacific to the spice islands of Asia. As respects North America beyond the Gulf of Mexico and the country to the North, dense ignorance still prevailed, and though a coast line had been followed from Florida to Cape Breton by Cabot, Gomez, and Verrazano, it was believed either to belong to a part of Asia or to be a mere prolongation of Greenland. If one belief prevailed more than another it was in the existence of a great sea, called on the maps "the sea of Verrazano," in what is now the upper basin of the Mississippi and the Great Lakes of the west, and which was only separated from the Atlantic by a narrow strip of land. Now that it was clear that no short passage to India and China could be found through the Gulf of Mexico, and that South America was a continental region, the attention of hopeful geographers and of enterprising sailors and adventurers was directed to the north, especially as Spain was relatively indifferent to enterprise in that region. No doubt the French King thought that Cartier would find his way to the sea of Verrazano, beyond which were probably the lands visited by Marco Polo, that enterprising merchant of Venice, whose stories of adventure in India and China read like stories of the Arabian Nights.

Jacques Cartier made three voyages to the continent of America between 1534 and 1542, and probably another in 1543. The first voyage, which took place in 1534 and lasted from April until September, was confined to the Gulf of St. Lawrence, which he

Jacques Cartier.

31

explored with some thoroughness after passing
through the strait of Belle Isle, then called the Gulf
of Castles (Chasteaux). The coast of Labrador he
described with perfect accuracy as extremely forbidding, covered with rocks and moss and " as very
likely the land given by God to Cain." In one of
the harbours of the Labrador coast he found a fishing vessel from La Rochelle, the famous Protestant
town of France, on its way to the port of Brest, then
and for some time after a place of call for the fishermen who were already thronging the Gulf, where
walrus, whales, and cod were so abundant. A good
deal of time has been expended by historical writers
on the itinerary of this voyage, the record of which
is somewhat puzzling at times when we come to fix
Cartier's names of places on a modern map. Confining ourselves to those localities of which there is
no doubt, we know he visited and named the isle of
Brion in honour of Admiral Philip de Chabot, Seigneur de Brion, who was a friend and companion of
Francis, and had received from him authority to
send out Cartier's expedition. The Breton saw the
great sand-dunes, and red cliffs of the Magdalens
rising from the sea like so many cones. It was one
of these islands he probably called Alezay, though
there are writers who recognise in his description a
headland of Prince Edward Island, but it is not certain that he visited or named any of the bays or
lagoons of that island which lies so snugly ensconced
in the Gulf. We recognise the bay of Miramichi
(St. Lunaire) and the still more beautiful scenery of
the much larger bay of Chaleur (Heat) which he so

named because he entered it on a very hot July day. There he had pleasant interviews with the natives, who danced and gave other demonstrations of joy when they received some presents in exchange for the food they brought to the strangers. These people were probably either Micmacs or Etchemins, one of the branches of the Algonquin nation who inhabited a large portion of the Northern continent. Cartier was enchanted with the natural beauties of " as fine a country as one would wish to see and live in, level and smooth, warmer than Spain, where there is abundance of wheat, which has an ear like that of rye, and again like oats, peas growing as thickly and as large as if they had been cultivated, red and white barberries, strawberries, red and white roses, and other flowers of a delightful and sweet perfume, meadows of rich grasses, and rivers full of salmon "—a perfectly true description of the beautiful country watered by the Restigouche and Metapedia rivers. Cartier also visited the picturesque bay of Gaspé, where the scenery is grand but the trees smaller and the land less fertile than in the neighbourhood of Chaleur and its rivers. On a point at the entrance of the harbour of Gaspé —an Indian name having probably reference to a split rock, which has long been a curiosity of the coast—Cartier raised a cross, thirty feet in height, on the middle of which there was a shield or escutcheon with three fleurs-de-lis, and the inscription, *Vive le Roy de France.* Cartier then returned to France by way of the strait of Belle Isle, without having seen the great river to whose mouth he had been so close

3

when he stood on the hills of Gaspé or passed around
the shores of desolate Anticosti.

Cartier brought back with him two sons of the
Indian chief of a tribe he saw at Gaspé, who seem
to have belonged to the Huron-Iroquois nation he
met at Stadacona, now Quebec, when he made the
second voyage which I have to describe. The accounts he gave of the country on the Gulf appear
to have been sufficiently encouraging to keep up the
interest of the King and the Admiral of France in
the scheme of discovery which they had planned.
In this second voyage of 1535–36, the most memorable of all he made to American waters, he had the
assistance of a little fleet of three vessels, the *Grande
Hermine*, the *Petite Hermine*, and the *Emérillon*, of
which the first had a burden of one hundred and
twenty tons—quite a large ship compared with the
two little vessels of sixty tons each that were given
him for his first venture. This fleet, which gave
Canada to France for two centuries and a quarter,
reached Newfoundland during the early part of July,
passed through the strait of Belle Isle, and on the
10th of August, came to a little bay or harbour on
the northern shore of the present province of Quebec, but then known as Labrador, to which he gave
the name of St. Laurent, in honour of the saint
whose festival happened to fall on the day of his
arrival. This bay is now generally believed to be
the port of Sainte Geneviève, and the name which
Cartier gave it was gradually transferred in the course
of a century to the whole gulf as well as to the river
itself which the Breton sailor was the first to place

definitely on the maps of those days of scanty
geographical knowledge. Cartier led his vessels
through the passage between the northern shores of
Canada and the island of Anticosti, which he called
Assomption, although it has long since resumed its
old name, which has been gradually changed from
the original Natiscotic to Naticousti, and finally to
Anticosti. When the adventurers came near the
neighbourhood of Trinity River on the north side of
the Gulf, the two Gaspé Indians who were on board
Cartier's vessel, the *Grande Hermine*, told them that
they were now at the entrance of the kingdom of
Saguenay where red copper was to be found, and
that away beyond flowed the great river of Hochelaga and Canada. This Saguenay kingdom extended
on the north side of the river as far as the neighbourhood of the present well-known Isle aux Coudres;
then came the kingdom of Canada, stretching as far
as the island of Montreal, where the King of Hochelaga exercised dominion over a number of tribes in
the adjacent country.

Cartier passed the gloomy portals of the Saguenay,
and stopped for a day or two at Isle aux Coudres
(Coudrières) over fifty miles below Quebec, where
mass was celebrated for the first time on the river of
Canada, and which he named on account of the
hazel-nuts he found " as large and better tasting
than those of France, though a little harder." Cartier then followed the north shore, with its lofty,
well-wooded mountains stretching away to the northward, and came at last to an anchorage not far from
Stadacona, somewhere between the present Isle of

Orleans and the mainland. Here he had an interview with the natives, who showed every confidence in the strangers when they found that the two Gaspé Indians, Taignoagny and Domagaya, were their companions. As soon as they were satisfied of this fact—and here we have a proof that these two Indians must have belonged to the same nation—"they showed their joy, danced, and performed various antics." Subsequently the lord of Donnacona, whose Indian title was Agouahana, came with twelve canoes and "made a speech according to the fashion, contorting the body and limbs in a remarkable way—a ceremony of joy and welcome." After looking about for a safe harbour, Cartier chose the mouth of the present St. Charles River, which he named the River of the Holy Cross (Sainte Croix) in honour of the day when he arrived. The fleet was anchored not far from the Indian village of Stadacona, and soon after its arrival one of the chiefs received the Frenchmen with a speech of welcome, "while the women danced and sang without ceasing, standing in the water up to their knees."

Moored in a safe haven, the French had abundant opportunity to make themselves acquainted with the surrounding country and its people. They visited the island close by, and were delighted with "its beautiful trees, the same as in France," and with the great quantities of vines "such as we had never before seen." Cartier called this attractive spot the Island of Bacchus, but changed the name subsequently to the Isle of Orleans, in honour of one of the royal sons of France. Cartier was equally charmed with the varied scenery and the fruitful soil of the country around Stadacona.

It was now the middle of September, and Cartier determined, since his men had fully recovered from the fatigues of the voyage, to proceed up the river as far as Hochelaga, of which he was constantly hearing accounts from the Indians. When they heard of this intention, Donnacona and other chiefs used their best efforts to dissuade him by inventing stories of the dangers of the navigation. The two Gaspé Indians lent themselves to the plans of the chief of Stadacona. Three Indians were dressed as devils, " with faces painted as black as coal, with horns as long as the arm, and covered with the skins of black and white dogs." These devils were declared to be emissaries of the Indian God at Hochelaga, called Cudragny, who warned the French that " there was so much snow and ice that all would die." The Gaspé Indians, who had so long an acquaintance with the religious customs and superstitions of the French, endeavoured to influence them by appeals to " Jesus" and " Jesus Maria." Cartier, however, only laughed at the tricks of the Indians, and told them that " their God Cudragny was a mere fool, and that Jesus would preserve them from all danger if they should believe in Him." The French at last started on the ascent of the river in the *Emérillon* and two large boats, but neither Taignoagny nor Domagaya could be induced to accompany the expedition to Hochelaga.

Cartier and his men reached the neighbourhood of Hochelaga, the Indian town on the island of Montreal, in about a fortnight's time. The appearance of the country bordering on the river between Stadacona and Hochelaga pleased the French on account of the springs of excellent water, the beautiful trees, and vines heavily laden with grapes, and the quantities of wild fowl that rose from every bay or creek as the voyagers passed by. At one place called Achelay, "a strait with a stony and dangerous current, full of rocks,"—probably the Richelieu Rapids* above Point au Platon—a number of Indians came on board the *Emérillon*, warned Cartier of the perils of the river, and the chief made him a present of two children, one of whom, a little girl of seven or eight years, he accepted and promised to take every care of. Somewhere on Lake St. Peter they found the water very shallow and decided to leave the *Emérillon* and proceed in the boats to Hochelaga, where they arrived on the second of October, and were met by more than "a thousand savages who gathered about them, men, women, and children, and received us as well as a parent does a child, showing great joy." After a display of friendly feeling on the part of the natives and their visitors, and the exchange of presents between them, Cartier returned to his boat in the stream. "All that night," says the narrative, "the savages remained on the shore near our boats, keeping up fires, dancing, crying out 'Aguaze,' which is their word for welcome and joy." The king or chief of this Indian domain was also called Agouahanna, and was a member of the Huron-Iroquois stock.

* The obstructions which created these rapids have been removed.

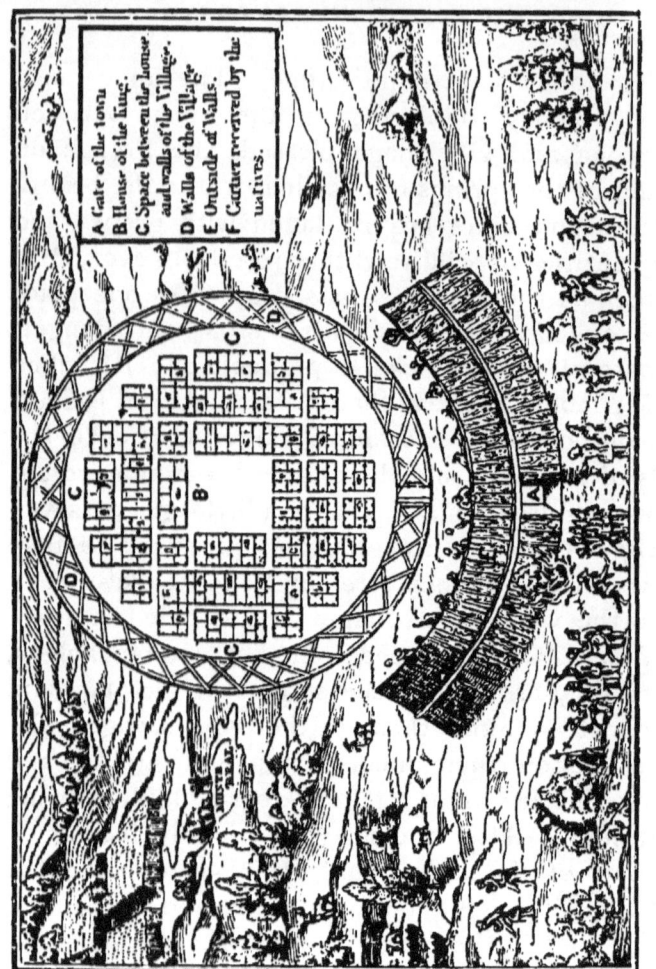

A Gate of the Town.
B House of the king.
C Space between the houses and walls of the Village.
D Walls of the Village.
E Outside of Walls.
F Cattle received by the natives.

ANCIENT HOCHELAGA (FROM RAMUSIO).

39

The French visitors were regarded by the Indians of Hochelaga as superior beings, endowed with supernatural powers. Cartier was called upon to touch the lame, blind, and wounded, and treat all the ailments with which the Indians were afflicted, " as if they thought that God had sent him to cure them."

Cartier's narrative describes the town as circular, inclosed by three rows of palisades arranged like a pyramid, crossed at the top, with the middle stakes standing perpendicular, and the others at an angle on each side, all being well joined and fastened after the Indian fashion. The inclosing wall was of the height of two lances, or about twenty feet, and there was only one entrance through a door generally kept barred. At several points within the inclosure there were platforms or stages reached by ladders, for the purpose of protecting the town with arrows, and rocks, piles of which were close at hand. The town contained fifty houses, each about one hundred feet in length and twenty-five or thirty in width, and constructed of wood, covered with bark and strips of board. These " long houses " were divided into several apartments, belonging to each family, but all of them assembled and ate in common. Storehouses for their grain and food were provided. They dried and smoked their fish, of which they had large quantities. They pounded the grain between flat stones and made it into dough which they cooked also on hot rocks. This tribe lived, Cartier tells us, " by ploughing and fishing alone," and were " not nomadic like the natives of Canada and the Saguenay."

Cartier and several of his companions were taken by the Indians to the mountain near the town of Hochelaga, and were the first Europeans to look on that noble panorama of river and forest which stretched then without a break over the whole continent, except where the Indian nations had made, as at Hochelaga, their villages and settlements. From that day to this the mountain, as well as the great city which it now overlooks in place of a humble Indian town, has borne the name which Cartier gave as a tribute to its unrivalled beauty. As we look from the royal mountain on the beautiful elms and maples rising in the meadows and gardens of an island, bathed by the waters of two noble rivers— the green of the St. Lawrence mingling with the blue of the Ottawa—on the many domes and towers of churches, convents, and colleges, on the stately mansions of the rich, on the tall chimneys of huge factories and blocks upon blocks of massive stores and warehouses, on the ocean steamers on their way to Europe by that very river which Cartier would not ascend with the *Emérillon;* as we look on this beauteous and inspiriting scene, we may well understand how it is that Canada has placed on Montreal the royal crown which Cartier first gave to the mountain he saw on a glorious October day when the foliage was wearing the golden and crimson tints of a Canadian autumn.

On Cartier's return to Stadacona he found that his officers had become suspicious of the intentions of the Indians and had raised a rude fort near the junction of the river of St. Croix and the little stream

called the Lairet. Here the French passed a long
and dreary winter, doubtful of the friendship of the
Indians, and suffering from the intense cold to which
they were unaccustomed. They were attacked by
that dreadful disease, the scurvy, which caused the
death of several men, and did not cease its ravages
until they learned from an Indian to use a drink
evidently made from spruce boughs. Then the
French recovered with great rapidity, and when the
spring arrived they made their preparations to return
to France. They abandoned the little *Hermine*, as
the crew had been so weakened by sickness and
death. They captured Donnacona and several
other chiefs and determined to take them to France
" to relate to the king the wonders of the world
Donnacona [evidently a great story-teller] had seen
in these western countries, for he had assured us
that he had been in the Saguenay kingdom, where
are infinite gold, rubies, and other riches, and white
men dressed in woollen clothing." In the vicinity
of the fort, at the meeting of the St. Croix and
Lairet, Cartier raised a cross, thirty-five feet in height
under the cross-bar of which there was a wooden
shield, showing the arms of France and the inscription

FRANCISCUS PRIMUS DEI GRATIA FRANCORUM
REX REGNAT.

When three centuries and a half had passed, a
hundred thousand French Canadians, in the presence
of an English governor-general of Canada, a French
Canadian lieutenant-governor and cardinal arch-

bishop, many ecclesiastical and civil dignitaries, assisted in the unveiling of a noble monument in memory of Jacques Cartier and his hardy companions of the voyage of 1535–36, and of Jean de Brebeuf, Ennemond Massé, and Charles Lalemant, the missionaries who built the first residence of the Jesuits nearly a century later on the site of the old French fort, and one of whom afterwards sacrificed his life for the faith to which they were all so devoted.

On the return voyage Cartier sailed to the southward of the Gulf, saw the picturesque headlands of northern Cape Breton, remained a few days in some harbours of Newfoundland, and finally reached St. Malo on the sixteenth of July, with the joyful news that he had discovered a great country and a noble river for France.

IV.

FROM CARTIER TO DE MONTS.

(1540–1603.)

THE third voyage made by Cartier to the new
world, in 1541, was relatively of little importance.
Donnacona and the other Indians of Stadacona,
whom the French carried away with them, never
returned to their forest homes, but died in France.
During the year Cartier remained in Canada he built a
fortified post at Cap Rouge, about seven miles west
of the heights of Quebec, and named it Charlesbourg
in honour of one of the sons of Francis the First.
He visited Hochelaga, and attempted to pass up
the river beyond the village, but was stopped by the
dangerous rapids now known as the St. Louis or
Lachine. He returned to France in the spring of
1542, with a few specimens of worthless metal resembling gold which he found among the rocks of
Cap Rouge, and some pieces of quartz crystal
which he believed were diamonds, and which have
given the name to the bold promontory on which
stand the ancient fortifications of Quebec.

THE "DAUPHIN MAP" OF CANADA, *circa*

CANADA

bell iſle

R. Cartier

Aſſumption

y.e de freiliꝫ

bacalliau

St. brion
o y de aux
marguile

aletay

St. Paul

TERRE DES
BRETONS

C. de Raz

C. aus bretons

MER DE FRANCE

y.e du breton   y.e de Jhan eſtienne

Leu m
o d'arable
les vous

encorporada

de guarca

Sete citades

S.ct

S.te anne

encorporada

MER   DESPAIGNE

ida

MER OCCEANE

u catholique

58
57
56
55
54
53
52
51
50
49
48
47
46
45
44
43
42
41
40
39
38
37
36
35
34
33
32
31
30
29
28
27
26

, SHOWING CARTIER'S DISCOVERIES.

Cartier is said to have returned on a fourth voyage to Canada in 1543—though no record exists—for the purpose of bringing back Monsieur Roberval, otherwise known to the history of those times as Jean François de la Roque, who had been appointed by Francis his lieutenant in Canada, Hochelaga, Saguenay, Newfoundland, Belle Isle, Carpunt, Labrador, the Great Bay (St. Lawrence), and Baccalaos, as well as lord of the mysterious region of Norumbega—an example of the lavish use of titles and the assumption of royal dominion in an unknown wilderness. Roberval and Cartier were to have sailed in company to Canada in 1541, but the former could not complete his arrangements and the latter sailed alone, as we have just read. On his return in 1542 Cartier is said to have met Roberval at a port of the Gulf, and to have secretly stolen away in the night and left his chief to go on to the St. Lawrence alone. But these are among historic questions in dispute, and it is useless to dwell on them here. What we do know to a certainty is that Roberval spent some months on the banks of the St. Lawrence,—probably from the spring of 1542 to late in the autumn of 1543,—and built a commodious fort at Charlesbourg, which he renamed France-Roy. He passed a miserable winter, as many of the colonists he had brought with him had been picked up amongst the lowest classes of France, and he had to govern his ill-assorted company with a rigid and even cruel hand. Roberval is said to have visited the Saguenay and explored its waters and surrounding country for a considerable distance, evidently hoping

to verify the fables of Donnacona and other Indians
that gold and precious stones were to be found
somewhere in that region.   His name has been given
to a little village at Lake St. John, on the assumption that he actually went so far on his Saguenay
expedition, while romantic tradition points to an isle
in the Gulf, the Isle de la Demoiselle, where he is said
to have abandoned his niece Marguérite,—who had
loved not wisely but too well—her lover, and an old
nurse.   This rocky spot appears to have become in
the story an isle of Demons who tormented the poor
wretches, exposed to all the rigours of Canadian win-
ters, and to starvation except when they could catch
fish or snare wild fowl.   The nurse and lover as well
as the infant died, but Marguérite is said to have
remained much longer on that lonely island until at
last Fate brought to her rescue a passing vessel and
carried her to France, where she is said to have told
the story of her adventures.

After this voyage Roberval disappeared from the
history of Canada.   Cartier is supposed to have
died about 1577 in his old manor house of Limoilou,
now in ruins, in the neighbourhood of St. Malo.
He was allowed by the King to bear always the
name of " Captain "—an appropriate title for a hardy
sailor who represented so well the heroism and enterprise of the men of St. Malo and the Breton coast.
The results of the voyages of Cartier, Roberval, and
the sailors and fishermen who frequented the waters
of the Great Bay, as the French long called it, can
be seen in the old maps that have come down to us,
and show the increasing geographical knowledge.

To this knowledge, a famous pilot, Captain Jehan Alfonce, a native of the little village of Saintonge in the grape district of Charente, made valuable contributions. He accompanied Roberval to Canada, and afterwards made voyages to the Saguenay, and appears to have explored the Gulf and the coasts of Cape Breton, Nova Scotia, and even Maine as far as the Penobscot, where he believed was the city of Norumbega.

After the death of Francis there came dark days for France, whose people were torn asunder by civil war and religious strife. With the return of peace in France the Marquis de la Roche received a commission from Henry the Fourth, as lieutenant-general of the King, to colonise Canada, but his ill-fated expedition of 1597 never got beyond the dangerous sandbanks of Sable Island. French fur-traders had now found their way to Anticosti and even Tadousac, at the mouth of the Saguenay, where the Indians were wont to assemble in large numbers from the great fur-region to which that melancholy river and its tributary lakes and rivers give access, but these traders like the fishermen made no attempt to settle the country.

From a very early date in the sixteenth century bold sailors from the west country of Devon were fishing in the Gulf and eventually made the safe and commodious port of St. John's, in Newfoundland, their headquarters. Some adventurous Englishmen even made a search for the land of Norumbega, and probably reached the bay of Penobscot. Near the close of the century, Frobisher attempted to open up

the secrets of the Arctic seas and find that passage
to the north which remained closed to venturesome
explorers until Sir Robert McClure, in 1850, successfully passed the icebergs and ice-floes that barred his
way from Bering Sea to Davis Strait.   In the reign
of the great Elizabeth, when Englishmen were at
last showing that ability for maritime enterprise
which was eventually to develop such remarkable
results, Sir Humphrey Gilbert, the half-brother of
Sir Walter Ralegh, the founder of Virginia, the Old
Dominion, took possession of Newfoundland with
much ceremony in the harbour of St. John's, and
erected a pillar on which were inscribed the Queen's
arms. Gilbert had none of the qualities of a coloniser,
and on his voyage back to England he was lost at
sea, and it was left to the men of Devon and the
West coast in later times to make a permanent
settlement on the great island of the Gulf.

The first years of the seventeenth century were
propitious for important schemes of colonisation and
trade in the western lands.   The sovereign of France
was Henry the Fourth, the intrepid Prince of Béarn,
as brave a soldier as he was a sagacious statesman.
Henry listened favourably—though his able minister,
Sully, held different views—to the schemes for opening up Canada to commerce and settlement that were
laid before him by an old veteran of the wars, and
a staunch friend, Aymar de Chastes, governor of
Dieppe.   Pontgravé, a rich Breton merchant of St.
Malo, had the charge of the two vessels which left
France in the spring of 1603, but it is a fact that a
great man, Samuel Champlain, accompanied the ex-

pedition that gives the chief interest to the voyage. Champlain, who was destined to be the founder of New France, was a native of Brouage in the Bay of Biscay, and belonged to a family of fishermen. During the war of the League he served in the army of Henry the Third, but when Henry of Navarre was proclaimed King of France on the assassination of his predecessor, and abjured the Protestant faith of which he had previously been the champion, Champlain, like other Frenchmen, who had followed the Duke of Guise, became an ardent supporter of the new régime and eventually a favourite of the Bernese prince. He visited the West Indies in a Spanish ship and made himself well acquainted with Mexico and other countries bordering on the Gulf. He has described all his voyages to the Indies and Canada in quaint quarto volumes, now very rare, and valuable on account of their minute and truthful narrative—despite his lively and credulous imagination—and the drawings and maps which he made rudely of the places he saw. His accounts of the Indians of Canada are among the most valuable that have come to us from the early days of American history. He had a fair knowledge of natural history for those times, though he believed in Mexican griffins, and was versed in geography and cartography.

In 1603 Pontgravé and Champlain ascended the River St. Lawrence as far as the island of Montreal, where they found only a few wandering Algonquins of the Ottawa and its tributaries, in place of the people who had inhabited the town of Hochelaga in the days of Cartier's visits. Champlain attempted to

4

pass the Lachine rapids but was soon forced to give up the perilous and impossible venture. During this voyage he explored the Saguenay for a considerable distance, and was able to add largely to the information that Cartier had given of Canada and the country around the Gulf. When the expedition reached France, Aymar de Chastes was dead, but two months had hardly elapsed after Champlain's return when a new company was formed on the usual basis of trade and colonisation. At its head was Sieur de Monts, Pierre du Guast, the governor of Pons, a Calvinist and a friend of the King. After much deliberation it was decided to venture south of Canada and explore that ill-defined region, called "La Cadie" in the royal commission given to De Monts as the King's lieutenant in Canada and adjacent countries, the first record we have of that Acadia where French and English were to contend during a century for the supremacy. For a few moments we must leave the valley of the St. Lawrence, where France was soon to enthrone herself on the heights of Quebec, and visit a beautiful bay on the western coast of Nova Scotia, where a sleepy old town, full of historic associations, still stands to recall the efforts of gentlemen-adventurers to establish a permanent settlement on the shores of the Atlantic.

V.

THE FRENCH OCCUPATION OF ACADIA AND THE FOUNDATION OF PORT ROYAL.

(1604–1614.)

IN the western valley of that part of French Acadia, now known as Nova Scotia, not only do we tread on historic ground, but we see in these days a landscape of more varied beauty than that which so delighted the gentlemen-adventurers of old France nearly three centuries ago. In this country, which the poem conceived by Longfellow amid the elms of Cambridge has made so famous, we see the rich lands reclaimed from the sea, which glistens a few miles to the north, and every day comes rushing up its estuaries. There to the north is dark, lofty Blomidon—whose name is probably a memorial of a Portuguese voyager—with its overhanging cliff under which the tumultuous tides struggle and foam. Here, in a meadow close by, is a long row of Lombardy poplars, pointing to another race and another country. There, on a slight acclivity, among the trees, is a pile of white college buildings, there a tall white spire

51

rises into the pure blue sky. We see cottages covered with honeysuckle and grapevine; with their gardens of roses and lilies, and many old-fashioned flowers. In the spring, the country is one mass of pink and white blossoms, which load the passing breeze with delicate fragrance; in autumn the trees bend beneath rosy and yellow apples.

We drive through a fertile valley, where runs a placid river amid many meadows, gardens, and orchards, until at last it empties into a picturesque basin, where the landscape shows a harmonious blending of mountain and water, of cultivated fields and ancient forest trees. Here we see a quiet old town, whose roofs are green with the moss of many years, where willows and grassy mounds tell of a historic past, where the bells of ox-teams tinkle in the streets, and commerce itself wears a look of reminiscence. For we have come to the banks of that basin where the French, in the first years of the seventeenth century, laid the foundations of a settlement which, despite all its early misfortunes, has lasted until the present time, though it is the English tongue that is now spoken and the Englishman who is now the occupant.

Early in the leafy month of June, 1604, the French under De Monts sailed into this spacious basin, and saw for the first time its grassy meadows, its numerous streams, its cascades tumbling from the hills, its forest-clad mountains. "This," said Champlain, who called it Port Royal, "was the most commodious and pleasant place that we had yet seen in this country."

It appears that the adventurers left France in the early part of April. When the King had been once won over to the project, he consented to give De Monts and his associates an entire monopoly of the fur-trade throughout the wide domain of which he was to be the viceroy. The expedition was chiefly supported by the merchants of the Protestant town of La Rochelle, and was regarded with much jealousy by other commercial cities. Protestants were to enjoy in the new colony all the advantages they were then allowed in France. The Catholics were appeased by the condition that the conversion of the natives should be reserved especially for the priests of their own church.

The man of most note, after De Monts and Champlain, was Jean de Biencourt, a rich nobleman of Picardy, better known in Acadian history as the Baron de Poutrincourt, who had distinguished himself as a soldier in the civil wars. A man of energy and enterprise, he was well fitted to assist in the establishment of a colony.

De Monts and his associates reached without accident the low fir-covered shores of Nova Scotia, visited several of its harbours, and finally sailed into the Bay of Fundy, which was named Baie Française. The French explored the coast of the bay after leaving Port Royal, and discovered the river which the Indians called Ouigoudi, or highway, and De Monts renamed St. John, as he saw it first on the festival of that saint. Proceeding along the northern shores of the bay the expedition came to a river which falls into Passamaquoddy Bay, and now forms the boun-

dary between the United States and the eastern
provinces of Canada. This river ever since has been
called the river of the Holy Cross (Sainte-Croix)
though the name was first given by De Monts to an
islet, well within the mouth of the stream, which he
chose as the site of the first French settlement on
the northeast coast of America. Buildings were
soon erected for the accommodation of some eighty
persons, as well as a small fort for their protection
on the rocky islet. *

While the French settlement was preparing for
the winter, Champlain explored the eastern coast
from the St. Croix to the Penobscot, where he came
to the conclusion that the story of a large city on its
banks was evidently a mere invention of the imagi-
native mind. He also was the first of Europeans, so
far as we know, to look on the mountains and cliffs
of the island—so famous as a summer resort in these
later times—which he very aptly named Monts-
Déserts. During the three years Champlain remained in Acadia he made explorations and surveys
of the southern coasts of Nova Scotia from Canseau
to Port Royal, of the shores of the Bay of Fundy,
and of the coast of New England from the St. Croix
to Vineyard Sound.

Poutrincourt, who had received from De Monts
a grant of the country around Port Royal, left his
companions in their dreary home in the latter part
of August and sailed for France, with the object of
making arrangements for settling his new domain in

---

* Now known as Douchet Island ; no relics remain of the French
occupation.

Acadia. He found that very little interest was taken in the new colony of which very unsatisfactory reports were brought back to France by his companions though he himself gave a glowing account of its beautiful scenery and resources.

While Poutrincourt was still in France, he was surprised to learn of the arrival of De Monts with very unsatisfactory accounts of the state of affairs in the infant colony. The adventurers had very soon found St. Croix entirely unfitted for a permament settlement, and after a most wretched winter had removed to the sunny banks of the Annapolis, which was then known as the Equille,* and subsequently as the Dauphin. Poutrincourt and De Monts went energetically to work, and succeeded in obtaining the services of all the mechanics and labourers they required. The new expedition was necessarily composed of very unruly characters, who sadly offended the staid folk of that orderly bulwark of Calvinism, the town of La Rochelle. At last on the 13th of May, 1606, the *Jonas*, with its unruly crew all on board, left for the new world under the command of Poutrincourt. Among the passengers was L'Escarbot, a Paris advocate, a poet, and an historian, to whom we are indebted for a very sprightly account of early French settlement in America. De Monts, however, was unable to leave with his friends.

On the 27th July, the *Jonas* entered the basin of Port Royal with the flood-tide. A peal from the rude bastion of the little fort bore testimony to the

---

* Champlain says the river was named after a little fish caught there, *de grandeur d'un esplan.*

joy of the two solitary Frenchmen, who, with a faithful old Indian chief, were the only inmates of the post at that time. These men, La Taille and Miquellet, explained that Pontgravé and Champlain, with the rest of the colony, had set sail for France a few days previously, in two small vessels which they had built themselves. But there was no time to spend in vain regrets. Poutrincourt opened a hogshead of wine, and the fort was soon the scene of mirth and festivity. Poutrincourt set energetically to improve the condition of things, by making additions to the buildings, and clearing the surrounding land, which is exceedingly rich. The fort stood on the north bank of the river—on what is now the Granville side—opposite Goat Island, or about six miles from the present town of Annapolis.

L'Escarbot appears to have been the very life of the little colony. If anything occurred to dampen their courage, his fertile mind soon devised some plan of chasing away forebodings of ill. When Poutrincourt and his party returned during the summer of 1606 in ill spirits from Malebarre, now Cape Cod, where several men had been surprised and killed by the savages, they were met on their landing by a procession of Tritons, with Neptune at their head, who saluted the adventurers with merry songs. As they entered the arched gateway, they saw above their heads another happy device of L'Escarbot, the arms of France and the King's motto, "*Duo protegit unus*," encircled with laurels. Under this were the arms of De Monts and Poutrincourt, with their respective mottoes—"*Dabit deus*

his quoque finem," and *" In viâ virtuti nulla est via,"*
—also surrounded with evergreens.

L'Escarbot's ingenious mind did not fail him,
even in respect to the daily supply of fresh provisions, for he created a new order for the especial
benefit of the principal table, at which Poutrincourt,
he himself, and thirteen others sat daily. These

CHAMPLAIN'S PLAN OF PORT ROYAL IN ACADIA IN 1605.

Key to illustration : A, Workmen's dwelling ; B, Platform for cannon ; C,
Storehouse ; D, Residence for Champlain and Pontgravé ; E, Blacksmith's forge ;
F, Palisade ; G, Bakehouse ; H, Kitchen ; I, Gardens ; K, Burying ground ; L,
St. Lawrence River ; M, Moat ; N, Dwelling of De Monts ; and O, Ships' store-
house.

fifteen gentlemen constituted themselves into *l'Ordre
de Bon Temps*, one of whom was grandmaster for a
day, and bound to cater for the company. Each
tried, of course, to excel the other in the quantity of
game and fish they were able to gather from the

surrounding country, and the consequence was, Poutrincourt's table never wanted any of the luxuries that the river or forest could supply. At the dinner hour the grandmaster, with the insignia of his order, a costly collar around his neck, a staff in his hand, and a napkin on his shoulder, came into the hall at the head of his brethren, each of whom carried some dish. The Indians were frequent guests at their feasts, especially old Membertou, a famous Micmac or Souriquois chief, who always retained a warm attachment for the pale-faced strangers. Songs of La Belle France were sung; many a toast was drunk in some rare vintage,—the flames flew up the huge chimney,—the Indians squatted on the floor, laughing like the merry Frenchmen. When the pipe went around — with its lobster-like bowl and tube elaborately worked with porcupine quills—stories were told, and none excelled the Indians themselves in this part of the entertainment. At last, when the tobacco was all exhausted, the grandmaster resigned his regalia of office to his successor, who lost no time in performing his duties. Thus the long winter evenings passed in that lonely French fort at the verge of an untamed continent.

Then came bad news from France. Late in the spring of 1607, a vessel sailed into the basin with letters from De Monts that the colony would have to be broken up, as his charter had been revoked, and the Company could no longer support Port Royal. The Breton and Basque merchants, who were very hostile to De Monts's monopoly, had succeeded in influencing the government to withdraw its patronage from him and his associates. Soon afterwards the little colony regretfully left Port Royal, which never looked so lovely in their eyes as they passed on to the Bay of Fundy, and saw the whole country in the glory of mid-summer. The Indians, especially Membertou, watched the depart-ure of their new friends with unfeigned regret, and promised to look carefully after the safety of the fort and its contents.

As soon as Poutrincourt reached his native coun-try he did his best to make friends at the Court, as he was resolved on returning to Acadia, while Champlain decided to venture to the St. Lawrence, where I shall take up his memorable story later. Poutrincourt's prospects, for a time, were exceed-ingly gloomy. De Monts was able to assist him but very little, and the adventurous Baron himself was involved in debt and litigations, but he eventually succeeded in obtaining a renewal of his grant from the King, and interesting some wealthy traders in the enterprise. Then some difficulties of a religious character threatened to interfere with the success of the expedition. The society of Jesuits was, at this time, exceedingly influential at court, and, in conse-quence of their representations, the King ordered that Pierre Biard, professor of theology at Lyons, should accompany the expedition. Though Poutrin-court was a good Catholic, he mistrusted this reli-gious order, and succeeded in deceiving Father Biard, who was waiting for him at Bordeaux, by taking his departure from Dieppe in company with

Father Fléché, who was not a member of the Jesuits.

The ship entered Port Royal basin in the beginning of June, 1610. Here they were agreeably surprised to find the buildings and their contents perfectly safe, and their old friend Membertou, now a centenarian, looking as hale as ever, and overwhelmed with joy at the return of the friendly palefaces. Among the first things that Poutrincourt did, after his arrival, was to make converts of the Indians. Father Fléché soon convinced Membertou and all his tribe of the truths of Christianity. Membertou was named Henri, after the king; his chief squaw Marie, after the queen. The Pope, the Dauphin, Marguérite de Valois, and other ladies and gentlemen famous in the history of their times, became sponsors for the Micmac converts who were gathered into mother church on St. John's day, with the most imposing ceremonies that the French could arrange in that wild country.

Conscious of the influence of the Jesuits at Court, and desirous of counteracting any prejudice that might have been created against him, Poutrincourt decided to send his son, a fine youth of eighteen years, in the ship returning to France, with a statement showing his zeal in converting the natives of the new colony.

When this youthful ambassador reached France, Henry of Navarre had perished by the knife of Ravaillac, and Marie de' Medici, that wily, cruel, and false Italian, was regent during the minority of her son, Louis XIII. The Jesuits were now all-powerful at the Louvre, and it was decided that Fathers Biard and Ennemond Massé should accompany Biencourt to Acadia. The ladies of the Court, especially Madame de Guercheville, wife of Duke de la Rochefoucauld de Liancourt, whose reputation could not be assailed by the tongue of scandal, even in a state of society when virtue was too often the exception, interested themselves in the work of converting the savages of Acadia. The business of the Protestant traders of Dieppe was purchased and made over to the Jesuits. Thus did these indefatigable priests, for the first time, engage in the work of converting the savage in the American wilderness.

The vessel which took Biencourt and his friends back to Port Royal arrived on the 22nd of July, 1611, off the fort, where Poutrincourt and his colonists were exceedingly short of supplies. His very first act was to appoint his son as vice-admiral, while he himself went on to France with the hope of obtaining further aid about the middle of July.

The total number of persons in the colony was only twenty-two, including the two Jesuits, who immediately commenced to learn Micmac, as the first step necessary to the success of the work they had in hand. The two priests suffered many hardships, but they bore their troubles with a patience and resignation which gained them even the admiration of those who were not prepossessed in their favour. Massé, who had gone to live among the Indians, was nearly starved and smoked to death in their rude camps; but still he appears to have persevered in that course of life as long as he possibly

could.   About this time the priests had the consola-
tion of performing the last offices for the veteran
Membertou, the staunch friend of the French colonists.   On his death-bed he expressed a strong desire
to be buried with his forefathers, but the arguments
of his priestly advisers overcame his superstition,
and his remains were finally laid in consecrated
ground.

Matters looked very gloomy by the end of February, when a ship arrived very opportunely from
France with a small store of supplies.   The news
from Poutrincourt was most discouraging.   Unable
to raise further funds on his own responsibility, he
had accepted the proffer of assistance from Mme. de
Guercheville, who, in her zeal, had also bought from
De Monts all his claims over the colony, with the
exception of Port Royal, which belonged to Poutrincourt.   The King not only consented to the
transfer but gave her a grant of the territory extending from Florida to Canada.   The society of Jesuits
was therefore virtually in possession of North America as far as a French deed could give it away.   But
the French king forgot when he was making this lavish gift of a continent, that the British laid claims to
the same region and had already established a colony in Virginia, which was then an undefined territory, extending from Florida to New France.   Both
France and England were now face to face on the
new continent, and a daring English adventurer was
about to strike in Acadia the first blow for English
supremacy.

Such was the position of affairs at the time of the

arrival of the new vessel and cargo, which were under the control of Simon Imbert, who had formerly been a servant to Poutrincourt. Among the passengers was another Jesuit father, Gilbert Du Thet, who came out in the interests of Mme. de Guercheville and his own order. The two agents quarrelled from the very day they set out until they arrived at Port Royal, and then the colony took the matter up. At last the difficulties were settled by Du Thet receiving permission to return to France.

A few months later, at the end of May, 1613, another French ship anchored off Port Royal. She had been sent out with a fine supply of stores, not by Poutrincourt, but by Mme. de Guercheville, and was under the orders of M. Saussaye, a gentleman by birth and a man of ability. On board were two Jesuits, Fathers Quentin and Gilbert Du Thet and a number of colonists. Poutrincourt, it appeared, was in prison and ill, unable to do anything whatever for his friends across the ocean. This was, indeed, sad news for Biencourt and his faithful allies, who had been anxiously expecting assistance from France.

At Port Royal the new vessel took on board the two priests Biard and Massé, and sailed towards the coast of New England; for Saussaye's instructions were to found a new colony in the vicinity of Pentagoët (Penobscot). In consequence of the prevalent sea-fogs, however, they were driven to the island of Monts-Déserts, where they found a harbour which, it was decided, would answer all their purposes on the western side of Soames's Sound. Saussaye and

his party had commenced to erect buildings for the
new colony, when an event occurred which placed a
very different complexion on matters.

A man-of-war came sailing into the harbour, and
from her masthead floated, not the fleur-de-lis, but
the blood-red flag of England. This new-comer was
Samuel Argall, a young English sea captain, a
coarse, passionate, and daring man, who had been
some time associated with the fortunes of Virginia.
In the spring of 1613 he set sail in a stout vessel of
130 tons, carrying 14 guns and 60 men, for a cruise
to the coast of Maine for a supply of cod-fish, and
whilst becalmed off Monts-Déserts, some Indians
came on board and informed him of the presence of
the French in the vicinity of that island. He looked
upon the French as encroaching upon British territory, and in a few hours had destroyed the infant
settlement of St. Sauveur. Saussaye was perfectly
paralysed, and attempted no defence when he saw
that Argall had hostile intentions; but the Jesuit
Du Thet did his utmost to rally the men to arms,
and was the first to fall a victim. Fifteen of the
prisoners, including Saussaye and Massé, were
turned adrift in an open boat; but fortunately, they
managed to cross the bay and reach the coast of
Nova Scotia, where they met with some trading
vessels belonging to St. Malo. Father Biard and
the others were taken to Virginia by Argall Biard
subsequently reached England, and was allowed to
return home. All the rest of the prisoners taken at
St. Sauveur also found their way to France.

But how prospered the fortunes of Poutrincourt

whilst the fate of Port Royal was hanging in the scale ? As we have previously stated, he had been put into prison by his creditors, and had there lain ill for some months. When he was at last liberated, and appeared once more among his friends he succeeded in obtaining some assistance, and fitting out a small vessel, with a limited supply of stores for his colony. In the spring of 1614 he entered the basin of Annapolis for the last time, to find his son and followers wanderers in the woods, and only piles of ashes marking the site of the buildings on which he and his friends had expended so much time and money. The fate of Port Royal may be very briefly told. The Governor of Virginia, Sir Thomas Dale, was exceedingly irate when he heard of the encroachments of France on what he considered to be British territory by right of prior discovery—that of John Cabot—and immediately sent Argall, after his return from St. Sauveur, on an expedition to the northward. Argall first touched at St. Sauveur, and completed the work of destruction, and next stopped at St. Croix, where he also destroyed the deserted buildings. To such an extent did he show his enmity, that he even erased the fleur-de-lis and the initial of De Monts and others from the massive stone on which they had been carved. Biencourt and nearly all the inmates of the fort were absent some distance in the country, and returned to see the English in complete possession.

The destruction of Port Royal by Argall ends the first period in the history of Acadia as a French colony. Poutrincourt bowed to the relentless fate that

5

drove him from the shores he loved so well, and
returned to France, where he took employment in
the service of the king. Two years later he was
killed at the siege of Méri on the upper Seine, during the civil war which followed the successful intrigues of Marie de' Medici with Spain, to marry the
boy king, Louis XIII., to Anne of Austria, and his
sister, the Princess Elisabeth, to a Spanish prince.
On his tomb at St. Just, in Champagne, there was
inscribed an elaborate Latin epitaph, of which the
following is a translation :

> "Ye people so dear to God,
> inhabitants of New France,
> whom I brought over to the
> Faith of Christ. I am Poutrincourt, your
> great chief, in whom was once your hope.
> If envy deceived you, mourn for me.
> My courage destroyed me. I could not
> hand to another the glory
> that I won among you.
> Cease not to mourn for me.

Port Royal, in later years, arose from its ashes,
and the fleur-de-lis, or the red cross, floated from its
walls, according as the French or the English were
the victors in the long struggle that ensued for the
possession of Acadia. But before we continue the
story of its varying fortunes in later times, we must
proceed to the banks of the St. Lawrence, where the
French had laid the foundation of Quebec and New
France in the great valley, while Poutrincourt was
struggling vainly to make a new home for himself
and family by the side of the river of Port Royal.

VI.

SAMUEL CHAMPLAIN IN THE VALLEY OF THE ST. LAWRENCE.

(1608–1635.)

WHEN Samuel Champlain entered the St. Lawrence River for the second time, in 1608, after his three years' explorations in Acadia, and laid the foundation of the present city of Quebec, the only Europeans on the Atlantic coast of America were a few Spaniards at St. Augustine, and a few Englishmen at Jamestown. The first attempt of the English, under the inspiration of the great Ralegh, to establish a colony in the fine country to the north of Spanish Florida, then known as Virginia, is only remembered for the mystery which must always surround the fate of Virginia Dare and the little band of colonists who were left on the island of Roanoke. Adventurous Englishmen, Gosnold, Pring, and Weymouth, had even explored the coast of the present United States as far as the Kennebec before the voyages of Champlain and Poutrincourt, and the first is said to have given the name of Cape

Cod to the point named Malebarre by the French.
It was not, however, until 1607 that Captain Newport, representing the great company of Virginia, to
whom King James II. gave a charter covering the
territory of an empire, brought the first permanent
English colony of one hundred persons up the
James River in Chesapeake Bay.

From this time forward France and England became rivals in America. In the first years of the
seventeenth century were laid the foundations not
only of the Old Dominion of Virginia, which was in
later times to form so important a state among the
American commonwealths, but also of the New
Dominion whose history may be said to commence
on the shores of Port Royal. But Acadia was not
destined to be the great colony of France—the centre of her imperial aspirations in America. The
story of the French in Acadia, from the days of De
Monts and Poutrincourt, until the beginning of the
eighteenth century when it became an English possession, is at most only a series of relatively unimportant episodes in the history of that scheme of
conquest which was planned in the eighteenth
century in the palace of Versailles and in the old
castle of St. Louis on the heights of Quebec, whose
interesting story I must now tell.

When Champlain returned to France in 1607 De
Monts obtained from Henry the Fourth a monopoly of the Canadian fur-trade for a year, and immediately fitted out two vessels, one of which was given
to Pontgravé, who had taken part in previous expeditions to the new world. Champlain was appointed

Champlain—

by De Monts as his representative, and practically
held the position of lieutenant-governor under different viceroys, with all necessary executive and
judicial powers, from this time until his death,
twenty-seven years later.

Champlain arrived on the 3rd of July off the
promontory of Quebec, which has ever since borne
the name given to it by the Algonquin tribes, in
whose language *Kebec* means such a strait or narrow-
ing of a river as actually occurs at this part of the
St. Lawrence. The French pioneers began at once
to clear away the trees and dig cellars on an accessible point of land which is now the site of Champlain
market in what is called " the lower town " of the
modern city. Champlain has left us a sketch of the
buildings he erected—*habitation* as he calls them—
and my readers will get from the illustration opposite an idea of the plan he followed. Champlain
made one of the buildings his headquarters for
twelve years, until he built a fort on the heights,
which was the beginning of that famous Fort and
Castle of St. Louis to which reference is so constantly made in the histories of New France.

Champlain was obliged immediately after his
arrival at Quebec to punish some conspirators who
had agreed to murder him and hand over the property of the post to the Basque fishermen frequenting
Tadousac. The leader, Jean du Val, was hanged
after a fair trial and three of his accomplices sent to
France, where they expiated their crime in the galleys. Great explorers had in those days to run such
risks among their followers and crews, not affected

by their own enthusiasm. Only three years later a
famous sailor and discoverer of new seas and lands,
was left to die among the waste of waters which ever
since have recalled the name of Henry Hudson.

HABITATION DE QUEBEC, FROM CHAMPLAIN'S SKETCH.
Key to illustration : A, Storehouse ; B, Dovecote ; C, Workmen's lodgings and
armoury ; D, Lodgings for mechanics ; E, Dial ; F, Blacksmith's shop and workmen's lodgings ; G, Galleries ; H, Champlain's residence ; I, Gate and draw-
bridge ; L, Walk ; M, Moat ; N, Platform for cannon ; O, Garden ; P, Kitchen ;
P, Vacant space ; R, St. Lawrence.

During the summer of 1609 Champlain decided to
join an expedition of the Algonquin and Huron
Indians of Canada against the Iroquois, whose country lay between the Hudson and Genesee rivers and
westward of a beautiful lake which he found could
be reached by the river, then known as the River of

the Iroquois—because it was their highway to the St. Lawrence—and now called the Richelieu.

Canada was to pay most dearly in later years, as these pages will show, for the alliance Champlain made with the inveterate enemies of the ablest and bravest Indians of North America. Nowhere in his own narrative of his doings in the colony does he give us an inkling of the motives that influenced him. We may, however, fairly believe that he underrated the strength and warlike qualities of the Iroquois, and believed that the allied nations of Canada would sooner or later, with his assistance, win the victory. If he had shown any hesitation to ally himself with the Indians of Canada, he might have hazarded the fortunes, and even ruined the fur-trade which was the sole basis of the little colony's existence for many years. The dominating purpose of his life in Canada, it is necessary to remember, was the exploration of the unknown region to which the rivers and lakes of Canada led, and that could never have been attempted, had he by any cold or unsympathetic conduct alienated the Indians who guarded the waterways over which he had to pass before he could unveil the mysteries of the western wilderness.

In the month of June Champlain and several Frenchmen commenced their ascent of the Richelieu in a large boat, in company with several bark canoes filled with sixty Canadian Indians. When they reached the rapids near the lovely basin of Chambly —named after a French officer and seignior in later times—the French boat could not be taken any fur-

ther.   It was sent back to Quebec while Champlain
and two others, armed with the arquebus, a short
gun with a matchlock, followed the Indians through
the woods to avoid this dangerous part of the river.
The party soon reached the safe waters of the Richelieu and embarked once more in their canoes.   For
the first time Champlain had abundant opportunities
to note the customs of the Indians on a war-path,
their appeals to evil spirits to help them against their
enemies, their faith in dreams, and their methods of
marching in a hostile country.   The party passed
into the beautiful lake which has ever since that day
borne the great Frenchman's name; they saw its
numerous islets, the Adirondacks in the west, and
the Green Mountains in the east.   Paddling cau-
tiously for some nights along the western shore, they
reached at last on the evening of the 29th of July a
point of land, identified in later days as the site of
Ticonderoga, so celebrated in the military annals of
America.   Here they found a party of Iroquois, who
received them with shouts of defiance, but retreated
to the woods for the night with the understanding
on both sides that the fight would take place as
soon as the sun rose next morning.   The allies remained in their canoes, dancing, singing, and hurling
insults at their foes, who did not fail to respond with
similar demonstrations.

Next morning, two hundred stalwart Iroquois
warriors, led by three chiefs with conspicuous plumes,
marched from their barricade of logs and were met
by the Canadian Indians.   Champlain immediately
fired on the chiefs with such success that two of

them fell dead and the other was wounded and died later. " Our Indians," writes Champlain, "shouted triumphantly, and then the arrows began to fly furiously from both parties. The Iroquois were clearly amazed that two chiefs should have been so suddenly killed although they were protected from arrows by a sort of armour made of strong twigs and filled with cotton. While I was reloading, one of my men, who was not seen by the enemy, fired a shot from the woods and so frightened the Iroquois, no longer led by their chiefs, that they lost courage and fled precipitately into the forest, where we followed and succeeded in killing a number and taking ten or twelve prisoners. On our side only ten or fifteen were wounded, and they very soon recovered."

On their return to the St. Lawrence, the Indians gave Champlain an illustration of their cruelty towards their captives. When they had harangued the Iroquois and narrated some of the tortures that his nation had inflicted on the Canadians in previous times, he was told to sing, and when he did so, as Champlain naïvely says, " the song was sad to hear."

A fire was lit, and when it was very hot, the Indians seized a burning brand and applied it to the naked body of their victim, who was tied to a tree. Sometimes they poured water on his wounds, tore off his nails, and poured hot gum on his head from which they had cut the scalp. They opened his arm near the wrists, and pulled at his tendons and when they would not come off, they used their knives. The poor wretch was forced to cry out now and then in his agony, and it made Champlain heartsick to see him so maltreated, but generally he exhibited so much courage and stoicism that he seemed as if he were not suffering at all. Champlain remonstrated with them, and was at last allowed to put a speedy end to the sufferings of the unhappy warrior. But even when he was dead, they cut the body into pieces and attempted to make the brother of the victim swallow his heart. Champlain might well say that it was better for an Indian to die on the battlefield or kill himself when wounded, than fall into the hands of such merciless enemies.

Soon after this memorable episode in the history of Canada, Champlain crossed the ocean to consult De Monts, who could not persuade the king and his minister to grant him a renewal of his charter. The merchants of the seaboard had combined to represent the injury the trade of the kingdom would sustain by continuing a monopoly of Canadian furs. De Monts, however, made the best arrangements he could under such unfavourable conditions, and Champlain returned to the St. Lawrence in the spring of 1610. During the summer he assisted the Canadian allies in a successful assault on a large body of the Iroquois who had raised a fortification at the mouth of the Richelieu, and all of whom were killed. It was on this occasion, when a large number of Canadian nations were assembled, that he commenced the useful experiment of sending Frenchmen into the Ottawa valley to learn the customs and language of the natives, and act as interpreters afterwards.

The French at Quebec heard of the assassination

of Henry the Fourth who had been a friend of the colony. Champlain went to France in the autumn of 1610, and returned to Canada in the following spring. In the course of the summer he passed some days on the island of Mont Royal where he proposed establishing a post where the allied nations could meet for purposes of trade and consultation, as he told the Ottawa Indians at a later time when he was in their country. He made a clearing on a little point to which he gave the name of Place Royale, now known as Pointe-à-Callières, on a portion of which the hospital of the Grey Nuns was subsequently built. It was not, however, until thirty years later that the first permanent settlement was made on the island, and the foundations laid of the great city which was first named Ville-Marie.

During the next twenty-four years Champlain passed some months in France at different times, according to the exigencies of the colony. One of the most important changes he brought about was the formation of a new commercial association, for the purpose of reconciling rival mercantile interests. To give strength and dignity to the enterprise, the Count de Soissons, Charles of Bourbon, one of the royal sons of France, was placed at the head, but he died suddenly, and was replaced by Prince de Condé, Henry of Bourbon, also a royal prince, best known as the father of the victor of Rocroy, and the opponent of Marie de' Medici during her intrigues with Spain. It was in this same year that he entered into an engagement with a rich Calvinist, Nicholas Boullé, to marry his daughter Helen, then a child,

when she had arrived at a suitable age, on the condition that the father would supply funds to help
the French in their Canadian experiment. The
marriage was not consummated until ten years later,
and Champlain's wife, whose Christian name he gave
to the pretty islet opposite Montreal harbour, spent
four years in the settlement. The happiness of a
domestic life was not possible in those early Canadian days, and a gentle French girl probably soon
found herself a mere luxury amid the savagery of
her surroundings. Helen Champlain has no place
in this narrative, and we leave her with the remark
that she was converted by her husband, and on his
death retired to the seclusion of an Ursuline convent in France. No child was born to bear the
name and possibly increase the fame of Champlain.

On his return to Canada, in the spring of 1613,
Champlain decided to explore the western waters of
Canada. L'Escarbot, who published his "New
France," soon after his return from Acadia, tells us
that "Champlain promised never to cease his efforts
until he has found there [in Canada] a western or
northern sea opening up the route to China which
so many have so far sought in vain." While at
Paris, during the winter of 1612, Champlain saw a
map which gave him some idea of the great sea
which Hudson had discovered. At the same time
he heard from a Frenchman, Nicholas de Vignau,
who had come to Paris direct from the Ottawa valley, that while among the Algonquin Indians he had
gone with a party to the north where they had found
a salt water sea, on whose shores were the remains

of an English ship. The Indians had also, according to Vignau, brought back an English lad, whom they intended to present to Champlain when he made his promised visit to the Upper Ottawa.

Champlain probably thought he was at last to realise the dream of his life. Accompanied by Vignau, four other Frenchmen, and an Indian guide, he ascended the great river, with its numerous lakes, cataracts, and islets. He saw the beautiful fall to which ever since has been given the name of Rideau —a name also extended to the river, whose waters make the descent at this point—on account of its striking resemblance to a white curtain. Next he looked into the deep chasm of mist, foam, and raging waters, which the Indians called Asticou or Cauldron (Chaudière), on whose sides and adjacent islets, then thickly wooded, now stand great mills where the electric light flashes amid the long steel saws as they cut into the huge pine logs which the forests of the Ottawa yearly contribute to the commerce and wealth of Canada. At the Chaudière the Indians evoked the spirits of the waters, and offered them gifts of tobacco if they would ward off misfortune. The expedition then passed up the noble expansion of the river known as the Chats, and saw other lakes and cataracts that gave variety and grandeur to the scenery of the river of the Algonquins, as it was then called, and reached at last, after a difficult portage, the country around Allumette lake, where Nicholas de Vignau had passed the previous winter. Two hundred and fifty-four years later, on an August day, a farmer unearthed on this old por-

tage route in the district of North Renfrew, an old
brass astrolabe of Paris make, dated 1603; the in-
strument used in those distant days for taking
astronomical observations and ascertaining the latitude. No doubt it had belonged to Champlain,
who lost it on this very portage by way of Muskrat

CHAMPLAIN'S LOST ASTROLABE.

and Mud lakes, as from this place he ceases to give
us the correct latitudes which he had previously
been able to do.

Among the Algonquin Indians of this district,
who lived in rudely-built bark cabins or camps, and
were hunters as well as cultivators of the soil, he
soon found out that there was not a word of truth
in the story which Nicholas de Vignau had told him

of a journey to a northern sea, but that it was the invention of " the most impudent liar whom I have seen for a long time." Champlain did not punish him, though the Indians urged him to put him to death.

Champlain remained a few days among the Indians, making arrangements for future explorations, and studying the customs of the people. He was especially struck with their method of burial. Posts supported a tablet or slab of wood on which was a rude carving supposed to represent the features of the dead. A plume decorated the head of a chief; his weapons meant a warrior; a small bow and one arrow, a boy; a kettle, a wooden spoon, an iron pot, and a paddle, a woman or girl. These figures were painted in red or yellow. The dead slept below, wrapped in furs and surrounded by hatchets, knives, or other treasures which they might like to have in the far-off country to which they had gone; for, as Champlain says, " they believe in the immortality of the soul."

Champlain made no attempt to proceed further up the river. Before leaving the Upper Ottawa, he made a cedar cross, showing the arms of France—a custom of the French explorers, as Cartier's narrative tells us—and fixed it on an elevation by the side of the lake. He also promised Tessouat to return in the following year and assist him against the Iroquois.

The next event of moment in the history of the colony was the arrival in 1615 of Fathers Denis Jamay, Jean d'Olbeau, and Joseph Le Caron, and the lay brother Pacifique du Plessis, who belonged to the mendicant order of the Recollets, or reformed branch of the Franciscans, so named from their founder, St. Francis d'Assisi. They built near the French post at Quebec a little chapel which was placed in charge of Father Jamay and Brother Du Plessis, while Jean d'Olbeau went to live among the Montagnais and Joseph Le Caron among the Hurons of the West.

During the summer of 1615 Champlain fulfilled his pledge to accompany the allied tribes on an expedition into the country of the Iroquois. This was the most important undertaking of Champlain's life in Canada, not only on account of the length of the journey, and the knowledge he obtained of the lake region, but of the loss of prestige he must have sustained among both Iroquois and Canadian Indians who had previously thought the Frenchman invincible. The enemy were reached not by the usual route of the Richelieu and Lake Champlain, considered too dangerous from their neighbourhood to the Iroquois, but by a long detour by way of the Ottawa valley, Georgian Bay, Lake Simcoe, and the portages, rivers, and lakes that lead into the River Trent, which falls into the pretty bay of Quinté, at the eastern end of Lake Ontario, whence they could pass rapidly into the country of the Five Nations.

Accompanied by Stephen Brulé, a noted Indian interpreter, a servant, and eight Indians, Champlain left Montreal about the middle of July, ascended the Ottawa, and paddled down the Mattawa to the lake of the Nipissings, where he had interviews with

6

the Indians who were dreaded by other tribes as sorcerers.

The canoes of the adventurous Frenchmen went down French River, and at last reached the waters of the great Fresh Water Sea, the *Mer Douce* of Champlain's maps, and now named Lake Huron in memory of the hapless race that once made their home in that wild region. Passing by the western shore of the picturesque district of Muskoka, the party landed at the foot of the bay and found themselves before long among the villages of the Hurons, whose country lay then between Nottawasaga Bay and Lake Simcoe. Here Champlain saw the triple palisades, long houses, containing several households, and other distinctive features of those Indian villages, one of which Cartier found at the foot of Mont Royal.

In the village of Carhagouaha, where the palisades were as high as thirty-five feet, Champlain met Father Le Caron, the pioneer of these intrepid missionaries who led the way to the head-waters and tributaries of the great lakes. For the first time in that western region the great Roman Catholic ceremony of the Mass was celebrated in the presence of Champlain and wondering Indian warriors. At the town of Cahiagué, the Indian capital, comprising two hundred cabins, and situated within the modern township of Orillia, he was received with great rejoicings, and preparations immediately made for the expedition against the Iroquois. Stephen Brulé undertook the dangerous mission of communicating with the Andastes, a friendly nation near the head-

waters of the Susquehanna, who had promised to
bring five hundred warriors to the assistance of the
Canadian allied forces.

The expedition reached the eastern end of Lake
Ontario at the beginning of October by the circuitous route I have already mentioned, crossed to the

ONONDAGA FORT IN THE IROQUOIS COUNTRY ; FROM CHAMPLAIN'S
SKETCH.

other side somewhere near Sackett's harbour, and
soon arrived in the neighbourhood of the Onondaga
fort, which is placed by the best authorities a few
miles to the south of Lake Oneida. It was on the
afternoon of the 10th of October, when the woods

wear their brightest foliage, that the allied Indians commenced the attack with all that impetuosity and imprudence peculiar to savages on such occasions. The fort was really a village protected by four concentric rows of palisades, made up of pieces of heavy timber, thirty feet in height, and supporting an inside gallery or parapet where the defenders were relatively safe from guns and arrows. The fort was by the side of a pond from which water was conducted to gutters under the control of the besieged for the purpose of protecting the outer walls from fire. Champlain had nine Frenchmen under his direction—eight of them having accompanied Father Le Caron to the Huron village. It was utterly impossible to give anything like method to the Indian assaults on the strong works of the enemy. Champlain had a high wooden platform built, and placed on it several of his gunners who could fire into the village, but the Iroquois kept well under cover and very little harm was done. The attempts to fire the palisades were fruitless on account of the want of method shown by the attacking parties. At last the allied Indians became disheartened when they saw Champlain himself was wounded and no impression was made on the fort. They returned to the cover of the woods, and awaited for a few days the arrival of Stephen Brulé and the expected reinforcements of Andastes. But when nearly a week had passed, and the scouts brought no news of Indians from the Susquehanna, the Canadians determined to return home without making another attack on the village. And here, I may mention, that Stephen Brulé was not seen at Quebec until three years later. It appeared then, from his account of his wanderings, that he succeeded after some vexatious delay in bringing the Andastes to Oneida Lake only to find that they had left the country of the Iroquois, who tortured him for a while, and then, pleased with his spirit, desisted, and eventually gave him his liberty. He is reported to have reached in his wanderings the neighbourhood of Lake Superior, where he found copper, but we have no satisfactory information on this point.*

On their return to Canada, the Indians carried Champlain and other wounded men in baskets made of withes. They reached the Huron villages on the 20th of December after a long and wearisome journey. Champlain remained in their country for four months, making himself acquainted with their customs and the nature of the region, of which he has given a graphic description. Towards the last of April, Champlain left the Huron villages, and arrived at Quebec near the end of June, to the great delight of his little colony, who were in doubt of his ever coming back.

Another important event in the history of those days was the coming into the country of several Jesuit missionaries in 1625, when the Duke of Ventadour, a staunch friend of the order, was made viceroy of the colony in place of the Duke of Montmorency, who had purchased the rights of the Prince of Condé when he was imprisoned in the

* Brulé was murdered by the Hurons in 1634 at Toanché, an Indian village in the West.

Bastile for having taken up arms against the King.
These Jesuit missionaries, Charles Lalemant, who
was the first superior in Canada, Jean de Brebeuf,
Ennemond Massé, the priest who had been in Acadia,
François Charton, and Gilbert Buret, the two latter
lay brothers, were received very coldly by the officials of Quebec, whose business interests were at
that time managed by the Huguenots, William and
Emeric Caen. They were, however, received by
the Recollets, who had removed to a convent,
Notre-Dame des Anges, which they had built by
the St. Charles, of sufficient strength to resist an
attack which, it is reported on sufficiently good
authority, the Iroquois made in 1622. The first
Jesuit establishment was built in 1625 on the point
at the meeting of the Lairet and St. Charles, where
Cartier had made his little fort ninety years before.

We come now to a critical point in the fortunes
of the poor and struggling colony. The ruling spirit
of France, Cardinal Richelieu, at last intervened in
Canadian affairs, and formed the Company of New
France, generally called the company of the Hundred Associates, who received a perpetual monopoly
of the fur-trade, and a control of all other commerce
for sixteen years, beside dominion over an immense
territory extending from Florida to the Arctic Seas,
and from the Gulf of St. Lawrence to the great
Fresh Water Sea, the extent of which was not yet
known. Richelieu placed himself at the head of the
enterprise. No Huguenot thenceforth was to be
allowed to enter the colony under any conditions.
The company was bound to send out immediately a

number of labourers and mechanics, with all their necessary tools, to the St. Lawrence, and four thousand other colonists in the course of fifteen years, and to support them for three years. Not only was the new association a great commercial corporation, but it was a feudal lord as well. Richelieu introduced in a modified form the old feudal tenure of France, with the object of creating a Canadian *noblesse* and encouraging men of good birth and means to emigrate and develop the resources of the country. This was the beginning of that seigniorial tenure which lasted for two centuries and a quarter.

Champlain was re-appointed lieutenant-governor and had every reason to believe that at last a new spirit would be infused into the affairs of the colony. Fate, however, was preparing for him a cruel blow. In the spring of 1628, the half-starved men of Quebec were anxiously looking for the provisions and men expected from France, when they were dismayed by the news that an English fleet was off the Saguenay. This disheartening report was immediately followed by a message to surrender the fort of Quebec to the English admiral, David Kirk. War had been declared between England and France, through the scheming chiefly of Buckingham, the rash favourite of Charles the First, and an intense hater of the French King for whose queen, Anne of Austria, he had developed an ardent and unrequited passion. English settlements were by this time established on Massachusetts Bay and England was ambitious of extending her dominion over North

America, even in those countries where France had preceded her.

Admiral Kirk, who was the son of a gentleman in Derbyshire, and one of the pioneers of the colonisation of Newfoundland, did not attempt the taking of Quebec in 1628, as he was quite satisfied with the capture off the Saguenay, of a French expedition, consisting of four armed vessels and eighteen transports, under the command of Claude de Roquemont, who had been sent by the new company to relieve Quebec. Next year, however, in July, he brought his fleet again to the Saguenay, and sent three ships to Quebec under his brothers, Lewis and Thomas. Champlain immediately surrendered, as his little garrison were half-starved and incapable of making any resistance, and the English flag floated for the first time on the fort of St. Louis. Champlain and his companions, excepting thirteen who remained with the English, went on board the English ships, and Lewis Kirk was left in charge of Quebec. On the way down the river, the English ships met a French vessel off Malbaie, under the command of Emeric Caen, and after a hot fight she became also an English prize.

When the fleet arrived in the harbour of Plymouth, the English Admiral heard to his amazement that peace had been declared some time before, and that all conquests made by the fleets or armies of either France or England after 24th April, 1629, must be restored. The Kirks and Alexander used every possible exertion to prevent the restoration of Quebec and Port Royal, which was also in the possession of the English. Three years elapsed before Champlain obtained a restitution of his property, which had been illegally seized. The King of England, Charles I., had not only renewed a charter, which his father had given to a favourite, Sir William Alexander, of the present province of Nova Scotia, then a part of Acadia, but had also extended it to the " county and lordship of Canada." Under these circumstances Charles delayed the negotiations for peace by every possible subterfuge. At last the French King, whose sister was married to Charles, agreed to pay the large sum of money which was still owing to the latter as the balance of the dower of his queen. Charles had already commenced that fight with his Commons, which was not to end until his head fell on the block, and was most anxious to get money wherever and as soon as he could. The result was the treaty of St. Germain-en-Laye, signed on March 29, 1632. Quebec as well as Port Royal —to whose history I shall refer in the following chapter—were restored to France, and Champlain was again in his fort on Cape Diamond in the last week of May, 1633. A number of Jesuits, who were favoured by Richelieu, accompanied him and henceforth took the place of the Recollets in the mission work of the colony. In 1634, there were altogether eight Jesuit priests in the country. They appear to have even borrowed the name of the Recollet convent, *Notre Dame des Anges*, and given it to their own establishment and seigniory by the St. Charles.

During the last three years of Champlain's life in Canada no events of importance occurred. The

Company of the Hundred Associates had been most seriously crippled by the capture of the expedition in 1628, and were not able to do very much for the colony. The indefatigable lieutenant-governor, true to his trust, succeeded in building a little fort in 1634 at the mouth of the St. Maurice, and founded the present city of Three Rivers, as a bulwark against the Iroquois. It had, however, been for years a trading place, where Brother Du Plessis spent some time in instructing the Indian children and people in the Catholic religion, and was instrumental in preventing a rising of the Montagnais Indians who had become discontented and proposed to destroy the French settlements.

On Christmas Day, 1635, Champlain died from a paralytic stroke in the fort, dominating the great river by whose banks he had toiled and struggled for so many years as a faithful servant of his king and country. Father Le Jeune pronounced the eulogy over his grave, the exact site of which is even now a matter of dispute.

What had the patient and courageous Frenchman of Brouage accomplished during the years—nearly three decades—since he landed at the foot of Cape Diamond ? On the verge of the heights a little fort of logs and a château of masonry, a few clumsy and wretched buildings on the point below, a cottage and clearing of the first Canadian farmer Hébert, the ruins of the Recollet convent and the mission house of the Jesuits on the St. Charles, the chapel of Notre-Dame de Recouvrance, which he had built close to the fort to commemorate the restoration of

Quebec to the French, the stone manor-house of the first seignior of Canada, Robert Giffard of Beauport, a post at Tadousac and another at Three Rivers, perhaps two hundred Frenchmen in the whole valley. These were the only visible signs of French dominion on the banks of the St. Lawrence, when the cold blasts of winter sighed Champlain's requiem on the heights whence his fancy had so often carried him to Cathay. The results look small when we think of the patience and energy shown by the great man whose aspirations took so ambitious and hopeful a range. It is evident by the last map he drew of the country, that he had some idea of the existence of a great lake beyond Lake Huron, and of the Niagara Falls, though he had seen neither. He died, however, ignorant of the magnitude, number, and position of the western lakes, and still deluded by visions, as others after him, of a road to Asia. No one, however, will deny that he was made of the heroic mould from which come founders of states, and the Jesuit historian Charlevoix has, with poetic justice, called him the " Father of New France."

VII.

GENTLEMEN-ADVENTURERS IN ACADIA.

(1614-1677.)

WE must now leave the lonely Canadian colonists on the snow-clad heights of Quebec to mourn the death of their great leader, and return to the shores of Acadia to follow the fortunes of Biencourt and his companions whom we last saw near the smoking ruins of their homes on the banks of the Annapolis. We have now come to a strange chapter of Canadian history, which has its picturesque aspect as well as its episodes of meanness, cupidity, and inhumanity. As we look back to those early years of Acadian history, we see rival chiefs with their bands of retainers engaged in deadly feuds, and storming each other's fortified posts as though they were the castles of barons living in mediæval times. We see savage Micmacs and Etchemins of Acadia, only too willing to aid in the quarrels and contests of the white men who hate each with a malignity that even the Indian cannot excel; closely shorn, ill-clad mendicant friars who see only good in those who

help their missions; grave and cautious Puritans trying to find their advantage in the rivalry of their
French neighbours; a Scotch nobleman and courtier
who would be a king in Acadia as well as a poet in
England; Frenchmen who claim to have noble blood
in their veins, and wish to be lords of a wide American domain; a courageous wife who lays aside the
gentleness of a woman's nature and fights as bravely
as any knight for the protection of her home and
what she believes to be her husband's rights. These
are among the figures that we see passing through
the shadowy vista which opens before us as we look
into the depths of the Acadian wilderness two centuries and a half ago.

Among the French adventurers, whose names are
intimately associated with the early history of
Acadia, no one occupies a more prominent position
than Charles de St. Etienne, the son of a Huguenot,
Claude de la Tour, who claimed to be of noble birth.
The La Tours had become so poor that they were
forced, like so many other nobles of those times, to
seek their fortune in the new world. Claude and his
son, then probably fourteen years of age, came to
Port Royal with Poutrincourt in 1610. In the various vicissitudes of the little settlement the father
and his son participated, and after it had been destroyed by Argall, they remained with Biencourt
and his companions. In the course of time, the
elder La Tour established a trading post on the
peninsula at the mouth of the Penobscot—in Acadian history a prominent place, as often in possession of the English as the French.

Biencourt and his companions appear to have had some accessions to their number during the years that followed the Virginian's visit. They built rude cabins on the banks of the Annapolis, and cultivated patches of ground after a fashion, beside raising a fort of logs and earth near Cape Sable, called indifferently Fort Louis or Lomeron. It has been generally believed that Biencourt died in Acadia about 1623, after making over all his rights to Charles La Tour, who was his personal friend and follower from his boyhood. Recently, however, the discovery of some old documents in Paris throws some doubt on the generally accepted statement of the place of his death.*

It is quite certain, however, whether Biencourt died in France or Acadia, young La Tour assumed after 1623 the control of Fort St. Louis and all other property previously held by the former. In 1626 the elder La Tour was driven from the Penobscot by English traders from Plymouth who took possession of the fort and held it for some years. He now recognised the urgent necessity of having his position in Acadia ratified and strengthened by the French king, and consequently went on a mission to France in 1627.

About this time the attention of prominent men in England was called to the fact that the French had settlements in Acadia. Sir William Alexander, afterwards the Earl of Stirling, a favourite of King James the Fourth of Scotland and First of England, and an author of several poetical tragedies, wished

* See *Trans. Roy. Soc. Canada*, vol. x., sec. 2, p. 93.

to follow the example of Sir Frederick Gorges, one of the promoters of the colonisation of New England. He had no difficulty in obtaining from James, as great a pedant as himself, a grant of Acadia, which he named Nova Scotia. When Charles the First became king, he renewed the patent, and also, at the persuasion of the ambitious poet, created an order of Nova Scotia baronets, who were obliged to assist in the settlement of the country, which was thereafter to be divided into " baronies." Sir William Alexander, however, did not succeed in making any settlement in Nova Scotia, and did not take any definite measures to drive the French from his princely, though savage, domain until about the time Claude de la Tour was engaged in advocating the claims of his son in Europe, where we must follow him.

The elder La Tour arrived at an opportune time in France. Cardinal Richelieu had just formed the Company of the Hundred Associates, and it was agreed that aid should at once be sent to Charles de la Tour, who was to be the King's lieutenant in Acadia. Men and supplies for the Acadian settlement were on board the squadron, commanded by Roquemont, who was captured by Kirk in the summer of 1628. On board one of the prizes was Claude de la Tour, who was carried to London as prisoner. Then to make the position for Charles de la Tour still more hazardous, Sir William Alexander's son arrived at Port Royal in the same year, and established on the Granville side a small Scotch colony as the commencement of a larger settlement in the

future.   Charles de la Tour does not appear to have
remained in Port Royal, but to have retired to the
protection of his own fort at Cape Sable, which
the English did not attempt to attack at that time.

In the meantime the elder La Tour was in high
favour at London.   He won the affections of one
of the Queen's maids of honour, and was easily persuaded by Alexander and others interested in
American colonisation, to pledge his allegiance to
the English king.   He and his son were made baronets of Nova Scotia, and received large grants of
land or " baronies " in the new province.   As Alexander was sending an expedition in 1630 with additional colonists and supplies for his colony in Nova
Scotia, Claude de la Tour agreed to go there for the
purpose of persuading his son to accept the honours
and advantages which the King of England had con-
ferred upon him.   The ambitious Scotch poet, it
was clear, still hoped that his arguments in favour
of retaining Acadia, despite the treaty of Susa,
made on the 24th of April, 1629, would prevail with
the King.   It was urged that as Port Royal was on
soil belonging to England by right of Cabot's
discovery, and the French had not formally claimed
the sovereignty of Acadia since the destruction of
their settlement by Argall, it did not fall within
the actual provisions of a treaty which referred only
to conquests made after its ratification.

Charles de la Tour would not yield to the appeals
of his father to give up the fort at Cape Sable, and
obliged the English vessels belonging to Alexander
to retire to the Scotch settlement by the Annapolis

basin. The elder La Tour went on to the same place, where he remained until his son persuaded him to join the French at Fort St. Louis, where the news had come that the King of France was determined on the restoration of Port Royal as well as Quebec. It was now decided to build a new fort on the River St. John, which would answer the double purpose of strengthening the French in Acadia, and driving the British out of Port Royal. Whilst this work was in course of construction, another vessel arrived from France with the welcome news that the loyalty of Charles de la Tour was appreciated by the King, who had appointed him as his lieutenant-governor over Fort Louis, Port La Tour, and dependencies.

By the treaty of St. Germain-en-Laye the French regained Acadia and were inclined to pay more attention to the work of colonisation. Richelieu sent out an expedition to take formal possession of New France, and Isaac de Launoy de Razilly, a military man of distinction, a Knight of Malta, and a friend of the great minister, was appointed governor of all Acadia. He brought with him a select colony, composed of artisans, farmers, several Capuchin friars, and some gentlemen, among whom were two whose names occupy a prominent place in the annals of Acadia and Cape Breton. One of them was Nicholas Denys, who became in later years the first governor of Cape Breton, where he made settlements at Saint Anne's and Saint Peter's, and also wrote an historical and descriptive account of the French Atlantic possessions. The most prominent

7

Frenchman after Razilly himself, was Charles de Menou, Chevalier d'Aunay and son of René de Menou, lord of Charnizay, who was of noble family, and became one of the members of the King's council of state at the time the disputes between his son and Charles de la Tour were at their height. Charles de Menou, or d'Aunay, as I shall generally name him, was made Razilly's deputy, and consequently at the outset of his career assumed a prominence in the country that must have deeply irritated young La Tour, who still remained one of the King's lieutenants and probably expected, until Razilly's arrival, to be the head of the colony.

Captain Forrester, in command of the Scotch colony at Port Royal, gave up the post to Razilly in accordance with the orders of the English king, who had acted with much duplicity throughout the negotiations. The fort was razed to the ground, and the majority of the Scotch, who had greatly suffered from disease and death, left Acadia, though several remained and married among the French colonists. This was the end of Alexander's experiment in colonising Acadia and founding a colonial *noblesse.*

Razilly made his settlement at La Hève, on the Atlantic shore of Nova Scotia, and Denys had a mill and trading establishment in the vicinity. Port Royal was improved and the post at Penobscot occupied. D'Aunay was given charge of the division west of the St. Croix, and during the summer of 1632 he came by sea to the Plymouth House on the Penobscot, and took forcible possession of the post with all its contents. A year later La Tour

also seized the " trading wigwam " at Machias, in
the present State of Maine, but not before two of
the English occupants were killed. La Tour had
by this time removed from Cape Sable to the mouth
of the River St. John, where he had built a strong
fort on, probably, Portland Point, on the east side
of the harbour of the present city of St. John, and
was engaged in a lucrative trade in furs until a quarrel broke out between him and D'Aunay.

Soon after Razilly's death in the autumn of 1635,
D'Aunay asserted his right, as lieutenant-governor
of Acadia and his late chief's deputy, to command
in the colony. He obtained from Claude de Razilly,
brother of the governor, all his rights in Acadia, and
removed the seat of government from La Hève to
Port Royal, where he built a fort on the site of the
present town of Annapolis. It was not long before
he and La Tour became bitter enemies.

La Tour considered, with much reason, that he
had superior rights on account of his long services
in the province that ought to have been acknowledged, and that D'Aunay was all the while working
to injure him in France. D'Aunay had certainly a
great advantage over his opponent, as he had powerful influence at the French Court, while La Tour was
not personally known and was regarded with some
suspicion on account of his father being a Huguenot, and friendly to England. As a matter of fact,
the younger La Tour was no Protestant, but a luke-
warm Catholic, who considered creed subservient to
his personal interests. This fact explains why the
Capuchin friars always had a good word to say for

his rival who was a zealous Catholic and did much to promote their mission.

The French Government attempted at first to decide between the two claimants and settle the dispute, but all in vain. La Tour made an attempt in 1640 to surprise D'Aunay at Port Royal, but the result was that he as well as his bride, who had just come from France, were themselves taken prisoners. The Capuchin friars induced D'Aunay to set them all at liberty on condition that La Tour should keep the peace in future. The only result was an aggravation of the difficulty and the reference of the disputes to France, where D'Aunay won the day both in the courts and with the royal authorities. La Tour's commission was revoked and D'Aunay eventually received an order to seize the property and person of his rival, when he proved contumacious and refused to obey the royal command, on the ground that it had been obtained by false representations. He retired to his fort on the St. John, where, with his resolute wife and a number of faithful Frenchmen and Indians, he set D'Aunay at defiance. In this crisis La Tour resolved to appeal to the government of Massachusetts for assistance. In 1630, the town of Boston was commenced on the peninsula of Shawmut, and was already a place of considerable commercial importance. Harvard College was already open, schools were established, town meetings were frequent, and a system of representative government was in existence. Not only so, the colonies of Massachusetts, Connecticut, New Haven, and Plymouth had formed themselves into a confederacy '' for preserving and propagating the truth and liberties of the Gospel, and for their own mutual safety and welfare.''

Much sympathy was felt in Boston for La Tour, who was a man of very pleasing manners, and was believed to be a Huguenot at heart. He explained the affair at Machias and his relations with the French Government to the satisfaction of the Boston people, though apparently with little regard to truth. The desire to encourage a man, who promised to be a good customer of their own, finally prevailed over their caution, and the cunning Puritans considered they got out of their quandary by the decision that, though the colony could not directly contribute assistance, yet it was lawful for private citizens to charter their vessels, and offer their services as volunteers to help La Tour. The New Englanders had not forgotten D'Aunay's action at Penobscot some years before, and evidently thought he was a more dangerous man than his rival.

Some Massachusetts merchants, under these circumstances, provided La Tour with four staunch armed vessels and seventy men, while he on his part gave them a lien over all his property. When D'Aunay had tidings of the expedition in the Bay of Fundy, he raised a blockade of Fort La Tour and escaped to the westward. La Tour, assisted by some of the New England volunteers, destroyed his rival's fortified mill, after a few lives were lost on either side. A pinnace, having on board a large quantity of D'Aunay's furs, was captured, and the booty divided between the Massachusetts men and La Tour.

From his wife, then in France, where she had gone to plead his cause, La Tour received the unwelcome news that his enemy was on his return to Acadia with an overwhelming force. Thereupon he presented himself again in Boston, and appealed to the authorities for further assistance, but they would not do more than send a remonstrance to D'Aunay and ask explanations of his conduct.

At this critical moment, La Tour's wife appeared on the scene. Unable to do anything in France for her husband, she had found her way to London, where she took passage on a vessel bound for Boston; but the master, instead of carrying her directly to Fort La Tour, as he had agreed, spent some months trading in the Gulf of St. Lawrence and on the coast of Nova Scotia. D'Aunay was cruising off Cape Sable, in the hope of intercepting her, and searched the vessel, but Madame La Tour was safely concealed in the hold, and the vessel was allowed to go on to Boston. On her arrival there, Madame La Tour brought an action against the master and consignee for a breach of contract, and succeeded in obtaining a judgment in her favour for two thousand pounds. When she found it impossible to come to a settlement, she seized the goods in the ship, and on this security hired three vessels and sailed to rejoin her husband. In the meantime an envoy from D'Aunay, a Monsieur Marie, always supposed to be a Capuchin friar, presented himself to the Massachusetts authorities, and after making a strong remon-

strance against the course heretofore pursued by the
colony, proffered terms of amity in the future on
the condition that no further aid was given to La
Tour. After some consideration the colonial government, of which Governor Endicott was now the
head, agreed to a treaty of friendship, which was not
ratified by D'Aunay for some time afterwards, when
La Tour was a fugitive. Then the terms were sanc-
tioned by the commissioners of the confederated
colonies.

Having succeeded in obtaining the neutrality of
the English colonists through his agent Marie,
D'Aunay then determined to attack La Tour's fort
on the St. John, as he had now under his control a
sufficient number of men and ships. In the spring
of the same year, however, when La Tour was absent, D'Aunay mustered all his vessels and men,
and laid siege to the fort, but he met with most
determined resistance from the garrison, nerved and
stimulated by the voice and example of the heroic
wife. The besiegers were almost disheartened, when
a traitor within the walls—a " mercenary Swiss,"
according to a contemporary writer—gave them
information which determined them to renew the
assault with still greater vigour. D'Aunay and his
men again attempted to scale the walls, but were
forced to retire with a considerable force. Then
D'Aunay offered fair terms if the fort was immediately given up. Madame La Tour, anxious to spare
the lives of her brave garrison, which was rapidly
thinning, agreed to the proposal, and surrendered
the fort ; and then D'Aunay is said to have broken

his solemn pledge, and hanged all the defenders except one, whose life was spared on the condition of
his acting as executioner.

One would fain not believe what the contemporary historian adds, that D'Aunay forced Madame
La Tour to remain with a rope round her own neck,
and witness the execution of the brave men who
had so nobly assisted her in defending the fort.
The poor lady did not long survive this tragedy, as
she died a prisoner a few weeks later. All the acts
of her adventurous and tragic career prove her to
have been a good woman and a courageous wife, and
may well be an inspiring theme for poetry and
romance.*

D'Aunay now reigned supreme in Acadia. He
had burdened himself heavily with debt in his efforts
to ruin his rival, but he had some compensation in

---

* This story of the capture of Fort La Tour rests on the authority
of Denys (*Description Géographique et Historique de l'Amérique
Septentrionale*, Paris, 1672), who was in Acadia at the time and must
have had an account from eyewitnesses of the tragedy. The details
which make D'Aunay so cruel and relentless are denied by a Mr.
Moreau in his *Histoire de l'Acadie Française* (Paris, 1873). This
book is confessedly written at the dictation of living members of the
D'Aunay family, and is, from the beginning to the end, an undis-
criminating eulogy of D'Aunay and an uncompromising attack on the
memory of La Tour and his wife. He attempts to deny that the fort
was seized by treachery, when on another page he has gone so far as
to accuse some Recollets of having made, at the instigation of
D'Aunay himself, an attempt to win the garrison from Madame La
Tour who was a Protestant and disliked by the priests. He also admits
that a number of the defenders of the fort were executed, while
others, probably the traitors, had their lives spared. The attacks on
Madame La Tour's character are not warranted by impartial history,
and clearly show the bias of the book.

the booty he found at St. John. By the capture of his fort La Tour lost jewels, plate, furniture, and goods valued at ten thousand pounds, and was for a time a bankrupt. His debts in Boston were very heavy, and Major Gibbons, who had sent vessels to Fort La Tour in 1643, was never able to recover the mortgage he had taken on his estate. Bereft of wife and possessions, La Tour left Acadia and sought aid from Sir David Kirk, who was then governor of Newfoundland, but to no purpose. Various stories are told of his career for two years or longer, and it is even reported that he robbed a Boston vessel in his necessities, " whereby it appeared, as the Scripture saith," mournfully exclaims Governor Winthrop, "that there is no confidence in any unfaithful or carnal man." Boston merchants and sailors had suffered a good deal from both D'Aunay and La Tour, and such a story would naturally obtain credence among men who found they had made a bad investment in Fort La Tour and its appendages. D'Aunay continued his work of improving Port Royal and surrounding country, and the colony he founded was the parent of those large settlements that in the course of time stretched as far as the isthmus of Chignecto. He was accidentally drowned in the Annapolis River some time in 1650. French Canadian writers call him cruel, vindictive, rapacious, and arbitrary, but he has never been the favourite of historians. His plans of settlement had a sound basis and might have led to a prosperous and populous Acadia, had he not wrecked them by the malignity with which he followed La Tour and his wife.

La Tour, in the year 1648, visited Quebec, where he was received with the most gratifying demonstrations of respect by his countrymen, who admired his conduct in the Acadian struggle. Then D'Aunay died and La Tour immediately went to France, where the government acknowledged the injustice with which it had treated him in the past, and appointed him governor of Acadia, with enlarged privileges and powers. In 1653 he married D'Aunay's widow, Jeanne de Motin, in the hope—to quote the contract—" to secure the peace and tranquillity of the country, and concord and union between the two families." Peace then reigned for some months in Acadia ; many new settlers came into the country, the forts were strengthened, and the people were hoping for an era of prosperity. But there was to be no peace or rest for the French in Acadia.

One of D'Aunay's creditors in France, named Le Borgne, came to America in 1654 at the head of a large force, with the object of obtaining possession of D'Aunay's property, and possibly of his position in Acadia. He made a prisoner of Denys, who was at that time engaged in trade in Cape Breton, and treated him with great harshness. After a short imprisonment at Port Royal, which was occupied by Le Borgne, Denys was allowed to go to France, where he succeeded eventually in obtaining a redress of his grievances, and an appointment as governor of Cape Breton.

Whilst Le Borgne was preparing to attack La Tour, the English appeared on the scene of action. By this time the civil war had been fought in England, the King beheaded, and Cromwell proclaimed Lord Protector of the Commonwealth. In 1653 very strong representations were made to the latter by the colonists of New England with respect to the movements of the French in Acadia, and the necessity of reducing the country to the dominion of England. Peace then nominally prevailed between France and Great Britain, but we have seen, as the case of Argall proved, that matters in America were often arranged without much reference to international obligations. A fleet, which had been sent out by Cromwell to operate against the Dutch colony at Manhattan, arrived at Boston in June, 1654, and the news came a few days later that peace had been proclaimed between the English and Dutch. Thereupon an expedition was organised against the French under the command of Major Robert Sedgewick of Massachusetts. Le Borgne at Port Royal and La Tour on the St. John immediately surrendered to this force, and in a few days all Acadia was once more in the hands of the English. Denys was almost ruined by these events and obliged to retire for a time from the country. La Tour was now far advanced in years, and did not attempt to resist the evil destiny that seemed to follow all the efforts of France to establish herself in Nova Scotia. No doubt the injuries he had received from his own countrymen, together with the apathy which the French Government always displayed in the affairs of Acadia, were strong arguments, if any were needed, to induce him to place himself under the protection of the English. The representations he made to the Protector met with a favourable response, and obtained for him letters patent, dated August 9, 1656, granting to him, Sir Charles La Tour, in conjunction with Sir Thomas Temple and William Crowne, the whole territory of Acadia, the mines and minerals alone being reserved for the government. Sir Thomas Temple, a man of generous disposition and remarkably free from religious prejudices, subsequently purchased La Tour's rights, and carried on a large trade in Acadia with much energy. La Tour now disappears from the scene, and is understood to have died in the country he loved in the year 1666, at the ripe age of seventy-four. He left several descendants, none of whom played a prominent part in Acadian history, though there are persons still in the maritime provinces of Canada who claim a connection with his family. His name clings to the little harbour near Cape Sable, where he built his post of Lomeron, and antiquaries now alone fight over the site of the more famous fort at the mouth of the St. John, where a large and enterprising city has grown up since the English occupation. About the figure of this bold gentleman-adventurer the romance of history has cast a veil of interest and generous appreciation on account of the devotion of his wife and of the obstinate fight he waged under tremendous disadvantages against a wealthy rival, supported by the authority of France. He was made of the same material as those brave men of the west coast of England who fought and robbed the Spaniard in the Spanish Main, but as he plundered only Puritans by giving them worthless mortgages, and fought only in the Acadian wilds, history has given him a relatively small space in its pages.

Acadia remained in possession of England until the Treaty of Breda, which was concluded in July of 1667, between Charles II. and Louis XIV. Temple, who had invested his fortune in the country, was nearly ruined, and never received any compensation for his efforts to develop Acadia. In a later chapter, when we continue the chequered history of Acadia, we shall see that her fortunes from this time become more closely connected with those of the greater and more favoured colony of France in the valley of the St. Lawrence.

VIII.

THE CANADIAN INDIANS AND THE IROQUOIS: THEIR ORGANISATION, CHARACTER, AND CUSTOMS.

AT the time of Champlain's death we see gathering in America the forces that were to influence the fortunes of French Canada—the English colonies growing up by the side of the Atlantic and the Iroquois, those dangerous foes, already irritated by the founder of Quebec. These Indians were able to buy firearms and ammunition from the Dutch traders at Fort Orange, now Albany, on the beautiful river which had been discovered by Hudson in 1609. From their warlike qualities and their strong natural position between the Hudson and Niagara rivers, they had now become most important factors in the early development of the French and English colonies, and it is consequently important to give some particulars of their character and organisation. In the first place, however, I shall refer to those Indian tribes who lived in Canada, and were closely identified with the interests of the French settlements. These Indians also became possessed of

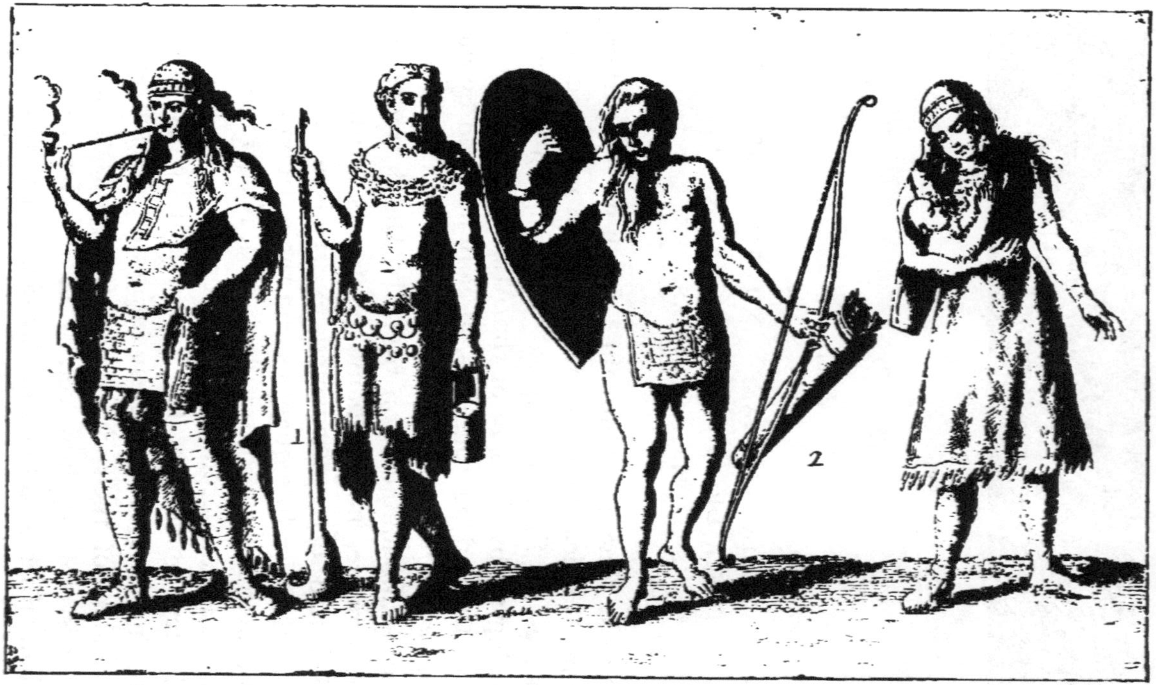

III INDIAN COSTUMES, FROM LAFITAU. 1, IROQUOIS; 2, ALGONQUIN.

firearms, sold to them from time to time by greedy
traders, despite the interdict of the French authorities in the early days of the colonies.

Champlain found no traces of the Indians of Cartier's time at Stadacona and Hochelaga.   The tribes
which had frequented the St. Lawrence seventy
years before had vanished, and in their place he saw
bands of wandering Algonquins.   It was only when
he reached the shores of Georgian Bay that he came
to Indian villages resembling that Hochelaga which
had disappeared so mysteriously.   The St. Lawrence
in Cartier's day had been frequented by tribes
speaking one or more of the dialects of the Huron-
Iroquois family, one of the seven great families that
then inhabited North America east of the Mississippi, from the Gulf of Mexico to the Hudson's Bay.
The short and imperfect vocabulary of Indian words
which Cartier left behind, his account of Hochelaga,
the intimacy of the two Gaspé Indians with the inhabitants of Stadacona—these and other facts go to
show that the barbarous tribes he met were of the
Iroquois stock.

The Indians have never had any written records,
in the European sense, to perpetuate the doings of
their nations or tribes.   From generation to generation, from century to century, however, tradition
has told of the deeds of ancestors, and given us
vague stories of the origin and history of the tribes.
It is only in this folk-lore—proved often on patient
investigation to be of historic value—that we can
find some threads to guide us through the labyrinth
of mystery to which we come in the prehistoric

times of Canada. Popular tradition tells us that the Hurons and Iroquois, branches of the same family, speaking dialects of one common language, were living at one time in villages not far from each other —the Hurons probably at Hochelaga and the Senecas on the opposite side of the mountain. It was against the law of the two communities for their men and women to intermarry, but the potent influence of true love, so rare in an Indian's bosom, soon broke this command. A Huron girl entered the cabin of an Iroquois chief as his wife. It was an unhappy marriage, the husband killed the wife in an angry moment. This was a serious matter, requiring a council meeting of the two tribes. Murder must be avenged, or liberal compensation given to the friends of the dead. The council decided that the woman deserved death, but the verdict did not please all her relatives, one of whom went off secretly and killed an Iroquois warrior. Then both tribes took up the hatchet and went on the warpath against each other, with the result that the village of Hochelaga, with all the women and children, was destroyed, and the Hurons, who were probably beaten, left the St. Lawrence, and eventually found a new home on Lake Huron.*

Leaving this realm of tradition, which has probably a basis of fact, we come to historic times. In Champlain's interesting narrative, and in the Jesuit *Relations*, we find very few facts relating to Indian history, though we have very full information re-

---

* See Horatio Hale's " Fall of Hochelaga," in *Journal of American Folklore*, Cambridge, Mass., 1894.

specting their customs, superstitions, and methods of living. The reports of the missionaries, in fact, form the basis of all the knowledge we have of the Canadian tribes as well as of the Five Nations themselves.

It is only necessary that we should here take account of the Algonquins and Huron-Iroquois, two great families separated from one another by radical differences of language, and not by special racial or physical characteristics. The Eskimo, Dacotah, Mandan, Pawnee, and Muskoki groups have no immediate connection with this Canadian story, although we shall meet representatives of these natural divisions in later chapters when we find the French in the Northwest, and on the waters of the Missouri and Mississippi. The Algonquins and Huron-Iroquois occupied the country extending, roughly speaking, from Virginia to Hudson's Bay, and from the Mississippi to the Atlantic. The Algonquins were by far the most numerous and widely distributed. Dialects of their common language were heard on the Atlantic coast all the way from Cape Fear to the Arctic region where the Eskimo hunted the seal or the walrus in his skin kayak. On the banks of the Kennebec and Penobscot in Acadia we find the Abenakis, who were firm friends of the French. They were hunters in the great forests of Maine, where even yet roam the deer and moose. The Etchemins or Canoemen, inhabited the country west and east of the St. Croix River, which had been named by De Monts. In Nova Scotia, Cape Breton, and Prince Edward Island, we see the Micmacs or Souriquois, a fierce, cruel race in early times, whose chief, Membertou, was the first convert of the Acadian missionaries. They were hunters and fishermen, and did not till the soil even in the lazy fashion of their Algonquin kindred in New England. The climate of Nova Scotia was not so congenial to the production of maize as that of the more southern countries. It was the culture of this very prolific plant, so easily sown, gathered, and dried, that largely modified and improved the savage conditions of Indian life elsewhere on the continent. It is where the maize was most abundant, in the valley of the Ohio, that we find relics of Indian arts—such as we never find in Acadia or Canada.

On the St. Lawrence, between the Gulf and Quebec, there were wandering Algonquin tribes, generally known as Montagnais or Mountaineers, living in rude camps covered with bark or brush, eking a precarious existence from the rivers and woods, and at times on the verge of starvation, when they did not hesitate at cannibalism. Between Quebec and the Upper Ottawa there were no village communities of any importance; for the *Petite Nation* of the river of that name was only a small band of Algonquins, living some distance from the Ottawa. On the Upper Ottawa we meet with the nation of the Isle (Allumette) and the Nipissings, both Algonquin tribes, mentioned in a previous chapter. They were chiefly hunters and fishermen, although the former cultivated some patches of ground. On Georgian Bay we come to a nation speaking one of the dialects of a language quite distinct from that

of the Algonquins. These were Hurons, numbering
in all some twenty thousand souls, of whom ten
thousand or more were adults, living in thirty-two
villages, comprising seven hundred dwellings of the
same style as Cartier saw at Hochelaga. These villages were protected by stockades or palisades, and
by some natural features of their situation—a river,
a lake, or a hill. Neither the long houses nor the
fortifications were as strongly or as cleverly constructed as those of the Iroquois. Maize, pumpkins,
and tobacco were the principal plants cultivated.
Sunflowers were also raised, chiefly for the oil with
which they greased their hair and bodies. Their
very name meant " Shock-heads "—a nickname
originating from the exclamation of some Frenchmen, when they first saw their grotesque way of
wearing their hair, "*Quelles hures !*" (What a head
of hair!) Champlain speaks of a tribe whom he met
after leaving Lake Nipissing, in 1615, and called the
Cheveux Relevés, or people with the stiff hair, but
they were wandering Algonquins. Champlain called
the Hurons, Attigouantans, though their true name
was Ouendat, afterwards corrupted to Wyandot,
which still clings to a remnant of the race in
America.

They were brave and warlike, with perhaps more
amiable qualities than the more ferocious, robust
Iroquois. The nation appears to have been a confederacy of tribes, each of which was divided into
clans or *gentes* on the Iroquois principle, which I
shall shortly explain. Two chiefs, one for peace and
one for war, assisted by a council of tribal chiefs,

constituted the general government. Each tribe had a system of local or self-government—to use a phrase applicable to modern federal conditions—consisting of chiefs and council. The federal organisation was not, however, so carefully framed and adjusted as that of their kin, the Iroquois. At council meetings all the principal men attended and votes were taken with the aid of reeds or sticks, the majority prevailing in all cases. The whole organisation was essentially a democracy, as the chiefs, although an oligarchy in appearance, were controlled by the voices and results of the councils. In this as in other American savage nations, the rule governing the transmission of hereditary honours and possessions was through the female line.

Beyond the Huron villages, south of Nottawasaga Bay—so named probably from the Nottaways, a branch of the same family, driven by war to the south—we come to the Tionotates or Tobacco tribe, who were kin in language and customs to their neighbours and afterwards joined their confederacy. The Neutral Nation, or Attiwandaronks of Iroquois stock, had their homes on the north shore of Lake Erie, and reached even as far as the Niagara. They were extremely cruel, and kept for a long while their position of neutrality between the Hurons and Five Nations. To the south of Lake Erie rose the smoke of the fires of the Eries, generally translated "Cats," but, properly speaking, the "Raccoons." Like the Andastes, near the Susquehanna, mentioned in a previous chapter, they were famous warriors, and for years held their own against the Iroquois, but eventually both these nations yielded to the fury of the relentless confederacy.

We have now come to the western door of the " long house " (*Ho-dé-no-sote*) of the Iroquois, who called themselves " the people of the long house " (*Ho-dé-no-sau-nee*), because they dwelt in a line of villages of " long houses," reaching from the Genesee to the Mohawk, where the eastern door looked toward the Hudson and Lake Champlain. The name by which they have been best known is considered by Charlevoix and other writers to be originally French; derived from " Hiro " (I have spoken)—the conclusion of all their harangues—and Koué, an exclamation of sorrow when it was prolonged, and of joy when pronounced shortly. They comprised five nations, living by the lakes, that still bear their names in the State of New York, in the following order as we go east from Niagara:

IROQUOIS NATIONS.	ENGLISH NAMES.	FRENCH NAMES.
Nundawäona Great hill people	Seneca	Tsonnontouans
Guéugwehono People of the marsh	Cayuga	Goyogouin
Onundägaono People of the hills	Onondaga	Onnontagué
Onayotékäono Granite people	Oneida	Onneyote
Gäneägaono Possessors of the flint	Mohawk	Agnier

Each tribe lived in a separate village of long houses, large enough to hold from five to twenty families. Each family was a clan or kin—resembling the *gens* of the Roman, the *γένος* of the Greek

—a group of males and females, whose kinship was reckoned only through females—the universal custom in archaic times in America. As among these people the marriage tie was easily sundered and chastity was the exception,—remarkably so among the Hurons, their kindred—it is not strange that all rank, titles, and property should be based on the rights of the woman alone. The child belonged consequently to the clan, not of the father, but of

IROQUOIS LONG HOUSE (FROM MORGAN).

the mother. Each of these tenement houses, as they may well be called, was occupied by related families, the mothers and their children belonging to the same clan, while the husbands and the fathers of these children belonged to other clans; consequently, the clan or kin of the mother easily predominated in the household.* Every clan had a name derived from the animal world, as a rule, and a rude picture

* In this necessarily very imperfect description of the organisation and customs of the Five Nations I depend mainly on those valuable and now rare books, *The League of the Iroquois*, and *Houses and Home Life of the Aborigines*, by Lewis H. Morgan. The reader should also consult Horatio Hale's *Iroquois Book of Rites*.

of the same was the " totem " or coat-of-arms of
the kin or *gens*, found over the door of a long house
or tattooed on the arms or bodies of its members.
The Tortoise, Bear, and Wolf, were for a long
time the most conspicuous totems of the Iroquois.
These people were originally a nation of one stock
of eight clans, and when they separated into five
tribes or sections, each contained parts of the original clans.   Consequently, " all the members of the
same clan, whatever tribe they belonged to, were
brothers or sisters to each other in virtue of their
descent from the same common female ancestor, and
they recognised each other as such with the fullest
cordiality."

Whatever was taken in the hunt, or raised in cultivation, by any member of the household—and the
Iroquois were good cultivators of maize, beans, and
squash—was used as a common stock for that particular household.   No woman could marry a member of her own clan or kin.   The marriage might be
severed at the will of either party.   Yet, while the
Iroquois women had so much importance in the
household and in the regulation of inheritance, she
was almost as much a drudge as the squaw of the
savage Micmacs of Acadia and the Gulf.

The tribe was simply a community of Indians of
a particular family or stock, speaking one of the
dialects of its language.   For instance, the Five
Nations or Tribes spoke different dialects of the
Iroquoian stock language, but each could understand
the other sufficiently for all purposes of deliberation
and discussion.   Each tribe was governed by its

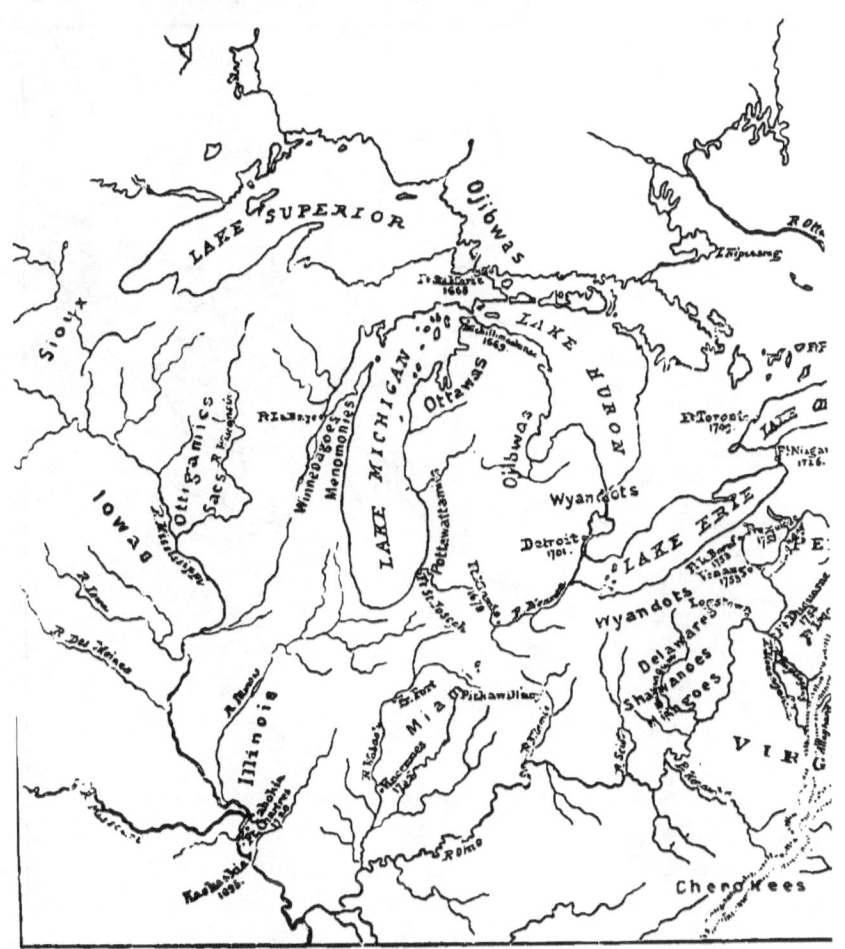

MAP OF FRENCH FO

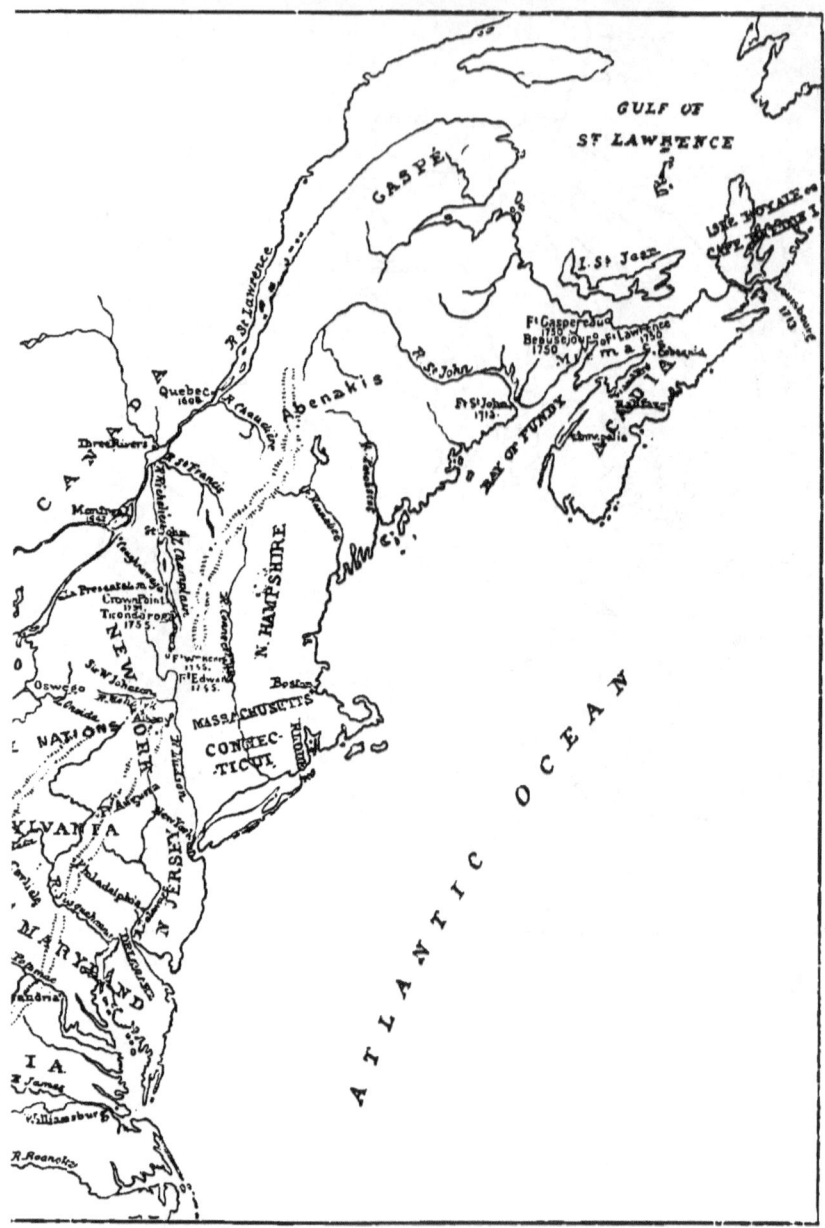

GULF OF
St LAWRENCE

GASPÉ

CANADA

Quebec
1608

R.St Lawrence

Abenakis

I. St Jean

Ft Gaspereau
1750
Beausejour
1750

Ft Lawrence 1750
Ft Lawrence

Mi c m a c s

Three Rivers

St Francis

R.Claudin

R.St John

Ft St John
1713

ACADIA

Montreal
1642

St Nicholette

La Prescata
Crown Point
1731
Ticonderoga
1755

R.Connecticut

N. HAMPSHIRE

Ft William
1755.
Ft Edward
1755.

BAY OF FUNDY

Annapolis

NEW YORK

Oswego

Ft Johnson

Albany

Boston

6 NATIONS

MASSACHUSETTS

CONNEC-
TICUT

ATLANTIC   OCEAN

PENNSYLVANIA

Philadelphia

NEW JERSEY

Delaware

MARYLAND

Potomac

Alexandria

Washington

VIRGINIA

R. James

Williamsburg

R. Roanoke

IN AMERICA, 1750–60.

own council of sachems and chiefs—the latter inferior in rank—elected by their respective clans, but
invested with office by the whole tribe. For all purposes of tribal government the tribes had separate
territories and jurisdiction. For common purposes
they united in a confederation in which each tribe
occupied a position of complete equality—the exception being the Tuscaroras—Dusgaóweh or " shirt-
wearing people "—who came from the south at the
beginning of the eighteenth century, and made up
the " Six Nations." If a tribe made peace it would
not bind the other tribes unless they had given their
consent in formal council, or by the presence of
their representatives. A general council of fifty
sachems, equal in rank and authority, administered
the affairs of the confederation. These sachems
were created in perpetuity in certain clans of the
several tribes and invested with office by the general council. They were also sachems in their respective tribes, and with other clan-chiefs formed the
council which was supreme over all matters apper-
taining to the tribe exclusively. Women, too, had
their clan and other councils, and could make their
wishes known through the delegates they appointed
to the council of the league. In the federal council
the sachems voted by tribes, and unanimity was
essential before action was taken or a conclusion
arrived at. The general council was open to the
whole community for the discussion of public questions, but the council alone decided. The council
of each tribe had power to convene the general
council, but the latter could not convene itself.

With the object of preventing the concentration of too much power in one man's hands, the federal council appointed two war chiefs, equal in authority. The council fire or brand was always burning in the valley of the Onondagas, where the central council met as a rule in the autumn, or whenever a tribe might consider a special meeting necessary. The Onondagas had also the custody of the " Wampum," or mnemonic record of their structure of government, and the Tadodä'ho, or most noble sachem of the league, was among the same tribe. The origin of the confederacy is attributed in legendary lore to Hä-yo-went'-hä, the Hiawatha of Longfellow's poem.

These are the main features of that famous polity of the Iroquois which gave them so remarkable a power of concentration in war, and was one reason of their decided superiority over all the other nations of America. In council, where all common and tribal affairs were decided, the Iroquois showed great capacity for calm deliberation, and became quite eloquent at times. Their language was extremely figurative, though incapable of the expression of abstract thought, as is the case with Indian tongues generally. The Indian—essentially a materialist—could only find his similes, metaphors, and illustrations in the objects of nature, but these he used with great skill. The Iroquois had a very keen appreciation of their interests, and were well able to protect them in their bargains or contracts with the white men. In war they were a terrible foe, and a whisper of their neighbourhood brought consternation to Indian camps and cabins, from the Kennebec to the Delaware, from the Susquehanna to the Illinois. They have been well described as "the scourge of God upon the aborigines of the continent." In their political organisation, their village life, their culture of the soil, their power of eloquence, their skill as politicians as well as warriors, they were superior to all the tribes in America as far as New Mexico, although in the making of pottery and other arts they were inferior to the mound-builders of the Ohio and the Mississippi—probably the Allegewi who gave their names to the Alleghanies and are believed by some writers to have been either exterminated by a combination of Algonquin and Iroquois or driven southward where they were absorbed in other nations. At no time could the Iroquois muster more than 3000 warriors; and yet they were the scourge and dread of all the scattered tribes of Algonquins, numbering in the aggregate probably 90,000 souls, and eventually crushed the Hurons and those other tribes of their own nationality, who did not belong to their confederacy and had evoked their wrath.

The Algonquin and Huron-Iroquois nations had many institutions and customs in common. Every clan had some such totem as I have described in the case of the Iroquois. Every tribe had its chiefs as military leaders and its councils for deliberation and decision. Consequently the democratic principle dominated the whole organisation. Eloquence was always prized and cultivated as a necessity of the system of government. Some tribes had their special orators among the chiefs. Though a general war was dependent on the action of the council, yet any number of warriors might go on the warpath at any time against the enemies of the tribe. They had no written records, but their memories were aided in council or otherwise by reeds or sticks and rude pictures; strings of wampum—cleverly manufactured from shells—served as annals, which the skilled men of a tribe could decipher and explain. The wampum belts performed an important part in the declaration of war or peace, and the pipe was equally effective in the deliberations of council and in the profession of amity. Murder might be expiated by presents to the family or relatives of the dead, and crime was rarely followed by death except there was a question of other nations, who would not be content unless the blood of their kinsman was washed away by blood. Charity and hospitality were among the virtues of the Indian race, especially among the Iroquois, and while there was food in a village no one need starve. The purity of love was unknown to a savage nature, chiefly animated by animal passion. Prisoners were treated with great ferocity, but the Iroquois exceeded all nations in the ingenuity of torture. Stoicism and endurance, even heroic, were characteristics of Indians generally, when in the hands of their enemies, and the cruellest insult that a warrior could receive was to be called a woman. Sometimes prisoners were spared and adopted into the tribe, and among most nations the wife or mother or sister of a dead chief might demand that he be replaced by a prisoner to whom they may have taken a fancy. After torture parts of the bodies of the victim would be eaten as a sort of mystic ceremony, but this custom was peculiar to the Hurons and Iroquois only. In their warlike expeditions they had no special discipline, and might be successfully met on the open field or under the protection of fortified works. Their favourite system was a surprise or furious onslaught. A siege soon exhausted their patience and resources. They were as treacherous as they were brave. In the shades of the forest, whose intricacies and secrets they understood so well, they were most to be feared. Behind every tree might lurk a warrior, when once a party was known to be on the warpath. To steal stealthily at night through the mazes of the woods, tomahawk their sleeping foes, and take many scalps, was the height of an Indian's bliss. Curious to say, the Indians took little precautions to guard against such surprises, but thought they were protected by their manitous or guardian spirits.

A spirit of materialism prevailed in all their superstitions. They had no conception of one all-pervading, omniscient divine being, governing and watching over humanity, when the missionaries first came among them. It was only by making use of their belief in the existence of a supreme chief for every race of animals, that the priests could lead their converts to the idea of a Great Spirit who ruled all creation. In their original state of savagery or barbarism, any conception an Indian might have of a supernatural being superior to himself was frittered away by his imagining that the whole material world was under the influence of innumerable mysterious powers. In the stirring of the leaves, in the glint of the sunbeam amid the foliage, in the shadow on his path, in the flash of the lightning, in the crash of the thunder, in the roar of the cataract, in the colours of the rainbow, in the very beat of his pulse, in the leap of the fish, in the flight of the birds, he saw some supernatural power to be evoked. The Indian companions of Champlain, we remember, threw tobacco to the genius or Manitou of the great fall of the Ottawa. The Manitou of the Algonquins, and the Okies or Otkons of the Hurons and Iroquois were not always superior, mysterious beings endowed with supernatural powers, like the Algonquin Manabozho, the Great Hare, the king of all animals; or a deified hero, like Hiawatha, the founder of the Iroquois confederacy, and Glooscap, the favourite of Micmac legends. The Manitou or Oki might even be a stone, a fish-bone, a bird's feather, or a serpent's skin, or some other thing in the animate or inanimate world, revealed to a young man in his dreams as his fetich or guardian through life. Dreams were respected as revelations from the spirit world. As Champlain tells us, during his first expedition to Lake Champlain, the Indians always questioned him as to his dreams, and at last he was able to tell them that he had seen in a vision some Iroquois drowning in the lake, and wished to help them, but was not permitted to do so by the Indians of his own party. This dream, in their opinion, was a portent in their favour.

A fetich became at last even the object of an Indian's worship—to be thanked, flattered, expostulated with, according to the emergency. It can be easily seen that in this Indian land of mysterious agencies, of manitous and spirits, the medicine-man and conjuror exercised a great power among old and young, chiefs and women. He had to be consulted in illness, in peace, in war, at every moment of importance to individual or nation. Even in case of illness and disease he found more value in secret communications with the supernatural world, and in working on the credulity of his tribesmen, than in the use of medicines made from plants. The grossest superstition dominated every community. All sorts of mystic ceremonies, some most cruel and repugnant to every sense of decency, were usual on occasions when supernatural influences had to be called into action.

Every respect was paid to the dead, who were supposed to have gone on a journey to a spirit land. Every one had such a separate scaffold or grave, generally speaking, as Champlain saw among the Ottawas, but it was the strange custom of the Hurons to collect the bones of their dead every few years and immure them in great pits or ossuaries with weirdlike ceremonies very minutely described in the *Relations*. In a passage previously quoted Champlain gave credit to the Indians for believing in the immortality of the soul. The world to which the Indian's imagination accompanied the dead was not the Heaven or Hell of the Jew or Christian. Among some tribes there was an impression rather than a belief that a distinction was made in the land of the Ponemah or Hereafter between the great or useful, and the weak or useless; but generally it was thought that all alike passed to the Spirit Land, and carried on their vocations as in life.   It was a Land of Shades where trees, flowers, animals, men, and all things were spirits.

> " By midnight moons, o'er moistening dews
>   In vestments for the chase arrayed
> The hunter still the deer pursues,
>   The hunter and the deer a shade."

IX.

CONVENTS AND HOSPITALS—VILLE-MARIE—MARTYRED MISSIONARIES—VICTORIOUS IROQUOIS—HAPLESS HURONS.

(1635--1652.)

A SCENE that was witnessed on the heights of Quebec on a fine June morning, two hundred and sixty years ago, illustrated the spirit that animated the founders of Canada. At the foot of a cross knelt the Governor, Charles Hault de Montmagny, Knight of Malta, who had come to take the place of his great predecessor, Samuel Champlain, whose remains were buried close by, if indeed this very cross did not indicate the spot. Jesuits in their black robes, soldiers in their gay uniforms, officials and inhabitants from the little town below, all followed the example of Montmagny, whose first words were, according to Father Le Jeune, the historian of those days : " Behold the first cross that I have seen in this country, let us worship the crucified Saviour in his image." Then, this act of devotion accomplished, the procession entered the

little church dedicated by Champlain to Notre
Dame de la Recouvrance, where the priests solemnly
chanted the *Te Deum* and offered up prayers for the
King of France.

The Church was first, the State second. After
the service the new governor entered the fort of St.
Louis, only a few steps from the sacred building,
received the keys amid salutes of cannon and musketry, and was officially installed as head of the civil
and military government of Canada, at this time
controlled by the Company of the Hundred Associates. Then he was called upon to act as god-father
for a dying Indian who desired baptism. In the
smoky cabin packed with Indians Montmagny stood
by the earnest Jesuit and named the Algonquin
Joseph. "I leave you to think," says Father Le
Jeune, "how greatly astonished were these people
to see so much crimson, so many handsomely
dressed persons beneath their bark roofs."

During the period of which I am now writing we
see the beginnings of the most famous educational
and religious institutions of the country. The
Hotel Dieu was founded in 1639, by the Sœurs
Hospitalières from the convent of St. Augustine, in
Dieppe, through the benefactions of the Duchess
d'Aiguillon, the niece of Cardinal Richelieu. Rich,
fascinating, and beautiful women contributed not
only their fortunes but their lives to the service of
the Church. Marie Madeleine de Chauvigny, who
belonged to a noble family in Normandy, married
at a very early age a M. de la Peltrie, who left her
a young widow of twenty-two years of age, without

MARIE GUYARD (MÈRE MARIE DE L'INCARNATION).

131

any children.   Deeply attached to her religion from
her youth, she decided to devote her life and her
wealth to the establishment of an institution for the
instruction of girls in Canada.   Her father and
friends threw all possible obstacles in the way of
what they believed was utter folly for a gentle cultured woman, but she succeeded by female wiles
and strategy in carrying out her plans.   On the first
of August, 1639, she arrived at Quebec, in company
with Marie Guyard, the daughter of a silk manufac-
turer of Tours, best known to Canadians as Mère de
l'Incarnation, the mother superior of the Ursulines,
whose spacious convent and grounds now cover
seven acres of land on Garden Street in the ancient capital.   She had a vision of a companion who
was to accompany her to a land of mists and mountains, to which the Virgin beckoned as the country
of her future life-work.   Canada was the land and
Madame de la Peltrie the companion foreshadowed
in that dream which gave Marie Guyard a vocation
which she filled for thirty years with remarkable
fidelity and ability.

Madame de la Peltrie and Marie Guyard were accompanied by Mdlle. de Savonnière de la Troche, who
belonged to a distinguished family of Anjou, and was
afterwards known in Canada as Mère de St. Joseph,
and also by another nun, called Mère Cécile de
Sainte-Croix.   A Jesuit, Father Vimont, afterwards
superior, and author of one of the *Rélations*, and the
three Hospital sisters, arrived in the same ship.

The company landed and " threw themselves on
their knees, blessed the God of Heaven, and kissed

the earth of their near country, as they now called it." A *Te Deum* followed in the Jesuits' church which was now completed on the heights near their college, commenced as early as 1635—one year before the building of Harvard College—through the generosity of Réné Rohault, eldest son of the Marquis de Gamache. The first visit of the nuns was to Sillery, four miles to the west of Quebec, on the north bank of the river, where an institution had been established for the instruction of the Algonquin and other Indians, through the liberality of Noël Brulart de Sillery, a Knight of Malta, and a member of an influential French family, who had taken a deep interest in the settlement of Canada and proved it by his bounty. Madame de la Peltrie and her companions, the Jesuit historian tells us naïvely, embraced the little Indian girls " without taking heed whether they were clean or not."

It was during Montmagny's term of office that the city of Montreal was founded by a number of religious enthusiasts. Jérôme le Royer de la Dauversière, receiver of taxes at La Flèche in Anjou, a noble and devotee, consulted with Jean Jacques Olier, then a priest of St. Sulpice in Paris, as to the best means of establishing a mission in Canada. Both declared they had visions which pointed to the island of Mont Royal as the future scene of their labours. They formed a company with large powers as seigniors as soon as they had obtained from M. de Lauzon, one of the members of the Company of Hundred Associates, a title to the island. They interested in the project Paul de Chomedey, Sieur de Maisonneuve, a devout and brave soldier, an honest and chivalric gentleman, who was appointed the first governor by the new company. Mdlle. Jeanne Mance, daughter of the attorney-general of Nogent-le-Roi, among the vine-clad hills of Champagne, who had bound herself to perpetual chastity from a remarkably early age, gladly joined in this religious undertaking. The company had in view the establishment of communities of secular priests, and of nuns to nurse the sick, and teach the children —the French as well as the savages. Madame de Bullion, the rich widow of a superintendent of finance, contributed largely towards the enterprise, and may be justly considered the founder of Hotel Dieu of Montreal.

Maisonneuve and Mdlle. Mance, accompanied by forty men and four women, arrived at Quebec in August, 1641, when it was far too late to attempt an establishment on the island. Governor de Montmagny and others at Quebec disapproved of the undertaking which had certainly elements of danger. The governor might well think it wisest to strengthen the colony by an establishment on the island of Orleans or in the immediate vicinity of Quebec, instead of laying the foundations of a new town in the most exposed part of Canada. However, all these objections availed nothing against the enthusiasm of devotees. In the spring of 1642, Maisonneuve and his company left Quebec. He was accompanied by Governor de Montmagny, Father Vimont, superior of the Jesuits, and Madame de la Peltrie, who left the Ursulines very abruptly and inconsiderately under the conviction that she had a mission to fill at Mont Royal.

On the 17th May, Maisonneuve and his compan-

PORTRAIT OF MAISONNEUVE.

ions landed on the little triangle of land, the Place Royale of Champlain, formed by the junction of a stream with the St. Lawrence. They fell immediately on their knees and gave their thanks to the

Most High.   After singing some hymns, they raised
an altar which was decorated by Madame de la Peltrie and Mdlle. Mance, and celebrated the first great
mass on the island.   Father Vimont, as he performed
this holy rite of his Church, addressed the new colonists with words which foreshadowed the success of
the Roman Catholic Church in the greatest Canadian
city, which was first named Ville-Marie.

A picket enclosure, mounted with cannon, protected the humble buildings erected for the use of
the first settlers on what is now the Custom-house
Square.   The little stream—not much more than a
rivulet except in spring—which for many years rip-
pled between green, mossy banks, now struggles
beneath the paved street.

An obelisk of gray Canadian granite now stands
on this historic ground.   Madame de la Peltrie did
not remain more than two years in Ville-Marie, but
returned to the convent at Quebec which she had
left in a moment of caprice.   Mdlle. Mance, who
was Madame de Bullion's friend, remained at the
head of the Hotel Dieu.   The Sulpicians eventually
obtained control of the spiritual welfare, and in fact
of the whole island, though from necessity and policy the Jesuits were at first in charge.   It was not
until 1653 that one of the most admirable figures in
the religious and educational history of Canada,
Margaret Bourgeoys, a maiden of Troyes, came to
Ville-Marie, and established the parent house in
Canada of the Congrégation de Notre-Dame, whose
schools have extended in the progress of centuries
from Sydney, on the island of Cape Breton, to the
Pacific coast.

Yet during these years, while convents and hospitals were founded, while brave gentlemen and cultured women gave up their lives to their country and their faith, while the bells were ever calling their congregations to mass and vespers, the country was defended by a mere handful of inhabitants, huddled together at Quebec, at Three Rivers, and at the little settlement of Ville-Marie. The canoes of the Iroquois were constantly passing on the lakes and rivers of Canada, from Georgian Bay to the Richelieu, and bands of those terrible foes of the French and their Indian allies were ever lurking in the woods that came so dangerously close to the white settlements and the Indian villages.

In 1642, Father Isaac Jogues was returning from the missions on Lake Huron, with Couture, an interpreter, and Goupil, a young medical attendant —both donnés or lay followers of the Jesuits. They were in the company of a number of Hurons who were bringing furs to the traders on the St. Lawrence, when the Iroquois surprised them at the western end of Lake St. Peter's. The prisoners were taken by the Richelieu to the Mohawk country and Father Jogues was the first Frenchman to pass through Lake George *—with its picturesque hills and islets—which in a subsequent journey he named Lac du Saint-Sacrament, because he reached it on the eve of Corpus Christi. The Frenchmen were carried from village to village of the Iroquois, and

* It was so called in 1753, after the reigning sovereign of England by an ambitious and politic Irishman, Sir William Johnson, whose name is constantly occurring in the history of the wars between England and France.

tortured with all the cruel ingenuity usual in such cases. Goupil's thumb was cut off with a clam shell, as one way of prolonging pain. At night the prisoners were stretched on their backs with their ankles and wrists bound to stakes. Couture was adopted into the tribe, and was found useful in later years as an intermediary between the French and Mohawks. Goupil was murdered and his body tossed into a stream rushing down a steep ravine. Despite his sufferings Father Jogues never desisted from his efforts to baptise children and administer the rites of his Church to the tortured prisoners. On one occasion he performed the sacred office for a dying Huron with some rain or dewdrops which were still clinging to an ear of green corn which had been thrown to him for food. After indescribable misery, he was taken to Fort Orange, where the Dutch helped him to escape to France, but he returned to Canada in the following year.

Bands of Iroquois continued to wage war with relentless fury on all the Algonquin tribes from the Chaudière Falls of the Ottawa to the upper waters of the Saguenay. Bressani, a highly cultured Italian priest, was taken prisoner on the St. Lawrence, while on his way to the Huron missions, and carried to the Mohawk villages, where he went through the customary ordeal of torture. He was eventually given to an old woman who had lost a member of her family, but when she saw his maimed hands—one split between the little finger and the ring-finger—she sent him to the Dutch, who ransomed and sent him to France, whence he came back like Jogues, a year later.

In 1645 the Mohawks made peace with the French, but the other members of the Five Nations refused to be bound by the treaty. Father Isaac Jogues ventured into their country in 1646, and after a successful negotiation returned to consult the governor at Quebec; but unhappily for him he left behind a small box, filled with some necessaries of his simple life, with which he did not wish to encumber himself on this flying visit. The medicine-men or sorcerers, who always hated the missionaries as the enemies of their vile superstitious practices, made the Indians believe that this box contained an evil spirit which was the origin of disease, misfortune, and death. When Father Jogues came back, he found the village divided into two parties—one wishing his death, the other inclined to show him mercy, and after infinite wrangling between the factions, he was suddenly killed by a blow from a tomahawk as he was entering a long-house, to attend a feast to which he had been invited. His body was treated with contumely, and his head affixed to a post of the palisades of the village. He was the first martyr who suffered death at the hands of the Iroquois.

The " black robe " was now to be seen in every Indian community of Canada; among the Hurons and Algonquins as far as Lake Huron, among the White Fish tribe at the head-waters of the Saguenay, and even among the Abenakis of the Kennebec. Father Gabriel Druillétes, who had served an apprenticeship among the Montagnais, was in charge of this Abenaki mission, and in the course of years visited Boston, Plymouth, and Salem, in the interests of the Canadian French, who wished to enter into commercial relations with New England, and also induce its governments to enter into an alliance against the Iroquois. The authorities of the New England confederacy eventually refused to evoke the hostility of the dangerous Five Nations. Father Druillétes, however, won for Canada the enduring friendship of the Abenakis, as Acadian history shows.

It is impossible within the limited space of this chapter to give any accurate idea of the spirit of patience, zeal, and self-sacrifice which the Jesuit Fathers exhibited in their missions among the hapless Hurons. For years they found these Indians very suspicious of their efforts to teach the lessons of their faith. It was only with difficulty the missionaries could baptise little children. They would give sugared water to a child, and, apparently by accident, drop some on its head, and at the same time pronounce the sacramental words. Some Indians believed for a long time that the books and strings of beads were the embodiment of witchcraft. But the persistency of the priests was at last rewarded by the conversion, or at all events the semblance of conversion, of large numbers of Hurons. It would seem, according as their fears of the Iroquois increased, the Hurons gave greater confidence to the French, and became more dependent on their counsel. In fact, in some respects, they lost their spirit of self-reliance. In some villages the converts at last exceeded the number of unbelievers. By

1647 there were eighteen priests engaged in the work of eleven missions, chiefly in the Huron country, but also among the Algonquin tribes on the east and northeast of Lake Huron or at the outlet of Lake Superior. Each mission had its little chapel, and a bell, generally hanging on a tree. One central mission house had been built at Ste. Marie close to a little river, now known as the Wye, which falls into Thunder Bay, an inlet of Matchedash Bay. This was a fortified station in the form of a parallelogram, constructed partly of masonry, and partly of wooden palisades, strengthened by two bastions containing magazines. The chapel and its pictures attracted the special admiration of the Indians, whose imagination was at last reached by the embellished ceremonies of the Jesuits' church. The priests, thoroughly understanding the superstitious character of the Indians, made a lavish use of pictorial representations of pain and sufferings and rewards, allotted to bad and good. Father Le Jeune tells us that " such holy pictures are most useful object-lessons for the Indians." On one occasion he made a special request for " three, four, or five devils, tormenting a soul with a variety of punishments—one using fire, another serpents, and another pincers." The mission house was also constantly full of Indians, not simply enjoying these pictures, but participating also in the generous hospitality of the Fathers.

It was in 1648 that the first blow descended on this unhappy people who were in three years' time to be blotted out as a warlike, united nation in

America. In that year the Iroquois attacked the mission of St. Joseph (Teanaustayé), fifteen miles from Ste. Marie, where in 1638 a famous Iroquois, Ononkwaya, had been tortured. All the people had been massacred or taken prisoners in the absence of the warriors who were mostly in pursuit of a band of Iroquois. Father Daniel, arrayed in the vestments of his vocation, was among the first to fall a victim to the furious savages, who instantly cast his body into the flames of his burning chapel,—a fitting pyre for the brave soldier of the Cross. St. Ignace, St. Louis, and other missions were attacked early in the following year. Fathers Jean de Brebeuf and Gabriel Lalemant were tortured and murdered at St. Ignace. From village after village the shrieks of helpless women and men and children, tied to stakes in burning houses, ascended to a seemingly pitiless Heaven. Many persons were tortured on the spot, but as many or more reserved for the sport of the Iroquois villages. Father Brebeuf was bound to a stake, and around his neck was thrown a necklace of red-hot tomahawks. They cut off his lower lip, and thrust a heated iron rod down his throat. It was doubtless their delight to force a groan or complaint from this stalwart priest, whose towering and noble figure had always been the admiration of the Canadian Indians, but both he and Lalemant, a relatively feeble man, showed themselves as brave as the most courageous Indian warriors under similar conditions.

When a party from Ste. Marie came a few days later to the ruins of St. Ignace, they found the tortured bodies of the dead missionaries on the ground, and carried them to the mission house, where they were buried in sacred earth. The skull of the generous, whole-souled Brebeuf is still to be seen within a silver bust in the Hotel Dieu of Quebec. Father Garnier was killed at the mission of St. Jean (Etarita), in the raids which the Iroquois made at a later time on the Tobacco Nation, the kindred of the Hurons. Father Chabanel, who was on his way from St. Jean to Ste. Marie, was never heard of, and it is generally believed that he was treacherously killed and robbed by a Huron.

The Hurons were still numerous despite the losses they had suffered—counting even then more families than the Five Nations—but as they looked on the smoking ruins of their villages and thought of the undying hatred which had followed them for so many years they lost all courage and decided to scatter and seek new homes elsewhere. Father Ragueneau, the superior of the Jesuits, after consultation with the Fathers and Frenchmen at Ste. Marie, some fifty persons altogether, felt they could no longer safely remain in their isolated position when the Hurons had left the country. They removed all their goods to the Isle of St. Joseph, now one of the Christian Islands, near the entrance of Matchedash Bay, where they erected a fortified post for the protection of several thousand Hurons who had sought refuge here. Before many months passed, the Hurons believed that their position would be untenable when the Iroquois renewed their attacks, and determined to leave the island. Some ventured even among the Iroquois and were formally received into the Senecas and other tribes. A remnant remained a few months longer on the island, but they soon left for Quebec after killing some thirty of the bravest Iroquois warriors, who had attempted to obtain possession of the fort by a base act of treachery. A number belonging to the Tobacco Nation eventually reached the upper waters of the Mississippi where they met the Sioux, or Dacotahs, a fierce nation belonging to a family quite distinct from the Algonquins and Iroquois, and generally found wandering between the head-waters of Lake Superior and the Falls of St. Anthony. After various vicissitudes these Hurons scattered, but some found their rest by the side of the Detroit River, where they have been always known as Wyandots. Some three hundred Hurons, old and young, left St. Joseph for Quebec, where they were most kindly received and given homes on the western end of the Isle of Orleans, where the Jesuits built a fort for their security; but even here, as we shall see, the Iroquois followed them, and they were eventually forced to hide themselves under the guns of Quebec. War and disease soon thinned them out, while not a few cast in their lot with the Iroquois who were at last themselves seeking recruits. The Huron remnant finally found a resting-place at Lorette on the banks of the St. Charles, a few miles from the heights of the Capital.

The only memorials now in Canada of a once powerful people, that numbered at least twenty thousand souls before the time of their ruin and dispersion, are a remnant still retaining the language of their tribe on the banks of the Detroit; a larger settlement on the banks of the St. Charles, but without the distinguishing characteristics of their ancestors who came there from Isle St. Joseph; the foundations of the old mission house of Ste. Marie, and the remarkable graves and ossuaries which interest the student and antiquary as they wander in the summer-time through the picturesque country where the nation was once supreme.

10

X.

YEARS OF GLOOM—THE KING COMES TO
THE RESCUE OF CANADA—THE
IROQUOIS HUMBLED.

(1652–1667.)

IT was noon on the 20th May, 1656, when the
residents of Quebec were startled by the remarkable
spectacle of a long line of bark canoes drawn up on
the river immediately in front of the town. They
could hear the shouts of the Mohawk warriors making
boast of the murder and capture of unhappy Hurons, whom they had surprised on the Isle of Orleans
close by. The voices of Huron girls—" the very
flower of the tribe," says the Jesuit narrator—were
raised in plaintive chants at the rude command of
their savage captors, who even forced them to dance
in sight of the French, on whose protection they
had relied. The governor, M. de Lauzon, a weak,
incapable man, only noted for his greed, was perfectly paralysed at a scene without example, even
in those days of terror, when the Iroquois were
virtually masters of the St. Lawrence valley from
Huron to Gaspé.

At this very time a number of Frenchmen—probably fifty in all—were in the power of the Iroquois, and the governor had no nerve to make even an effort to save the Hurons from their fate. To understand the situation of affairs, it is necessary to go back for a few years. After the dispersion of the Hurons, the Iroquois, principally the Mohawks, became bolder than ever on the St. Lawrence. M. du Plessis-Bochat, the governor of Three Rivers, lost his life in a courageous but ill-advised attempt to chastise a band of warriors that were in ambush not far from the fort. Father Buteux was killed on his way to his mission of the Attikamegs or White Fish tribe, at the headwaters of the St. Maurice. In 1653, Father Poucet was carried off to a Mohawk village, where he was tortured in the usual fashion, and then sent back to Canada with offers of peace. The Senecas and Cayugas were then busily engaged in exterminating the Eries, who had burned one of their most famous chiefs, whose last words at the stake were prophetic: " Eries, you burn in me an entire nation ! "

A peace, or rather a truce, was declared formally in the fall of 1653. Then, at the request of the Onondagas, Father Simon le Moyne, a missionary of great tact and courage, who was the first Frenchman to ascend the St. Lawrence as far as the Thousand Isles, ventured into the Iroquois country, where he soon became a favourite. As a result of the negotiations which followed this mission, Governor de Lauzon was persuaded to send a colony to the villages of the Onondagas. This colony was composed of Captain Dupuy, an officer of the garrison, ten soldiers, and between thirty and forty volunteers. Father Dablon, who had previously gone with Father Chaumonot among the Onondagas, and had brought back the request for a colony, accompanied the expedition, which left Quebec in the month of June, 1656. On the way up the river the Onondagas were attacked by a band of Mohawks, when the boats carrying the French had gone ahead and were not within sight. Some of the Onondagas were killed and wounded, and then the Mohawks found out that they had surprised and injured warriors belonging to a tribe of their own confederacy. They endeavoured to explain this very serious act of hostility against their own friends and allies by the excuse that they had mistaken them for Hurons, whom they were on the way to attack. There is little doubt that they well understood the character of the expedition, and attacked it through envy of the success of the Onondagas in obtaining the settlement of Frenchmen in their villages.

When the Mohawks had made their explanations, they allowed the angry Onondagas to proceed on their journey, while they themselves went on to Quebec where, as we have already seen, they showed their contempt of the French by assailing the Hurons under the very guns of the fort of St. Louis. As soon as the French colony arrived at the Onondaga villages, they took possession of the country in the name of Jesus. On an eminence overlooking the lake they erected the mission of St. Mary of Gannentaha, the correct Iroquois name for Onondaga, in the vicinity of the present city of Syracuse. The Onondagas generally appeared delighted at the presence of the French, though at this very time the Mohawks continued to paddle up and down the St. Lawrence to the consternation of the French and Canadian Indians alike. The Jesuit priest Garreau was killed in one of these excursions while accompanying a party of Ottawas to Lake Superior.

The colonists at Gannentaha at last found that their own lives were threatened by a conspiracy to destroy them, but they succeeded in deceiving the Indians and in escaping to Canada in the month of March, after living only two years among the Onondagas. Whilst the Indians were sleeping away the effects of one of those mystic feasts, at which they invariably stuffed themselves to repletion, the Frenchmen escaped at night and reached the Oswego River, which they successfully descended by the aid of flat-boats which they had secretly constructed after the discovery of the plot. The party reached the French settlement with the loss of three men, drowned in the descent of the rapids of the St. Lawrence, probably the Cedars. The enterprise was most hazardous at this season when the ice had to be broken on the rivers before the boats could be used. But this very fact had its advantage, since the bark canoes of the Indians would have been useless had they followed the party. This exploit is one of the most remarkable ever performed by the French in those early days, and shows of what excellent material those pioneers of French colonisation were made.

In the spring of 1660 it was discovered that an

organised attack was to be made on all the settlements by a large force of over a thousand Iroquois, who were to assemble at the junction of the Ottawa and St. Lawrence rivers. It is stated on credible authority that Montreal—Canada in fact—was saved at this critical juncture by the heroism of a few devoted Frenchmen. Among the officers of the little garrison that then protected Montreal, was Adam Daulac or Dollard, Sieur des Ormeaux, who obtained leave from Maisonneuve, the governor, to lead a party of volunteers against the Iroquois, who were wintering in large numbers on the upper Ottawa. Sixteen brave fellows, whose names are all recorded in the early records of Montreal, took a solemn oath to accept and give no quarter, and after settling their private affairs and receiving the sacrament, they set out on their mission of inevitable death. Dollard and his band soon reached the impetuous rapids of the Long Sault of the Ottawa, destined to be their Thermopylæ. There, among the woods, they found an old circular inclosure of logs, which had been built by some Indians for defensive purposes. This was only a wretched bulwark, but the Frenchmen were in a state of exalted enthusiasm, and proceeded to strengthen it. Only two or three days after their arrival, they heard that the Iroquois were descending the river. The first attacks of the Iroquois were repulsed, and then they sent out scouts to bring up a large force of five hundred warriors who were at the mouth of the Richelieu. In the meantime they continued harassing the inmates of the fort, who were suffering for food and water. A band of Hurons who had joined the French just before the arrival of the Iroquois, now deserted them, with the exception of their chief, who as well as four Algonquins, remained faithful to the end. The forests soon resounded with the yells of the Iroquois, when reinforced. Still Dollard and his brave companions never faltered, but day after day beat back the astonished assailants, who knew the weakness of the defenders, and had anticipated an easy victory. At last a general assault was made, and in the struggle Dollard was killed. Even then the survivors kept up the fight, and when the Iroquois stood within the inclosure there was no one to meet them. Four Frenchmen, still alive, were picked up from the pile of corpses. Three of these were instantly burned, while the fourth was reserved for continuous torture a day or so later. The faithless Hurons gained nothing by their desertion, for they were put to death, with the exception of five who eluded their captors, and took an account of this remarkable episode to the French at Montreal. The Iroquois were obviously amazed at the courage of a few Frenchmen, and decided to give up, for the present, their project of attacking settlements defended by men so dauntless.

Even the forces of nature seemed at this time to conspire against the unfortunate colony. A remarkable earthquake, the effects of which can still be seen on the St. Lawrence,—at picturesque Les Eboulements, which means " earth slips," for instance,—commenced in the month of February, 1663, and did not cease entirely until the following summer.

Fervent appeals for assistance were made to the King by Pierre Boucher, the governor of Three Rivers, by Monseigneur Laval, the first bishop, by the Jesuit Fathers, and by the governors of New France, especially by M. d'Avaugour, who recommended that three thousand soldiers be sent to the colony, and allowed to become settlers after a certain term of service. By 1663, the total population of Canada did not exceed two thousand souls, the large majority of whom were at Quebec, Montreal, and Three Rivers. It was at the risk of their lives that men ventured beyond the guns of Montreal. The fur-trade was in the hands of monopolists. The people could not raise enough food to feed themselves, but had to depend on the French ships to a large extent. The Company of the Hundred Associates had been found quite unequal to the work of settling and developing the country, or providing adequate means of defence. Under the advice of the great Colbert, the King, young Louis Quatorze, decided to assume the control of New France and make it a royal province. The immediate result of the new policy was the coming of the Marquis de Tracy, a veteran soldier, as lieutenant-general, with full powers to inquire into the state of Canada. He arrived at Quebec on the 30th June, 1665, attended by a brilliant retinue. The Carignan-Salières Regiment, which had distinguished itself against the Turks, was also sent as a proof of the intention of the King to defend his long-neglected colony. In a few weeks, more than two thousand persons, soldiers and settlers, had come to Canada. Among

the number were M. de Courcelles, the first governor, and M. Talon, the first intendant, under the
new régime. Both were fond of state and ceremony,
and the French taste of the Canadians was now
gratified by a plentiful display of gold lace, ribbons,
wigs, ornamented swords, and slouched hats. Probably the most interesting feature of the immigration
was the number of young women as wives for the
bachelors—as the future mothers of a Canadian
people.

The new authorities went energetically to work.
The fortifications at Quebec, Three Rivers, and
Montreal were strengthened, and four new forts
erected from the mouth of the Richelieu to Isle La
Mothe on Lake Champlain. The Iroquois saw the
significance of this new condition of things. The
Onondagas, led by Garacontié, a friend of the Jesuits, made overtures of peace, which were favourably
heard by "Onontio," as the governor of Canada
had been called ever since the days of Montmagny,
whose name, "Great Mountain," the Iroquois so
translated. The Mohawks, the most dangerous tribe,
sent no envoys, and Courcelles, in the inclement
month of January, went into their country with a
large force of regular soldiers and fur hunters, but
missed the trail to their villages, and found himself
at the Dutch settlements, where he learned, to his
dismay, that the English had become the possessors
of the New Netherlands. On its return, the expedition suffered terribly from the severe cold, and lost
a number of persons who were killed by the Indians,
always hovering in the rear. The Mohawks then

thought it prudent to send a deputation to treat for peace, but the Marquis de Tracy and Governor de Courcelles were suspicious of their good faith, and sent a Jesuit priest to their country to ascertain the real sentiment of the tribe. He was recalled, while on the way, on account of the news that several French officers—one of them a relative of the lieutenant-general—had been murdered by the Mohawks. The lieutenant-general and governor at once organised a powerful expedition of the regular forces and Canadian inhabitants—some thirteen hundred in all—who left Quebec, with those two distinguished officers in command, on the day of the Exaltation of the Cross, the 14th September, 1666, as every effort was made to give a religious aspect to an army, intended to avenge the death of martyred missionaries, as well as to afford Canada some guarantees of peace. It took the expedition nearly a month to reach the first village of the Mohawks, but only to find it deserted. It was the same result in three other villages visited by the French. The Mohawks had made preparations for defence, but their courage failed them as they heard of the formidable character of the force that had come into the country. They deserted their homes and great stores of provisions. Villages and provisions were burned, and the Iroquois saw only ashes when they returned after the departure of the French. It was a great blow to these formidable foes of the French. Peace was soon made between the Five Nations and the French. The Marquis de Tracy then returned to France, and for twenty years

Canada had a respite from the raids which had so seriously disturbed her tranquillity, and was enabled at last to organise her new government, extend her settlements, and develop her strength for days of future trial.

XI.

CANADA AS A ROYAL PROVINCE—CHURCH AND STATE.

(1663-1759.)

WE have now come to that period of Canadian history when the political and social conditions of the people assumed those forms which they retained, with a few modifications from time to time, during the whole of the French régime. Four men now made a permanent impress on the struggling colony so long neglected by the French Government. First, was the King, Louis Quatorze, then full of the arrogance and confidence of a youthful prince, imbued with the most extravagant idea of his kingly attributes. By his side was the great successor of Mazarin, Jean Baptiste Colbert, whose knowledge of finance, earnest desire to foster the best resources of the kingdom, acknowledged rectitude, as well as admirable tact, gave him not only great influence in France, but enabled him to sway the mind of the autocratic king at most critical junctures. Happily for Colbert and Canada, Louis was a most industrious as well as pleasure-seeking sovereign, and studied the documents, which his various servants, from Colbert to the intendants in the colonies, sent him from time to time respecting their affairs.

In Canada itself the great minister had the aid of the ablest intendant ever sent by the King to Canada. This was Jean Baptiste Talon, who was not inferior to Colbert for his knowledge of commerce and finance, and clearness of intellect.

We see also in the picture of those times the piercing eyes and prominent nose of the ascetic face of the eminent divine who, even more than Colbert and Talon, has moulded the opinions of the Canadian people in certain important respects down to the present time. Monseigneur Laval was known in France as the Abbé de Montigny, and when the Jesuits induced him to come to Canada he was appointed grand vicar by the Pope, with the title of Bishop of Petræa.

Before the Canadian bishops and their agents in France decided on the Abbé de Montigny as a bishop they had made an experiment with the Abbé Queylus, one of the four Sulpician priests who came to Montreal in 1657, to look after the spiritual, and subsequently its temporal, interests. The Abbé had been appointed vicar-general of Canada by the Archbishop of Rouen, who claimed a certain ecclesiastical jurisdiction in the country, and the Jesuits at Quebec were at first disposed to make him bishop had they found him sufficiently ductile. After some experience of his opinions and character, they came to the conclusion that he was not a friend of their order, and used all their influence thenceforth to drive him from Canada. Then they chose the Abbé de Montigny, between whom and the Abbé Queylus there ensued a conflict of authority, which ended eventually in the defeat of the latter, as well as of the Archbishop of Rouen. The Abbé, divested of his former dignity and pretensions, returned in later years to the island of Montreal, of which the Sulpicians had become the seigniorial proprietors, when the original company were too weak to carry out the objects of their formation. The same order remains in possession of their most valuable lands in the city and island, where their seminary for the education of priests and youth generally occupies a high position among the educational institutions of the province.

Bishop Laval was endowed with an inflexible will, and eminently fitted to assert those ultramontane principles which would make all temporal power subordinate to the Pope and his vicegerents on earth. His claim to take precedence even of the governor on certain public occasions indicates the extremes to which this resolute dignitary of the Church was prepared to go on behalf of its supremacy.

No question can be raised as to Bishop Laval's charity and generosity. He accumulated no riches for himself—he spent nothing on the luxuries, hardly anything on the conveniences of life, but gave freely to the establishment of those famous seminaries at Quebec, which have been ever since identified with the religious and secular instruction of the French Canadians, and now form part of the noble university which bears his name.

With a man like Laval at the head of the Church in Canada at this early period, it necessarily exercised a powerful influence at the council board, and

PORTRAIT OF LAVAL, FIRST CANADIAN BISHOP.

in the affairs of the country generally. If he was sometimes too arbitrary, too arrogant in the assertion of his ecclesiastical dignity, yet he was also

animated by very conscientious motives with respect
to temporal questions. In the quarrel he had with
the governor, Baron Dubois d'Avaugour, an old
soldier, as to the sale of brandy to the Indians, he
showed that his zeal in the discharge of what he
believed to be a Christian and patriotic duty predominated above all such mercenary and commercial
considerations as animated the governor and officials,
who believed that the trading interests of the country were injured by prohibition. Laval saw that the
very life-blood of the Indians was being poisoned by
this traffic, and succeeded in obtaining the removal
of D'Avaugour. But all the efforts of himself and
his successor, Saint-Vallier, could not practically
restrain the sale of spirituous liquors, as long as the
fur-trade so largely depended on their consumption.

At this time, and for a long time afterwards, Prot-
estantism was unknown in Canada, for the King and
Jesuits had decided to keep the colony entirely free
from heresy. The French Protestants, after the
revocation of the edict of Nantes, gave to England
and the Netherlands the benefit of their great industry and manufacturing knowledge. Some of them
even found their way to America, and stimulated
the gathering strength of the southern colonies of
Virginia and the Carolinas.

The new régime under Colbert was essentially
parental. All emigration was under the direction of
the French authorities. Wives were sent by ship-
loads for the settlers, newly-wedded couples received
liberal presents suitable to their condition in a new
country; early marriages and large families were

CANADA AS A ROYAL PROVINCE. 161

encouraged by bounties. Every possible care was
taken by the officials and religious communities who
had charge of such matters, that the women were of
good morals, and suitable for the struggles of a
colonial existence.

While State and Church were providing a population for the country, Colbert and Talon were
devoting themselves to the encouragement of manu-
factures and commerce. When the Company of the
Hundred Associates, who appear to have been
robbed by their agents in the colony, fell to pieces,
they were replaced by a large organisation, known
as the Company of the West, to which was given
very important privileges throughout all the French
colonies and dependencies. The company, however, never prospered, and came to an end in 1674,
after ten years' existence, during which it inflicted
much injury on the countries where it was given so
many privileges. The government hereafter controlled all commerce and finance. Various manufac-
tures, like shipbuilding, leather, hemp, and beer,
were encouraged, but at no time did Canada show
any manufacturing or commercial enterprise. Under
the system of monopolies and bounties fostered by
Colbert and his successors, a spirit of self-reliance
was never stimulated. The whole system of government tended to peculation and jobbery—to the
enrichment of worthless officials. The people were
always extremely poor. Money was rarely seen in
the shape of specie. The few coins that came to
the colony soon found their way back to France.
From 1685 down to 1759 the government issued a

11

paper currency, known as "card money," because common playing cards were used. This currency bore the crown and fleur-de-lis and signatures of officials, and gradually became depreciated and worthless.

CARD ISSUE OF 1729, FOR 12 LIVRES.

While the townsfolk of Massachusetts were discussing affairs in town-meetings, the French inhabitants of Canada were never allowed to take part in public assemblies but were taught to depend in the most trivial matters on a paternal government. Canada was governed as far as possible like a province of France. In the early days of the colony, when it was under the rule of the Company of the Hundred Associates, the governors practically exercised arbitrary power, with the assistance of a nominal council chosen by themselves. When, however, the King took the government of the colony into his own hands, he appointed a governor, an intendant, and a supreme or—as it was subsequently called—a sovereign council, of which the bishop was a member, to administer under his own direction the affairs of the country. The governor, who was generally a soldier, was nominally at the head of affairs, and had the direction of the defences of the colony, but to all intents and purposes the intendant, who was a man of legal attainments, had the greater influence. He was the finance minister, and made

FIFTEEN SOL PIECE.

special reports to the King on all Canadian matters. He had the power of issuing ordinances which had the effect of law, and showed the arbitrary nature of the government to which the people were subject. Every effort to assemble the people for public purposes was systematically crushed by the orders of the government. A public meeting of the parishioners to consider the cost of a new church could not be held without the special permission of the intendant. Count Frontenac, immediately after his arrival, in 1672, attempted to assemble the different orders of the colony, the clergy, the *noblesse* or *seigneurs*, the judiciary, and the third estate, in imitation of the old institutions of France. The French king promptly rebuked the haughty governor for this attempt to establish a semblance of popular government.

From that moment we hear no more of the assembling of " Canadian Estates," and an effort to elect a mayor and aldermen for Quebec also failed through the opposition of the authorities. An attempt was then made to elect a syndic—a representative of popular rights in towns—but M. de Mésy, then governor, could not obtain the consent of the bishop, who knew that his views were those of the King. The result of the difficulties that followed was the dismissal of the governor, who died soon afterwards, but not until he had confessed his error, and made his peace with the haughty bishop whom he had dared to oppose.

The administration of local affairs throughout the province was exclusively under the control of the King's officers at Quebec. The ordinances of the intendant and of the council were the law. The country was eventually subdivided into the following divisions for purposes of government, settlement, and justice: 1. Districts. 2. Seigniories. 3. Parishes. The districts were simply established for judicial and legal purposes, and each of them bore the name of the principal town within its limits— viz., Quebec, also called the *Prévoté de Québec*, Montreal, and Three Rivers. In each of these districts there was a judge, appointed by the king, to adjudicate on all civil and criminal matters. An appeal was allowed in the most trivial cases to the supreme or superior council, which also exercised original jurisdiction. The customary law of Paris, which is based on the civil law of Rome, was the fundamental law of Canada, and still governs the civil rights of the people.

The greater part of Canada was divided into large estates or seigniories, with the view of creating a colonial *noblesse*, and of stimulating settlement in a wilderness. It was not necessary to be of noble birth to be a Canadian seigneur. Any trader with a few louis d'or and influence could obtain a patent for a Canadian lordship. The seignior on his accession to his estate was required to pay homage to the King, or to his feudal superior in case the lands were granted by another than the King. The seignior received his land gratuitously from the crown, and granted them to his vassals, who were generally known as *habitants*, or cultivators of the soil, on condition of their making small annual payments in money or produce known as *cens et rente*. The *habitant* was obliged to grind his corn at the seignior's mill *(moulin banal)*, bake his bread in the seignior's oven, give his lord a tithe of the fish caught in his waters, and comply with other conditions at no time onerous or strictly enforced in the days of the French régime. This system had some advantages in a new country like Canada, where the government managed everything, and colonisation was not left to chance. The seignior was obliged to cultivate his estate at a risk of forfeiture, consequently it was absolutely necessary that he should exert himself to bring settlers upon his lands. The obligation of the *habitant* to grind his corn in the seignior's mill was clearly an advantage for the settlers. In the early days of the colony, however, the seigniors were generally too poor to fulfil this condition, and the *habitants* had to grind corn between stones, or in rude hand mills. The seigniors had the right of dispensing justice in certain cases, though it was one he very rarely exercised. As respects civil affairs, however, both lord and vassal were to all intents and purposes on the same footing, for they were equally ignored in matters of government.

In the days of the French régime, the only towns for many years were Quebec, Montreal, and Three Rivers. In remote and exposed places—like those on the Richelieu, where officers and soldiers of the Carignan-Salières Regiment had been induced to settle—palisaded villages had been built. The principal settlements were, in course of time, established on the banks of the St. Lawrence, as affording in those days the easiest means of intercommunication. As the lots of a seigniorial grant were limited in area—four arpents in front by forty in depth— the farms in the course of time assumed the appearance of a continuous settlement on the river. These various settlements became known in local phraseology as *Côtes*, apparently from their natural situation on the banks of the river. This is the origin of Côte des Neiges, Côte St. Louis, Côte St. Paul, and of many picturesque villages in the neighbourhood of Montreal and Quebec. As the country became settled, parishes were established for ecclesiastical purposes and the administration of local affairs. Here the influential men were the curé, the seignior, and the captain of the militia. The seignior, from his social position, exercised a considerable weight in the community, but not to the degree that the representative of the Church enjoyed. The church in the parishes was kept up by tithes, regulated by ordinances, and first imposed by Bishop Laval for the support of the Quebec Seminary and the clergy. Next to the curé in importance was the captain of the militia. The whole province was formed into a militia district, so that, in times of war, the inhabitants might be obliged to perform military service under the French governor. In times of peace these militia officers in the parishes executed the orders of the governor and intendant in all matters affecting the King. In case it was considered necessary to build a church or presbytery, the intendant authorised the *habitants* to assemble for the purpose of choosing from among themselves four persons to make, with the curé, the seignior, and the captain of the militia, an estimate of the expense of the structure. It was the special care of the captain of the militia to look after the work, and see that each parishioner did his full share. It was only in church matters, in fact, that the people of a parish had a voice, and even in these, as we see, they did not take the initiative. The Quebec authorities must in all such cases first issue an ordinance.

Under these circumstances it is quite intelligible that the people of Canada were obliged to seek in the clearing of the forest, in the cultivation of the field, in the chase, and in adventure, the means of livelihood, and hardly ever busied themselves about public matters in which they were not allowed to take even a humble part.

XII.

THE PERIOD OF EXPLORATION AND DISCOVERY:
PRIESTS, FUR-TRADERS, AND COUREURS
DE BOIS IN THE WEST.

(1634–1687.)

WE have now come to that interesting period in
the history of Canada, when the enterprise and courage of French adventurers gave France a claim to
an immense domain, stretching from the Gulf of
St. Lawrence indefinitely beyond the Great Lakes,
and from the basin of those island seas as far as the
Gulf of Mexico. The eminent intendant, Talon,
appears to have immediately understood the importance of the discovery which had been made by
the interpreter and trader, Jean Nicolet, of Three
Rivers, who, before the death of Champlain, probably in 1634, ventured into the region of the lakes,
and heard of " a great water "—no doubt the Mississippi—while among the Mascoutins, a branch of
the Algonquin stock, whose villages were generally
found in the valley of the Fox River. He is considered to have been the first European who reached
Sault Ste. Marie—the strait between Superior and

Huron—though there is no evidence that he ventured beyond the rapids, and saw the great expanse of lake which had been, in all probability, visited some years before by Etienne Brulé, after his escape from the Iroquois. Nicolet also was the first Frenchman who passed through the straits of Mackinac or Michillimackinac, though he did not realise the importance of its situation in relation to the lakes of the western country. It is told of him that he made his appearance among the Winnebagos in a robe of brilliant China damask, decorated with flowers and birds of varied colours, and holding a pistol in each hand. This theatrical display in the western forest is adduced as evidence of his belief in the story that he had heard among the Nipissings, at the head-waters of the Ottawa, that there were tribes in the west, without hair and beards, like the Chinese. No doubt, he thought he was coming to a country where, at last, he would find that short route to the Chinese seas which had been the dream of many Frenchmen since the days of Cartier. We have no answer to give to the question that naturally suggests itself, whether Champlain ever saw Nicolet on his return, and heard from him the interesting story of his adventures. It was not until 1641, or five years after Champlain's death, that Father Vimont gave to the world an account of Nicolet's journey, which, no doubt, stimulated the interest that was felt in the mysterious region of the west. From year to year the Jesuit and the trader added something to the geographical knowledge of the western lakes, where the secret was soon to be unlocked by means of the rivers which fed those remarkable reservoirs of the continent. In 1641 Fathers Raymbault and Jogues preached their Faith to a large concourse of Indians at the Sault between Huron and Superior, where, for the first time, they heard of the Sioux or Dacotah, those vagrants of the northwest, and where the former died without realising the hope he had cherished, of reaching China across the western wilderness. Then came those years of terror, when trade and enterprise were paralysed by those raids of the Iroquois, which culminated in the dispersion of the Hurons. For years the Ottawa valley was almost deserted, and very few traders or *coureurs de bois* ventured into the country around the western lakes. An enterprising trader of Three Rivers, Médard Chouart, Sieur de Grosseilliers, is believed to have reached the shores of Lake Superior in 1658, and also to have visited La Pointe, now Ashland, at its western extremity, in the summer of 1659, in company with Pierre d'Esprit, Sieur Radisson, whose sister he had married. Some critical historians do not altogether discredit the assumption that these two venturesome traders ascended the Fox and Wisconsin rivers, and even reached the Mississippi, twelve years before Jolliet and Marquette.

With the peace that followed the destruction of the Mohawk villages by Tracy and Courcelles, and the influx of a considerable population into Canada, the conditions became more favourable for exploration and the fur trade. The tame and steady life of the farm had little charm for many restless spirits, who had fought for France in the Carignan Regiment. Not a few of them followed the roving Canadian youth into the forest, where they had learned to love the free life of the Indians. The priest, the *gentilhomme*, and the *coureur de bois*, each in his way, became explorers of the western wilderness.

From the moment the French landed on the shores of Canada, they seemed to enter into the spirit of forest life. Men of noble birth and courtly associations adapted themselves immediately to the customs of the Indians, and found that charm in the forest and river which seemed wanting in the tamer life of the towns and settlements. The English colonisers of New England were never able to win the affections of the Indian tribes, and adapt themselves so readily to the habits of forest life as the French Canadian adventurer.

A very remarkable instance of the infatuation which led away so many young men into the forest, is to be found in the life of Baron de Saint-Castin, a native of the romantic Bernese country, who came to Canada with the Carignan Regiment during 1665, and established himself for a time on the Richelieu. But he soon became tired of his inactive life, and leaving his Canadian home, settled on a peninsula of Penobscot Bay (then Pentagoët), which still bears his name. Here he fraternised with the Abenaquis, and led the life of a forest chief, whose name was long the terror of the New England settlers. He married the daughter of Madocawando, the implacable enemy of the English, and so influential did he become that, at his summons, all the tribes on

the frontier between Acadia and New England
would proceed on the warpath.   He amassed a fortune of three hundred thousand crowns in " good
dry gold," but we are told he only used the greater
part of it to buy presents for his Indian followers,
who paid him back in beaver skins.   His life at Pentagoët, for years, was very active and adventurous,
as the annals of New England show.   In 1781 he
returned to France, where he had an estate, and
thenceforth disappeared from history.   His son, by
his Abenaqui Baroness, then took command of his
fort and savage retainers, and after assisting in the
defence of Port Royal, and making more than one
onslaught on the English settlers of Massachusetts,
he returned to Europe on the death of his father.
The poet Longfellow has made use of this romantic
episode in the early life of the Acadian settlements:

> " The warm winds blow on the hills of Spain,
> The birds are building and the leaves are green,
> The Baron Castine, of St. Castine,
> Hath come at last to his own again."

Year after year saw the settlements almost de-
nuded of their young men, who had been lured away
by the fascinations of the fur trade in the forest
fastnesses of the west.   The government found all
their plans for increasing the population and colonising the country thwarted by the nomadic habits of
a restless youth.   The young man, whether son of
the *gentilhomme*, or of the humble *habitant*, was carried away by his love for forest life, and no enact-
ments, however severe—not even the penalty of

Canadiens en Raquette allant en guerre sur la nege

CANADIAN TRAPPER, FROM LA POTHERIE.

173

death—had the effect of restraining his restlessness. That the majority of the *coureurs de bois* were a reckless, dare-devil set of fellows, it is needless to say. On their return from their forest haunts, after months of savage liberty, they too often threw off all restraint, and indulged in the most furious orgies. Montreal was their favourite place of resort, for here were held the great fairs for the sale of furs. The Ottawas, Hurons, and other tribes came from distant parts of the North and West, and camped on the shores in the immediate vicinity of the town. When the fair was in full operation, a scene was represented well worthy of the bold brush of a Doré. The royal mountain, then as now, formed a background of rare sylvan beauty. The old town was huddled together on the low lands near the river, and was for years a mere collection of low wooden houses and churches, all surrounded by palisades. On the fair ground were to be seen Indians tricked out in their savage finery; *coureurs de bois* in equally gorgeous apparel; black-robed priests and busy merchants from all the towns, intent on wheedling the Indians and bush rangers out of their choicest furs.

The principal rendezvous in the west was Mackinac or Michillimackinac. Few places possessed a more interesting history than this old headquarters of the Indian tribes and French voyageurs. Mackinac may be considered, in some respects, the key of the upper lakes. Here the tribes from the north to the south could assemble at a very short notice and decide on questions of trade or war. It was long the metropolis of a large portion of the Huron and Ottawa nations, and many a council, fraught with the peace of Canada, was held there in the olden times. It was on the north side of the straits that Father Marquette—whose name must ever live in the west—some time in 1671 founded the mission of St. Ignace, where gradually grew up the most important settlement which the French had to the northwest of Fort Frontenac or Cataraqui. The French built a chapel and fort, and the Hurons and Ottawas lived in palisaded villages in the neighbourhood. The *coureurs de bois* were always to be seen at a point where they could be sure to find Indians in large numbers. Contemporary writers state that the presence of so many unruly elements at this distant outpost frequently threw the whole settlement into a sad state of confusion and excitement, which the priests were at times entirely unable to restrain. Indians, soldiers, and traders became at last so demoralised, that one of the priests wrote, in his despair, that there seemed no course open except " deserting the missions and giving them up to the brandy-sellers as a domain of drunkenness and debauchery."

But it would be a mistake to judge all the *coureurs de bois* by the behaviour of a majority, who were made up necessarily from the ruder elements of the Canadian population. Even the most reckless of their class had their work to do in the opening up of this continent. Despising danger in every form, they wandered over rivers and lakes and through virgin forests, and " blazed " a track, as it were, for the future pioneer. They were the first to lift the veil of mystery that hung, until they came, on many a solitary river and forest. The posts they raised by the side of the western lakes and rivers, were so many videttes of that army of colonisers who have built up great commonwealths in that vast country, where the bushranger was the only European two centuries ago. The most famous amongst their leaders was the quick-witted Nicholas Perrot—the explorer of the interior of the continent. Another was Daniel Greysolon Duluth, who became a Canadian Robin Hood, and had his band of bushrangers like any forest chieftain. For years he wandered through the forests of the West, and founded various posts at important points, where the fur trade could be prosecuted to advantage. Posterity has been more generous to him than it has been to others equally famous as pioneers, for it has given his name to a city at the head of Lake Superior. Like many a forest which they first saw in its primeval vastness, these pioneers have disappeared into the shadowy domain of an almost forgotten past, and their memory is only recalled as we pass by some storm-beat cape, or land-locked bay, or silent river, to which may still cling the names they gave as they swept along in the days of the old régime.

XIII.

THE PERIOD OF EXPLORATION AND DISCOVERY: FRANCE IN THE VALLEY OF THE MISSISSIPPI.

(1672–1687.)

SAULT STE. MARIE was the scene of a memorable episode in the history of New France during the summer of 1671. Simon François Daumont, Sieur St. Lusson, received a commission from the government of Quebec to proceed to Lake Superior to search for copper mines, and also to take formal possession of the basin of the lakes and its tributary rivers. With him were two men, who became more famous than himself—Nicholas Perrot and Louis Jolliet, the noted explorers and rangers of the West. On an elevation overlooking the rapids, around which modern enterprise has built two ship-canals, St. Lusson erected a cross and post of cedar, with the arms of France, in the presence of priests in their black robes, Indians bedecked with tawdry finery, and bushrangers in motley dress. In the name of the " most high, mighty, and redoubted monarch, Louis XIV. of that name, most Christian King of France and of

Navarre," he declared France the owner of Sault Ste. Marie, Lakes Huron and Superior, and Isle of Mackinac, and " all of adjacent countries, rivers, and lakes, and contiguous streams." As far as boastful words and priestly blessings could go, France was mistress of an empire in the great West.

Three names stand out in bold letters on the records of western discovery: Jolliet, the enterprising trader, Marquette, the faithful missionary, and La Salle, the bold explorer. The story of their adventures takes up many pages in the histories of this fascinating epoch. Talon may be fairly considered to have laid the foundations of western exploration, and it was left for Louis de Baude, Comte de Frontenac, who succeeded Courcelles as governor in 1672, to carry out the plans of the able intendant when he left the St. Lawrence.

Jolliet, a Canadian by birth, was wisely chosen by Talon—and Frontenac approved of the choice—to explore the West and find the " great water," of which vague stories were constantly brought back by traders and bushrangers. Jolliet was one of the best specimens of a trader and pioneer that Canadian history gives us. His roving inclinations were qualified by a cool, collected brain, which carried him safely through many a perilous adventure. He had for his companion Father Marquette, who was then stationed at the mission of St. Ignace, and had gathered from the Indians at his western missions—especially at La Pointe on Lake Superior—valuable information respecting the " great water " then called the " Missipi." Both had many sympathies in common. Jolliet had been educated by the Jesuits in Canada, but unlike La Salle, he was in full accord with their objects. Marquette possessed those qualities of self-sacrifice and religious devotion which entitle him to rank with Lalemant, Jogues, and Brebeuf. While Jolliet was inspired by purely ambitious and trading instincts, the missionary had no other hope or desire than to bring a great region and its savage communities under the benign influence of the divine being whose heavenly face seemed ever present, encouraging him to fresh efforts in her service. It was in the spring of 1673 that these two men started with five companions in two canoes on their journey through that wilderness, which stretched beyond Green Bay—an English corruption of Grande Baie. Like Nicolet, they ascended the Fox River to the country of the Mascoutins, Foxes, and Kickapoos, where they obtained guides to lead them across the portage to the Wisconsin. The adventurers had now reached the low "divide" between the valleys of the Lakes and the Mississippi. The Fox River and its affluents flowed tranquilly to the great reservoirs of the St. Lawrence, while the Wisconsin, on which they now launched their canoes, carried them to a mighty river, which ended they knew not where. A month after leaving St. Ignace they found themselves " with a great and inexpressible joy "—to quote Marquette's words— on the rapid current of a river which they recognised as the Missipi. As they proceeded they saw the low-lying natural meadows and prairies where herds of buffalo were grazing, marshes with a luxuriant growth of wild rice, the ruined castles which nature had in the course of many centuries formed out of the rocks of the western shores, and the hideous manitous which Indian ingenuity had pictured on the time-worn cliffs. They had pleasant interviews with the Indians that were hunting the roebuck and buffalo in this land of rich grasses. Their canoes struggled through the muddy current, which the Missouri gave as its tribute to the Missipi, passed the low marshy shores of the Ohio, and at last came near the mouth of the Arkansas, where they landed at an Indian village which the natives called Akamsea. Here they gathered sufficient information to enable them to form the conclusion that the great river before their eyes found its way, not to the Atlantic or Pacific oceans, but to the Gulf of Mexico. Then they decided not to pursue their expeditions further at that time, but to return home and relate the story of their discovery. When they came to the mouth of the Illinois River, they took that route in preference to the one by which they had come, followed the Des Plaines River,—where a hill still bears Jolliet's name—crossed the Chicago portage, and at last found themselves at the southern extremity of Lake Michigan. It was then the end of September, and Jolliet did not reach Canada until the following summer. When nearly at his journey's end, Fate dealt him a cruel blow, his canoe was capsized after running the Lachine Rapids just above Montreal, and he lost all the original notes of his journey. Frontenac, however, received from him a full account of his explorations, and sent it to France.

Two centuries later than this memorable voyage of Jolliet, a French Canadian poet-laureate described it in verse fully worthy of the subject, as the following passage and equally spirited translation * go to show:

LA DÉCOUVERTE DU MISSISSIPPI.	THE DISCOVERY OF THE MISSISSIPPI.
Jolliet . . . Jolliet . . . quel spectacle féérique Dut frapper ton regard, quand ta nef historique Bondit sur les flots d'or du grand fleuve inconnu . . . Quel éclair triomphant, à cet instant de fièvre, Dut resplendir sur ton front nu ? . . .	O, Jolliet, what splendid faery dream Met thy regard, when on that mighty stream, Bursting upon its lonely unknown flow, Thy keel historic cleft its golden tide :— Blossomed thy lip with what stern smile of pride? What conquering light shone on thy lofty brow ?
Le voyez-vous là-bas, debout comme un prophète, L'œil tout illuminé d'audace satisfaite, La main tendue au loin vers l'Occident bronzé, Prendre possession de ce domaine immense, Au nom du Dieu vivant, au nom roi de France, Et du monde civilisé? . . .	Behold him there, a prophet, lifted high, Heart-satisfied, with bold, illumined eye, His hand outstretched toward the sunset furled, Taking possession of this domain immense, In the name of the living God, in the name of the King of France, And the mighty modern world.
Puis, bercé par la houle, et bercé par ses rêves, L'oreille ouverte aux bruits harmonieux des grèves,	Rocked by the tides, wrapt in his glorious moods, Breathing perfumes of lofty odorous woods,

* Mr. W. Wilfrid Campbell, F.R.S.C., a well-known English-Canadian poet, has translated for " The Story of Canada " these verses of his French contemporary Fréchette.

Humant l'acre parfum des grands
  bois odorants,
Rasant les îlots verts et les dunes
  d'opale,
De méandre en méandre, au fil
  l'onde pâle,
    Suivre le cours des flots
    errants. . . .

A son aspect, du sein des flottan-
  tes ramures,
Montait comme un concert de
  chants et de murmures ;
Des vols d'oiseaux marins s'éle-
  vaient des roseaux,
Et, pour montrer la route à la
  pirogue frêle,
S'enfuyaient en avant, traînant
  leur ombre grêle
    Dans le pli lumineux des
    eaux.

Et, pendant qu'il allait voguant
  à la dérive,
On aurait dit qu'au loin, les
  arbres de la rive,
En arceaux parfumés penchés sur
  son chemin,
Saluaient le héros dont l'éner-
  gique audace
Venait d'inscrire encor le nom de
  notre race
    Aux fastes de l'esprit
    humain.

Ears opened to the shores' harmonious tunes,
Following in their dreams and
  voices mellow,
To wander and wander in the
  thread of the pale billow,
Past islands hushed and opales-
  cent dunes.

Lo, as he comes, from out the
  waving boughs,
A rising concert of murmurous
  song upflows,
Of winging sea-fowl lifting from
  the reeds ;
Pointing the route to his swift
  dripping blade,
Then skimming before, tracing
  their slender shade
In luminous foldings of the
  watery meads.

And as he journeys, drifting with
  its flow,
The forests lifting their glad
  roofs aglow,
In perfumed arches o'er his keel's
  swift swell,
Salute the hero, whose undaunted
  soul
Had graved anew " LA FRANCE"
  on that proud scroll
Of human genius, bright, imperishable.

Jolliet's companion, the Jesuit missionary, never
realised his dream of many years of usefulness in
new missions among the tribes of the immense
region claimed by France. In the spring of 1675 he
died by the side of a little stream which finds its
outlet on the western shore of Lake Michigan, soon
after his return from a painful journey he had taken,
while in a feeble state of health, to the Indian communities of Kaskaskia between the Illinois and

Wabash rivers. A few months later his remains were removed by some Ottawas, who knew and loved him well, and carried to St. Ignace, where they were buried beneath the little mission chapel. His memory has been perpetuated in the nomenclature of the western region, and his statue stands in the rotunda of that marble capitol which represents, not the power and greatness of that France which he loved only less than his Church, but the national development of those English colonies which, in his time, were only a narrow fringe on the Atlantic coast, separated from the great West by mountain ranges which none of the most venturesome of their people had yet dared to cross.

The work that was commenced by Jolliet and Marquette, of solving the mystery that had so long surrounded the Mississippi, was completed by Réné Robert Cavalier, Sieur de la Salle, a native of Rouen, who came to Canada when quite a young man, and obtained a grant of land from the Sulpician proprietors of Montreal at the head of the rapids, then known as St. Louis. Like so many Canadians of those days he was soon carried away by a spirit of adventure. He had heard of the " great water " in the west, which he believed, in common with others, might lead to the Gulf of California. In the summer of 1669 he accompanied two Sulpician priests, of Montreal, Dollier de Casson and Gallinée, on an expedition they made, under the authority of Governor Courcelles, to the extreme western end of Ontario, where he met Jolliet, apparently for the first time, and probably had many conversations

with him respecting the west and south, and their
unknown rivers. He decided to leave the party and
attempt an exploration by a southerly route, while
the priests went on to the upper lakes as far as the
Sault. Of La Salle's movements for the next two
years we are largely in the dark—in some respects
entirely so. It has been claimed by some that he
first discovered the Ohio, and even reached the
Mississippi, but so careful an historian as Justin
Winsor agrees with Shea's conclusion that La Salle
" reached the Illinois or some other affluent of the
Mississippi, but made no report and made no claim,
having failed to reach the great river." It was on
his return from these mysterious wanderings, that
his seigniory is said to have received the name of
La Chine as a derisive comment on his failure to find
a road to China. In the course of years the name
was very commonly given, not only to the lake but
to the rapids of St. Louis.

We now come to sure ground when we follow La
Salle's later explorations, on which his fame entirely
rests. Frontenac entered heartily into his plans of
following the Mississippi to its mouth, and setting
at rest the doubts that existed as to its course. He
received from the King a grant of Fort Frontenac
and its surrounding lands as a seigniory. This fort
had been built by the governor in 1673 at Cataraqui,
now Kingston, as an advanced trading and defensive
post on Lake Ontario. La Salle considered it a
most advantageous position for carrying on his ambitious projects of exploration. He visited France
in 1677 and received from the King letters-patent

185

authorising him to build forts south and west in that region "through which it would seem a passage to Mexico can be discovered." On his return to Canada he was accompanied by a Recollet friar, Father Louis Hennepin, and by Henry de Tonty, the son of an Italian resident of Paris, both of whom have associated their names with western exploration. Of all his friends and followers, Tonty, who had a copper hand in the place of the one blown off in an Italian war, was the most faithful and honest, through the varying fortunes of the explorer's career from this time forward. To Father Hennepin I refer in another place.

Both Hennepin and Tonty accompanied La Salle on his expedition of 1678 to the Niagara district, where, above the great falls, near the mouth of Cayuga Creek, he built the first vessel that ever ventured on the lakes, and which he named the "Griffin" in honour of Frontenac, whose coat-of-arms bore such a heraldic device. The loss of this vessel, while returning with a cargo of furs from Green Bay to Niagara, was a great blow to La Salle, who, from this time until his death, suffered many misfortunes which might well have discouraged one of less indomitable will and fixity of purpose. On the banks of the Illinois River, a little below the present city of Peoria, he built Fort Crèveccœur, probably as a memorial of a famous fort in the Netherlands, not long before captured by the French. While on a visit to Canada, this post was destroyed by some of his own men in the absence of Tonty, who had been left in charge. These men were subsequently captured not far from Cataraqui, and severely punished.

In the meantime, three Frenchmen, Father Hennepin, Michel Accaut, and one Du Gay, in obedience to La Salle's orders, had ventured to the upper waters of the Mississippi, and were made prisoners by a wandering tribe of Sioux. Not far from the falls of St. Anthony Father Hennepin met with the famous forest ranger, Duluth, who was better acquainted with the Sioux country than any other living Frenchman, and was forming ambitious designs to explore the whole western region beyond Lake Superior. Father Hennepin, who had been adopted by an aged Sioux chief, was free to follow Duluth back to the French post at the Straits of Mackinac. This adventure of Father Hennepin is famous in history, not on account of any discoveries he actually made, but on account of the claim he attempted to establish some years after his journey, of having followed the Mississippi to the Gulf. In the first edition of his book, printed in 1683—*Description de la Louisiane*—no such claim was ever suggested, and it was only in 1697 that the same work appeared in an enlarged form,—*La Nouvelle Découverte*—crediting Hennepin with having descended the great river to its outlet. It is not necessary here to puncture a falsehood which was long ago exposed by historical writers. His history of having reached the Gulf of Mexico is as visionary as the traveller's tales of Norumbega. Indeed, he could not even claim a gift of fertile invention in this case, as the very account of his alleged discovery was obviously plagiarised from Father Membré's narrative of La Salle's voyage of 1682, which appears in Le Clercq's *Premier Établissement de la Foy*.

When La Salle was again able to venture into the west he found the villages of the Illinois only blackened heaps of ruins—sure evidence of the Iroquois having been on the warpath. During the winter of 1681 he remained at a post he had built on the banks of the St. Joseph in the Miami country, and heard no news of his faithful Tonty. It was not until the spring, whilst on his way to Canada for men and supplies, that he discovered his friend at Mackinac, after having passed through some critical experiences among the Iroquois, who, in conjunction with the Miamis, had destroyed the villages of the Illinois, and killed a number of those Indians with their customary ferocity. Tonty had finally found rest and security in a village of the Pottawattomies at the head of Green Bay.

On the 6th of February, 1682, La Salle passed down the swift current of the Mississippi on that memorable voyage which led him to the Gulf of Mexico. He was accompanied by Tonty, and Father Membré, one of the Recollet order, whom he always preferred to the Jesuits. The Indians of the expedition were Abenakis and Mohegans, who had left the far-off Atlantic coast and Acadian rivers, and wandered into the great west after the unsuccessful war in New England, which was waged by the Sachem Metacomet, better known as King Philip, and only ended with his death in 1676, and the destruction of many settlements in the colony of Plymouth.

They met with a kindly reception from the Indians encamped by the side of the river, and, for the first time, saw the villages of the Taënsas and Natchez, who were worshippers of the sun. At last on the 6th of April, La Salle, Tonty, and Dautray, went separately in canoes through the three channels of the Mississippi, and emerged on the bosom of the great Gulf. Not far from the mouth of the river where the ground was relatively high and dry, a column was raised with the inscription :

> *" Louis le Grand, roy de France et de Navarre, règne ; le neuviesme Avril, 1682."*

And La Salle took possession of the country with just such ceremonies as had distinguished a similar proceeding at Sault Ste. Marie eleven years before. It can be said that Frenchmen had at least fairly laid a basis for future empire from the Lakes to the Gulf. It was for France to show her appreciation of the enterprise of her sons and make good her claim to such a vast imperial domain. The future was to show that she was unequal to the task.

The few remaining years of La Salle's life were crowded with misfortunes. Duchesneau, the intendant, who had succeeded Talon, was an enemy of both Frontenac and the explorer. The distinguished governor was recalled by his royal master, who was tired of the constant complaints of his enemies against him, and misled by their accusations. La Barre, the incompetent governor who followed Frontenac, took possession of Fort St. Louis, which La Salle had succeeded, after his return from the Gulf of Mexico, in erecting at Starved Rock on the banks of the Illinois not far from the present city of Ottawa, where a large number of Indians had returned to their favourite home. In France, however, the importance of his discovery was fully recognised, and when he visited his native country in 1683-4 he met with a very cordial reception from the King, and Seignelay, who had succeeded his father, Colbert, when he resigned. The King ordered that La Salle's forts be restored to him, and gave him a commission to found colonies in Louisiana, as the new country through which the Mississippi flowed had been called since 1682. By a strange irony of Fate, the expedition of 1684 passed the mouth of the Mississippi, and La Salle made the first French settlement on the Gulf somewhere in the vicinity of Matagorda Bay, in the present State of Texas. Misery was the lot of the little colony from the very first moment it landed on that lonely shore. When his misfortunes were most grievous, La Salle decided to make an effort to reach the Illinois country, but he was assassinated by two of his own men—Duhaut and Liotot—near a branch of the Trinity River. His nephew Moranget, Nika, a faithful Shawnee who had been by his side for years, and Sayet, his own servant, suffered the same fate. The leader of the murderers was killed soon afterwards by one of his accomplices, and the others found a refuge among the Indians; but of their subsequent fate we know nothing positively, except that they were never brought to justice, if any one of them returned to Canada or France. The few Frenchmen remaining in Texas were either killed or captured by unfriendly Indians, before the Spaniards could reach the place to expel these intruders on their domain. La Salle himself never found a burial place, for his body was left to wolves and birds of prey. His name has not been perpetuated in Louisiana, though it has been given to a county of Texas as well as to a city and county of Illinois, which was originally included in French Louisiana. The most noteworthy tribute to his memory has been paid by the historian Parkman, who has elevated him almost to the dignity of a hero. La Salle's indomitable energy, his remarkable courage in the face of disaster, his inflexibility of purpose under the most adverse circumstances, must be always fully recognised, but at the same time one may think that more tact and skill in managing men, more readiness to bend and conciliate, might have spared him much bitterness and trouble, and even saved his life at the end. That he did good service for France all will admit, though his achievement in reaching the Mississippi was rendered relatively easy after the preliminary expedition of Jolliet and Marquette.

XIV.

CANADA AND ACADIA: FROM FRONTENAC TO THE
TREATY OF UTRECHT.

(1672–1713.)

In the previous chapter I have shown the important part that the Count de Frontenac took in stimulating the enterprise of La Salle and other explorers, and it now remains for me to review those other features of the administration of that great governor, which more or less influenced the fortunes of the province committed to his charge.

A brave and bold soldier, a man of infinite resources in times of difficulty, as bold to conceive as he was quick to carry out a design, dignified and fascinating in his manner when it pleased him, arrogant and obstinate when others thwarted him, having a keen appreciation of the Indian character, selfish where his personal gain was concerned, and yet never losing sight of the substantial interests of France in America, the Count de Frontenac was able, for nineteen years, to administer the affairs of New France with remarkable ability, despite his

Frontenac

Frontenac, from Hébert's Statue at Quebec.

personal weaknesses, to stimulate and concentrate
her energies and resources, and to make her when
he died a power in America far beyond what her
population or actual strength seemed to justify.
The Iroquois learned at last to tremble at his name,
and the Indian allies of Canada, from the Abenakis
of Acadia to the Illinois of the West, could trust in
his desire and ability to assist them against their
ferocious enemy. As is the case with all great men,
his faults and virtues have been equally exaggerated.
The Recollets, whom he always favoured, could
never speak too well of him, whilst the Jesuits,
whom he distrusted, did all they could to tarnish
his reputation.

It is not profitable or necessary in this story of
Canada to dwell on the details of Frontenac's administration of public affairs during the first years
of his régime (1672–1682), which were chiefly noted
for the display of his faults of character—especially
his obstinacy and impatience of all opposition. He
was constantly at conflict with the bishop, who was
always asserting the supremacy of his Church, with
the intendant Duchesneau, who was simply a spy
on his actions, with the Jesuits, whom he disliked
and accused of even being interested in the sale of
brandy, and with traders like Governor Perrot of
Montreal who eventually found himself in the Bastile for a few days for having defied the edict of the
King against the *coureurs de bois* who were under his
influence and helped him in the fur trade.

The complaints against Frontenac from influential
people in Canada at last became so numerous that

he was recalled to France in 1682. His successor, La Barre, proved himself thoroughly incapable. The interests of the province were seriously threatened at that time by the intention of the Iroquois to destroy the Illinois and divert the western traffic to the Dutch and English, whose carriers they wished to become. La Barre was well aware how much depended on the protection of the Illinois and the fidelity of the Indians on the lakes. La Hontan, a talkative but not always veracious writer, who was in Canada at this time, gives us an insight into the weakness of the governor, whose efforts to awe the Iroquois ended in an abortive expedition which was attacked by disease and did not get beyond La Famine, now Salmon River, in the Iroquois country. The famous "La Grande Gueule," or Big Mouth, —so called on account of his eloquence,—made a mockery of the French efforts to deceive him by a pretence of strength, and openly declared the intention of the Iroquois to destroy the Illinois, while La Barre dared not utter a defiant word in behalf of his allies. This incapable governor was soon recalled and the Marquis de Denonville, an officer of dragoons, sent in his place. One of the most notable incidents of the new administration was the capture of the fortified trading-posts belonging to the English Company of Hudson's Bay, by the Chevalier de Troyes and a number of Canadians from Montreal, among whom were the three famous sons of Charles Le Moyne, Iberville, Sainte-Hélène, and Maricourt, the former of whom became ere long the most distinguished French Canadian of his time. The next

event of importance was the invasion of the country
of the Senecas, and the destruction of their villages
and stores of provisions.   This was a most doubtful
triumph, since it left the Senecas themselves un-
hurt.   How ineffectual it was even to awe the Iroquois, was evident from the massacre of La Chine,
near Montreal, in the August of 1689, when a large
band fell upon the village during a stormy night,
burned the houses, butchered two hundred men,
women and children, and probably carried off at
least one hundred and twenty prisoners before they
left the island of Montreal, where the authorities
and people seemed paralysed for the moment.   The
whole history of Canada has no more mournful story
to tell than this massacre of this unhappy settlement
by the side of the beautiful lake of St. Louis.   The
Iroquois had never forgiven the treachery of the
governor during the winter of 1687, at Fort Frontenac, where he had seized a large number of
friendly Indians of the Five Nations who had settled
in the neutral villages of Kenté (now Quinté) and
Ganneious (now Gananoque), not many miles from
the fort.   Some of the men were distributed among
the missions of Quebec, and others actually sent to
labour in the royal galleys of France, where they
remained until the survivors were brought back by
Frontenac, when he and other Frenchmen recognised the enormity of the crime that had been committed by Denonville, who is immediately responsible
for the massacre of La Chine.   The Iroquois never
forgot or forgave.

The French authorities soon recognised the fact

that Denonville was entirely unequal to the critical condition of things in Canada, and decided in 1689 to send Frontenac back. During his second term, which lasted for nearly ten years, there was now and then some friction between himself and the intendant, on matters of internal government, and between himself and the bishop and the Jesuits with respect to amusements which the clergy always discountenanced; but he displayed on the whole more tact and judgment in his administration of public affairs. Undoubtedly the responsibilities now resting upon him tasked the energies of a man of seventy-two years of age to the utmost. In Acadia, whose interests were now immediately connected with those of Canada, he had to guard against the aggressive movements of New England. The English of New York and the adjacent colonies were intriguing with the Iroquois and the Foxes, always jealous of French encroachments in the northwest, and encouraging them to harass the French settlers. The efforts of the English to establish themselves in Hudson's Bay and Newfoundland, had to be met by vigorous action on the part of Canadians. In fact, we see on all sides the increasing difficulties of France in America, on account of the rapid growth of the English colonies.

When Frontenac arrived in Canada, war had been declared between France and England. James II. had been deposed and William of Orange was on the English throne. Before the governor left France a plan had been devised at the suggestion of Callières, the governor of Montreal, for the conquest

of New York.   An expedition of regular troops and
Canadian volunteers were to descend from Canada
and assault New York by land, simultaneously with
an attack by a French squadron from the sea.   Un-
foreseen delays prevented the enterprise from being
carried out, when success was possible.   Had New
York and Albany been captured, Callières was to
have been the new governor.   Catholics alone
would be allowed to remain in the province, and all
the other inhabitants would be exiled—an atrocious
design which was to be successfully executed sixty
years later, by the English authorities, in the Acadian settlements of Nova Scotia.

Count de Frontenac organised three expeditions
in 1690 against the English colonies, with the view
of raising the depressed spirits of the Canadians and
showing their Indian allies how far Onontio's arm
would reach,.   The first party, led by Mantet and
Sainte-Hélène, and comprising among the volunteers
Iberville, marched in the depth of winter on Corlaer
(Schenectady), surprised the sleeping and negligent
inhabitants, killed a considerable number, took
many prisoners, and then burned nearly all the
houses.   The second party, under the command of
François Hertel, destroyed the small settlement of
Salmon Falls on the Piscataqua, and later formed a
junction with the third party, led by Portneuf of
Quebec, and with a number of Abenakis under
Baron de Saint-Castin.   The settlement at Casco
Bay, defended by Fort Loyal (Portland) surrendered
after a short struggle to these combined forces, and
the garrison was treated with great inhumanity.   The

cruelties practised by the Indian allies invested these raids with additional terrors.

While Frontenac was congratulating himself on the success of this ruthless border warfare, and on the arrival at Montreal of a richly laden fleet of canoes from the west, the English colonies concerted measures of retaliation in a congress held at New York. The blow first fell on Acadia, which had been in the possession of France since the treaty of Breda. Port Royal was taken without difficulty in 1690 by Sir William Phips, and the shore settlements at La Hève and Cape Sable ravaged by his orders.

Another expedition organised in New York and Connecticut to attack Montreal, was a failure, although a raid was made by Captain John Schuyler into the country, south of Montreal, and a number of persons killed at La Prairie. A more important expedition was now given to the command of Phips, a sturdy figure in colonial annals, who had sprung from humble parentage in Maine, and won both money and distinction by the recovery of the riches of a Spanish galleon which had been wrecked on the Spanish Main half a century before. His fleet, consisting of thirty-two vessels—including several men-of-war, and carrying 2300 troops, exclusively provincials, fishermen, farmers, and sailors—appeared in the middle of October, 1690, off Quebec, whose defences had been strengthened by Frontenac, and where a large force had assembled from the French towns and settlements. As soon as the fleet came to an anchorage, just below the town, Phips sent a messenger to present a letter to Frontenac, asking him to surrender the fort. This envoy was led blindfolded up the heights and brought into the presence of the governor, who was awaiting him in the fort, surrounded by a number of officers dressed in the brilliant uniform of the French army. As soon as he had recovered from the surprise which for the moment he felt, when the bandage was taken off his eyes, and he saw so brilliant an array of soldierly men, he read the letter, which, " by the orders of the King and Queen of England and of the government of the colony of New England," demanded " the surrender of the forts and castles undemolished, and of all munitions untouched, as also an immediate surrender of your persons and property at my discretion." The envoy, when the whole letter was read, took out his watch, and remarking that it was ten o'clock, asked that he be sent back by eleven. Count de Frontenac's answer was defiant. He refused to recognise William of Orange as the lawful sovereign of England, and declared him an " usurper." The haughty governor continued in the same strain for a few moments longer, and when he had closed, Phips's messenger asked that the answer be given in writing. " No," he replied, " I have none to give but by the mouth of my cannon; and let your general learn that this is no way to send a summons to a man like me. Let him do the best on his side, as I am resolved to do on mine."

Phips and his officers determined to attack Quebec in the rear by the way of Beauport, simultaneously with a fierce cannonading by the fleet. A considerable force, under the command of Major Walley, landed, and after some days of unhappy experiences, during which Phips showed his incapacity to manage the siege, the former was obliged to find refuge in the ships, without having succeeded in crossing the St. Charles. By this time Frontenac had at least three thousand men, many of them veterans, in Quebec, and Phips considered it his only prudent course to return to Boston, where he arrived with the loss of many vessels and men, chiefly from disasters at sea. The French had lost very few men by the cannonading and in the skirmishing on the St. Charles—probably not more than sixty killed and wounded—and celebrated their victory with great enthusiasm. Religious processions marched through the streets to the cathedral and churches, *Te Deums* were chanted, the colonial admiral's flag, which had been cut down by a lucky shot from the fort, was borne aloft in triumph, a new church was consecrated to *Notre Dame de la Victoire*, and a medal was struck in Paris in commemoration of the event. In Boston, the people received with dismay the news of the failure of an expedition which had ended so ignobly and involved them so heavily in debt.

The Iroquois, in league with the English of New York, where the able governor Dongan and his successor Andros, carefully watched over the interests of their colony, continued to be a constant menace to the French on the St. Lawrence, and to their allies in the West. In order to strengthen

themselves with the Five Nations, the New York
authorities sent Major Peter Schuyler, with a force
of Mohawks, Dutch, and English, to harass the
settlements near Montreal.   An obstinate fight
occurred at La Prairie between him and a considerable force of troops, Canadians, Hurons, and Iroquois
of the Canadian mission under Varennes, an able
officer, but Schuyler succeeded in breaking through
the ranks of his enemies and reaching the Richelieu,
whence he returned to Albany without further losses.
In Acadia, however, the French gained an advantage
by the recovery of Port Royal by Villebon.

At this time occurred an interesting episode.   A
young girl of only fourteen years, Madelaine, daughter of the seigneur of Verchères, on the south side
of the St. Lawrence, ten miles from Montreal, successfully held her father's fort and block-house
against a band of Iroquois, with the aid of only six
persons, two of whom were boys, and one an old
man.   Day and night, for a week, she was on the
watch against surprise by the Indians, who were
entirely deceived by her actions, and supposed the
fort was held by a garrison.   At last a reinforcement
came to the succour of the brave girl, and the Indians
retreated.   The courage displayed by this Canadian
heroine is an evidence of the courage shown by the
people of Canada generally, under the trying circumstances that so constantly surrounded them
throughout the whole of the French régime.

In 1693 the Mohawks were punished by an expedition composed of regulars, militia, and bushrangers, with a large Indian contingent, chiefly

drawn from the Iroquois mission near Montreal, the modern settlement of Caughnawaga. This force was led by Mantet, Courtemanche, and La Noue, who succeeded in destroying the Mohawk villages after a fierce fight, in killing a large number, and in capturing several hundreds. The English, who had early information of the invasion, sent Major Peter Schuyler to pursue the retreating force, but it was too late. The immediate result of this success was a revival of trade. A large fleet of canoes came down from the upper lakes with a rich store of furs, that had been accumulating at Mackinac and other posts for nearly three years, on account of the Iroquois. Frontenac's triumph was complete, and he was called far and wide " the father of the people, the preserver of the country."

Returning for the moment to the Atlantic shores of Acadia, we find that the French arms triumphed in 1696 at Pemaquid, always an important point in those days of border warfare.

The fort, which was of some pretensions, was captured by the French under Iberville and the Abenakis under Saint-Castin, and after its destruction Iberville went on to Newfoundland, where the French ruined the English settlements at St. John and other places. Then the fleet proceeded to Hudson's Bay, where the French recaptured the trading posts which had been retaken a short time previously by the English.

In the meantime Frontenac had decided on an expedition against the Onondagas. Early in July, 1696, despite his age, he led the expedition to Fort

Frontenac, which he had restored, and after a delay of a few days he went on to the Onondaga town, which he destroyed with all its stores of provisions, and its standing fields of maize. The Oneida village was also destroyed, and a number of men taken prisoners as hostages for their good behaviour. The Onondagas had fled, and the only one captured was an aged chief, who was wantonly tortured to death. It was now clear to the Iroquois that the English of New York could not defend them from the constant raids of the French, and they now made offers of peace, provided it did not include the western allies of France. Frontenac, however, was resolved to make no peace, except on terms which would ensure the security of the French for many years. He died in the November of 1698 amid the regrets of the people of all classes who admired his great qualities as a leader of men.

Callières, of Montreal, an able and brave soldier, who succeeded him, soon brought the Iroquois difficulty to an issue. The calumet was smoked and peace duly signed, in a great council held in the August of 1701, at Montreal, where assembled representatives of the Indian nations of the West, of the Abenakis, and of the Iroquois. From that time forward, Canada had no reason to fear the Iroquois, who saw that the French were their masters. The trade with the West was now free from the interruptions which had so long crippled it.

The Treaty of Ryswick, which was ratified in 1697, lasted for only five years. Then broke out the great conflict known in Europe as the War of

CAPTURE OF FORT NELSON, IN HUDSON'S BAY, BY THE FRENCH ; FROM LA POTHERIE.

A. French boats.   B. Camp.   C. Mortar.   D. Skirmishers.   E. Fort Nelson.

205

the Spanish Succession. The reckless ambition of Louis XIV., then in the plenitude of his power, had coveted the throne of Spain for his own family, and brought him into conflict with England when he recognised the Pretender as the rightful heir to the English Crown. Queen Anne, the daughter of James II. and sister of Mary, queen of William III., had succeeded to the throne, and the war which was declared on the 15th May, 1702, was thereafter known in America by her name. The Abenakis, who had promised peace, broke their pledges, and joined the French Canadian bands in attacking Wells, Saco, and Haverhill, and the annals of New England tell many a sad story of burning homes, of murdered men and women. The people of New England retaliated on Acadia, and several ineffective attempts were made to take Port Royal by Colonels Church and Wainwright, who proved their incapacity. A movement was then made for the conquest of Canada by the English colonists, but it failed in consequence of an European emergency having diverted the British squadron intended for America to the shores of Portugal. An expedition was next organised in 1710, under the command of Colonel Nicholson, a man of much sagacity and audacity, though of little or no military experience, for the capture of Port Royal, which was surrendered by the governor, Subercase, and from that day this historic place has been known as Annapolis Royal, in honour of the reigning sovereign. It was not until the following year that the British Government yielded to the urgent representations of the colonies, and sent to America a powerful armament to attempt the conquest of Canada. The fleet was under the orders of Sir Hovenden Walker, whose incapacity was only equalled by that of the commander of the troops, Colonel Hill. After the loss of eight transports and nearly nine hundred men in a storm near the Isle aux Œufs, at the entrance of the St. Lawrence, the incapable admiral decided to give up the project of besieging Quebec, and without even venturing to attack the little French post of Plaisance, he returned to England, where he was received with marks of disfavour on all sides, and forced soon afterwards to retire to South Carolina. While New England was sadly disappointed by this second failure to take Quebec, the French of Canada considered it a providential interposition in their behalf, and the church, which had been first named after the defeat of Phips, was now dedicated to *Notre Dame des Victoires.*

All this while the French dominion was slowly and surely extending into the great valleys of the West and South. A fort had been built opposite to the Jesuit mission of St. Ignace, on the other side of the Strait of Michillimackinac, and it was now also proposed to make the French headquarters at Detroit, which had been founded by Antoine de la Mothe-Cadillac, despite the opposition of the Jesuits, who wished to have the mission field of the West in their own hands, and resented the intention to establish Recollets and other priests at the new post. As soon as the French established themselves permanently at this key to the Lakes and West, the

English practically gave up for fifty years the hope
of acquiring the Northwest, and controlling the
Indian trade. French pioneers were pushing their
way into the valleys of the Illinois and the Wabash.
Perrot and Le Sueur had taken possession of the
region watered by the upper Mississippi and its
affluents. Iberville and Bienville had made small
settlements at Biloxi, Mobile, and on the banks of
the Mississippi, and with them was associated one
of the most admirable figures of Canadian history,
Henry de Tonty, who had left his fort on the Illinois. In 1711 Louisiana was made a separate government, with Mobile as the capital, and included
the whole region from the Lakes to the Gulf, and
from the Alleghanies to the Rocky Mountains. By
the time of the Treaty of Utrecht the Indian tribes
of the West were, for the most part, in the interest
of the French, with the exception of the Sioux,
Sauks, and Foxes, whose hostility was for a long
time an impediment to their progress on the upper
reaches of the Mississippi.

Louis XIV. was humbled by Marlborough on the
battlefields of Blenheim, Ramillies, and Oudenarde,
and obliged to agree to the Treaty of Utrecht,
which was a triumph for England, since it gave her
possession of Acadia, Hudson's Bay, Newfoundland
(subject to the rights of France in the fisheries), and
made the important concession that France should
never molest the Five Nations under the dominion
of Great Britain. Such questions as the limits of
Acadia, and the bounds of the territory of the Iroquois, were to be among the subjects of fruitful
controversy for half a century.

CHEVALIER D'IBERVILLE.

209

XV.

ACADIA AND ÎLE ROYALE, FROM THE TREATY OF UTRECHT TO THE TREATY OF AIX-LA-CHAPELLE.

(1713–1748.)

THE attention of Louis XIV. and his ministers was now naturally directed to Cape Breton, which, like the greater island of Newfoundland, guards the eastern approaches to the valley of the St. Lawrence. Cape Breton had been neglected since the days of Denys, though its harbours had been for over two centuries frequented by sailors of all nationalities. Plaisance, the Placentia of the Portuguese, had been for years the headquarters of the French fisheries in the Gulf of St. Lawrence, but when Newfoundland was ceded to the English, all the French officials and fishermen removed to English Harbour, on the eastern coast of Cape Breton, ever since known as Louisbourg. The island itself was called Île Royale, and its first governor was M. de Costabelle, who had held a similar position at Plaisance. It was not, however, until 1720, that France commenced the construction of the fortifications of Louisbourg, which eventually cost her over ten million dollars of modern money, and even then, they were never completed in accordance with the original design, on account of the enormous expense which far exceeded the original estimates. The fortifications were built on an oblong neck of land on the southern shore of the port, which lies only two leagues from that famous cape from which the island takes its name. The fortress occupied an area of over one hundred acres, and was planned on the best system of Vauban and other great masters of engineering skill, who intended it should be, as indeed it was, despite some faulty details of construction, the most complete example of a strongly fortified city in America. The harbour was also defended by batteries on an island at the entrance, and at other important points, while there were fortified works and small garrisons at Port Toulouse (St. Peter's) and Port Dauphin (St. Anne's). The government of the island was modelled on that of Canada, to which it was subordinate, and the governor was generally a military man. During the years the fortress was in possession of the French, there were probably, on an average, nearly two thousand people living in the town and vicinity, but this number was increased in the time of war by the inhabitants of the adjacent ports and bays.

During the thirty years that elapsed between the Treaty of Utrecht and the breaking out of war between France and Great Britain, the people of New England found that the merely nominal possession of Acadia by the English was of little security to them, while the French still held the island of Cape Breton and had the fealty of the Indians and Acadians, who were looking forward to the restoration of the country to its former owners.   England systematically neglected Nova Scotia, where, until the foundation of Halifax, her only sign of sovereignty was the dilapidated fort at Annapolis, with an insignificant garrison, utterly unable to awe the Acadian French, and bring them completely under the authority of the British Crown.   French emissaries, chiefly priests, —notably the treacherous Le Loutre —were constantly at work among the Acadians, Micmacs, and Abenakis, telling them that France would soon regain her dominion in Acadia.   For years the Abenakis tomahawked the helpless English colonists that had made their homes in the present State of Maine, in the vicinity of the Kennebec and the Penobscot.   The insidious policy of Vaudreuil and other governors of Canada, acting under instructions from France, was to keep alive the hostility of the Abenakis so as to prevent the settlement of that region known as Northern New England, one of whose rivers, the Kennebec, gave easy access to the St. Lawrence near Quebec.   From Annapolis to Canseau the Micmacs destroyed life and property, and kept the English posts in constant fear.

New England took a signal revenge at last on the cruel and treacherous Abenakis, and inflicted on them a blow from which they never recovered.   At Norridgewock perished the famous missionary, Sebastian Rale, beneath whose black robe beat the heart of a dauntless soldier, whose highest aspirations were to establish his creed and promote the ambitious designs of France in Acadia. A peace was made in 1726 between the colonists and the Abenakis, but New England felt she had no efficient security for its continuance while Acadian and Indian could see in the great fortress of Cape Breton powerful evidence that France was not yet willing to give up the contest for dominion in Acadia. Northern New England became now of relatively little importance in view of the obvious designs of France to regain Nova Scotia.

We have now come to an important period in the history of America as well as of Europe. In 1739 Walpole was forced to go to war with Spain, at the dictation of the commercial classes, who wished to obtain control of the Spanish Main. Then followed the War of the Austrian Succession, in which France broke her solemn pledge to Charles VI., Emperor of Germany, that she would support his daughter, Maria Theresa, in her rights to reign over his hereditary dominions. But when the Emperor was dead, France and other Powers proceeded to promote their own ambitious and selfish designs. France wished to possess the rich Netherlands, and Spain, Milan; Frederick of Prussia had no higher desire than to seize Silesia, and to drive Austria from Germany. Bavaria claimed the Austrian duchy of Bohemia. Maria Theresa was to have only Hungary and the duchy of Austria. The King of England was jealous of Prussia, and thought more of his Hanoverian throne than of his English crown. It became the interest of England to assist Austria and prevent the success of France, now the ally of Spain, forced to defend her colonial possessions in America. The complications in Europe at last compelled France and England to fight at Dettingen in 1743, and George II. won a doubtful victory, but war was not actually declared between these two nations until some months later. England had no reason to congratulate herself on the results, either in Europe or America. Her fleet met only with disaster, and her commerce was destroyed on the Spanish Main. Four years later she won a victory over the Spanish fleet in the Mediterranean, but hardly had her people ceased celebrating the event, than they heard that the combined forces of Hanover, Holland, and England, under the Duke of Cumberland, had been badly beaten by Marshal Saxe at Fontenoy.

It was at this time, when the prospects of England were so gloomy on the continent of Europe, that Englishmen heard, with surprise and gratification, that the strong fortress of Louisbourg in French America had surrendered to the audacious attack of four thousand colonists of New England.

A combination of events had aided the success of the brave enterprise. The news of the declaration of war reached Louisbourg at least two months before it was known in Boston, and the French Governor, M. Duquesnel, immediately sent out expeditions to capture the English posts in Nova Scotia. Canseau, at the entrance of the strait of that name, was easily taken, and the garrison carried to Louisbourg, but Annapolis Royal was successfully defended by Colonel Mascarene, then governor of

Nova Scotia. All these events had their direct influence on the expedition which New England sent in the spring of 1745 against Louisbourg. The prisoners who had been captured at Canseau had remained until the autumn in Louisbourg, and the accounts they brought back of its condition gave Shirley and others reason to believe that if an expedition was, without loss of time, sent against it, there would be a fair chance of success. Not only did they learn that the garrison was small, but that it was discontented, and a mutiny had actually broken out on account of the soldiers not having received the usual additions to their regular pay for work on the fortifications. The ramparts were stated to be defective in more than one place, while gales and other causes had delayed the arrival of the ships which arrived every year with provisions and reinforcements. These facts gave additional confidence to Governor Shirley of Massachusetts, William Vaughan of New Hampshire, and many influential men who had already conceived the idea of striking a blow at the French which would give the English control of the whole coast from Cape Sable to the entrance of the St. Lawrence.

The expedition against Louisbourg consisted of over four thousand men, of whom Massachusetts, which then included the present State of Maine, contributed nearly one-third. Colonel Pepperrell of Kittery on the Piscataqua, who had command, with the title of lieutenant-general, was a man of wealth and influence, though without any military experience. His excellent judgment and undaunted

courage, however, contributed largely to the success
of this bold venture. Captain Edward Tyng, a
capable colonial sailor, was the commodore of the
little fleet of thirteen vessels, carrying in all about
two hundred guns. The Puritan spirit of New England had much influence in organising an expedition, and whose flag had a motto suggested by the
Methodist revivalist, Whitfield : " *Nil desperandum
Christo duce*." The story of the success of the
New England troops, in conjunction with the small
English fleet, under the command of Commodore
Warren, has been often told, and we need not dwell
on its details. M. Duchambon was at the time governor of Louisbourg, and maintained the defence for
nearly forty days. The capitulation of the fortress
was hastened by the fact that the English fleet captured the French frigate *Vigilante*, on whose arrival
the garrison had been depending for weeks. On
the afternoon of June 17th, General Pepperrell
marched at the head of his army through the West
or Dauphin gate into the town, and received the
keys from the commandant, who, with his garrison
drawn up in line, received him in the King's bastion.
One hundred and fifty years later a granite column
was raised on the same historic ground in honour of
this famous victory, which caused such rejoicings
throughout England and America.

By the articles of capitulation, the garrison and
residents of Louisbourg, probably two thousand persons in all, were transported to France. The settlement of Port Toulouse and Port Dauphin had
been captured, the first before, and the other during

the siege. The leader of the New England expedition was rewarded with a baronetcy, the first distinction of the kind ever given to a colonist, while Warren was promoted to the rank of rear-admiral of the blue.

If the English Government had fully understood the necessities of their American colonies, they would have immediately followed the advice of Governor Shirley, who was a man of statesmanlike views and bold conception, though he possessed no capacity as a leader of military operations, as his later career in America proved. He suggested that an expedition should attack Montreal by the usual route of Lake Champlain, while an English fleet ascended the St. Lawrence and besieged Quebec. All the colonies set to work with considerable energy to carry out this scheme, but it came to nought, in consequence of the failure of the Duke of Newcastle, the most incapable statesman ever at the head of imperial affairs, to redeem his promise. It was then proposed to attack Fort Frederick at Crown Point, on the western side of Lake Champlain, where it contracts to a narrow river, but its progress was arrested by the startling news that the French were sending out a fleet to take Cape Breton and Acadia, and attack Boston and other places on the Atlantic sea-board.

France had heard with dismay of the loss of Cape Breton, which she recognised as a key to the St. Lawrence, and made two efforts to recover it before the war closed in 1748. One of the noblest fleets that ever sailed from the shores of France left Ro-

chelle in 1746 for Cape Breton, under the command
of M. de la Rochefoucauld, the Duke d'Anville, an
able, sensitive man, who, however, had had no
naval experience.   Storm and pestilence attacked
the fleet, which found a refuge in the harbour of
Chebouctou, afterwards Halifax, where the unfortunate Admiral died from an apopleptic seizure.   His
successor, M. d'Estournelle, committed suicide in
a fit of despondency caused by the responsibility
thrown upon him, when men were dying by hundreds every day on those lonely Acadian shores.
The French lost between two and three thousand
men by disease or casualties, and the remnant of
the great fleet, which was to have restored the fortunes of France in America, returned home under
the command of M. de la Jonquière without having
even attempted to capture the half-ruined fort at
Annapolis.   Another fleet in 1747, under M. de St.
George and the Marquis de la Jonquière, the latter
of whom became subsequently Governor of Canada,
never reached its destination, but was defeated off
Cape Finisterre by a more powerful fleet under Ad-
mirals Anson and Warren.

The Canadian Government, of which the Marquis
de Beauharnois was then the head, had confidently
expected to regain Acadia, when they heard of the
arrival of the Duke d'Anville's fleet, and immediately sent M. de Ramesay to excite the Acadians,
now very numerous—probably ten thousand altogether—to rise in arms against the few Englishmen
at Port Royal.   He had with him a considerable
force of Indians and Canadians, among the latter

such distinguished men as Beaujeu, Saint-Ours, Boishébert, Lanaudière, but the news of the disasters that had crippled the fleet, forced him to give up his plan of attacking Annapolis, and to withdraw to the isthmus of Chignecto, where he built a small fort at Baie Verte. In the following year, 1747, he succeeded in surprising and capturing Colonel Arthur Noble and a considerable force of New England troops who had taken possession of the houses of the Acadian French at Grand Pré, one of the most fertile and beautiful districts of the province, afterwards still more famous in poetry and history. This exploit, however, did not materially change the aspect of things in Acadia, where the French Acadians had entirely disappointed the hopes of Ramesay and his government. Had they been as active or enterprising as their compatriots on the banks of the St. Lawrence, they might easily, at that time, have won back Acadia for France. As it was, however, Ramesay was not able to gain a firm foothold beyond the isthmus. Even the success he won was neutralised by the activity of Governor Shirley, who was ever alive to the importance of Nova Scotia, and immediately sent another force to occupy the meadows of Grand Pré.

In 1748 English diplomacy, careless of colonial interests, restored the island of Cape Breton to France by the Treaty of Aix-la-Chapelle, in return for the commercial post of Madras, which had been taken by the French in the East Indies where England and France were now rivals for the supremacy. It was the persistency of the French to regain pos-

session of so valuable a bulwark to their great
dominion of Canada, that forced the English cabi-
net to restore it at a time when the nation was
threatened by a Catholic pretender, and disheartened at the results of the war on the continent.
Weary of the struggle and anxious for a breathing
space, England deserted Maria Theresa and made
peace with France.

XVI.

THE STRUGGLE FOR DOMINION IN THE GREAT VALLEYS OF NORTH AMERICA—PRELUDE.

(1748–1756.)

THE map that is placed at the beginning of this chapter outlines the ambitious designs conceived by French statesmen soon after the Treaty of Aix-la-Chapelle. We see the names of many posts and forts intended to keep up communications between Canada and Louisiana, and overawe the English colonies then confined to a relatively narrow strip of territory on the Atlantic coast. Conscious of the mistake that they had made in giving up Acadia, the French now claimed that its " ancient limits " did not extend beyond the isthmus of Chignecto—in other words, included only Nova Scotia. Accordingly they proceeded to construct the forts of Gaspereau and Beauséjour on that neck of land, and also one on the St. John River, so that they might control the land and sea approaches to Cape Breton from the St. Lawrence where Quebec, enthroned on her picturesque heights, and Montreal at the confluence of the Ottawa and the St. Lawrence, held the keys to Canada. The approaches by the way of Lake Champlain and the Richelieu were defended by the fort of St. John near the northern extremity of the lake, and by the more formidable works known as Fort Frederick or Crown Point—to give the better known English name—on a peninsula at the narrows towards the south. The latter was the most advanced post of the French until they built Fort Ticonderoga or Carillon on a high, rocky promontory at the head of Lake Sacrement, afterwards called Lake George by General Johnson—a sheet of water always famed for its picturesque charms. At the foot of this lake, associated with so many memorable episodes in American history, General Johnson, a clever, ambitious Irishman, a nephew of Sir Peter Warren, in 1755, erected Fort William Henry, about fourteen miles from Fort Edward or Lyman, at the great carrying place on the upper waters of the Hudson. Returning to the St. Lawrence and the lakes, we find Fort Frontenac or Cataraqui at the eastern end of Lake Ontario, where the old city of Kingston now stands. Within the limits of the present city of Toronto, La Galissonnière built Fort Rouillé as an attempt to control the trade of the Indians of the North, who were finding their way to the English fort at Choueguen (Oswego), which had been commenced with the consent of the Iroquois by Governor Burnet of New York and was now a menace to the French dominion of Lake Ontario. At the other extremity of this lake was Fort Niagara, the key to the West.

At Detroit, Mackinac, and Sault Ste. Marie the French continued to hold possession of the Great Lakes and the country to the west and south. Their communications, then, between the West and Quebec were established, but between the great valleys of the St. Lawrence and the Mississippi, over which they claimed exclusive rights, there was another valley which became of importance in the execution of their scheme of continental dominion. In the years succeeding the treaty of Aix-la-Chapelle the English colonists awakened to the importance of the valley of the Ohio, and adventurous frontiersmen of Virginia and Pennsylvania were already forcing their way into its wilderness, when France's ambition barred the way to their further progress. That astute Canadian, Governor La Galissonnière, in 1749, recognised the importance of the Ohio in relation to the Illinois and Mississippi, and sent Céloron, a captain in the French service, to claim possession of the valley of the former river and its tributaries. This officer made a long and enterprising journey, in the course of which he affixed at different points the arms of France to trees, and buried leaden plates bearing the inscription, that they were memorials of the " renewal of the possession of the Ohio and all its affluents " originally established by arms and treaties, particularly those of Ryswick, Utrecht, and Aix-la-Chapelle. Under the instructions of Governor Duquesne, who possessed all the sagacity of La Galissonnière, forts were established at Presqu'ile (Erie) and on French Creek, a tributary of the Alleghany. Virginians saw with dismay the entrance

of the French into a region on which they were now
casting a longing eye. Their government had secured from the Iroquois a doubtful deed which gave
them, as they urged, a title to the Great West, and
a company was even formed to occupy the Ohio.
In 1754 the English commenced the construction
of a fort at the forks of the Ohio, but it was easily
captured by Contrecœur, who completed and renamed it in honour of the Governor of Canada,
Duquesne. Washington, who now first appears in
American history, was defeated by Chevalier de Vil-
liers at Fort Necessity, a mere intrenchment at Great
Meadows, and the French held entire possession of
the Ohio valley, where no English trader or pioneer
dared show himself. By 1755 the French dominion
was complete from the Ohio to the Illinois, and from
the Great Lakes to the Gulf of Mexico, so far as a
slender line of communication by means of widely
separated posts and settlements could make it so.
On the St. Joseph, the Maumee, the Wabash, and
the Illinois, there were small forts. Fort Chartres
in the Illinois country was the only post of any
thorough construction. At Cahokia, opposite the
modern city of St. Louis, and at Kaskaskia, at the
junction of the river of that name with the Mississippi, there were small and relatively prosperous
French villages. In Louisiana the French had the
towns of Mobile, Biloxi, New Orleans, and a few
other settlements, where the African blacks far outnumbered the whites. That colony had had many
difficulties to surmount before it could be considered
established. Wars with the Natchez and Chicka-

saws had been constant. Crozat's experiment had been followed by the establishment of the Mississippi or Western Company, which was to develop gold mines, that never existed except in the imaginations of its reckless promoter, John Law, a Scotchman. When the Mississippi bubble burst, and so many thousands were ruined in France, Louisiana still continued under the control of the company, which was eventually obliged to give up its charter after heavy expenditures which had produced very small results, and the colony became a royal province. With its chequered future must be always associated the name of the Canadian Bienville, who was for some years its governor and justly earned the title of "Father of Louisiana." Insignificant as was its progress, France prized its possession, and had she been alive to her opportunities she might have colonised it with Huguenots and made it a power in the conflict between herself and England in America.

France, busy with her ambitious designs in Europe, gave but a meagre and too often half-hearted support to the men who had dreams of founding a mighty empire in America. When France and England met for the great struggle on that continent, the thirteen colonies had reached a population of nearly a million and a quarter of souls, exclusive of the negroes in the South, while the total number of the people in Canada and Louisiana did not exceed eighty thousand. In wealth and comfort there was the same disproportion between the French and English colonies. In fact at the time of the last

15

war, Canadian commerce was entirely paralysed, farms neglected, and the towns barely able to live. In 1757 food was so scarce in Quebec and Montreal that the soldiers and people had to use horse flesh. The combined forces of Canadian militia and regular troops were always much inferior in number to the British and colonial armies when united for the invasion of Canada, with the support of a powerful fleet; but the great strength of the French colony lay in the natural barriers between the English colonies and the keys to New France, Quebec, and Montreal, and in the skill with which the approaches by way of Lake Champlain had been defended by forts at every important point.   If the French force was insignificant in number, it was, as a rule, skilfully managed, and in the early part of the struggle the English had no commander to compare with Montcalm for military genius.   In some respects the French Canadians were more manageable in war than the English colonists.   No legislative bodies existed in Canada to interfere with and thwart the plans and orders of military commanders, but the whole Canadian people acted as a unit to be moved and directed at the will of the King's officers. The Indian tribes from Acadia to the Mississippi, the Ohio, and the Illinois, were, with the exception of the Five Nations, always friendly to the French since the days of Champlain—the warm allies of a people who fraternised naturally with them; and it would have been an unhappy day for the English colonists had eighty or a hundred thousand Canadians been able to arm and, under the skilful generalship of Montcalm, swoop down with their savage allies on the English colonial settlements. But the French of Canada were never able, as a rule, to do more than harass by sudden raids and skirmishes— by a system of *petite guerre*, or petty warfare—the English of America, and at no time in colonial history was the capture of Boston or of New York actually attempted by a land force from Canada, though it was suggested more than once. At the outbreak of the war the Mohawks were the only Indian tribe on whom the English could place much dependence, and that was largely owing to the energy and discretion of Sir William Johnson, who had long lived in their country and gained not only their confidence but even their affection. The tribes in the Ohio valley had been won by the success of the French in driving out the Virginians, while in the further west the Foxes and other communities who had been unfriendly to the French had been beaten into submission—the Foxes in fact almost destroyed —by the raids of the French and their Indian allies. The great current of active thought and enterprise which develops a nation was always with the English colonies, and though large schemes of ambition stimulated the energies of the bold and adventurous men to whom the destinies of France were entrusted from the days of La Salle to those of Montcalm, their ability to found a new empire in America under the lilies of France was ever hindered by the slow development of the French settlements, by the incapacity of the King and his ministers in France to grasp the importance of the situation on this conti-

nent, and by their refusal to carry out the projects
of men like La Galissonnière, who at once recognised
the consequences of such neglect and indifference,
but found no one ready to favour his scheme of establishing large settlements of French peasantry in
Canada and Louisiana.   France, we see now, had
her great opportunity in America, and lost it forever
at Quebec in 1759.

Before we proceed to the record of the events
which led to the conquest of Canada, it is necessary
that we should briefly review the history of the
period which elapsed between the Treaty of Aix-la-
Chapelle and the commencement of the Seven Years'
War.   When English statesmen were informed of
the mistake they had made in restoring Cape Breton
to France with such reckless haste, they began to
reflect on the best means of retrieving it as far as
possible ; and at the suggestion of Shirley and other
colonists they set to work to bring an English population into Nova Scotia, and to make it a source of
strength instead of weakness to the New England
communities.   In 1749, the year of the formal surrender of Louisbourg, the city of Halifax was
founded on the west side of the admirable harbour,
long known in Acadian history as Chebouctou.
Here, under the direction of Governor Cornwallis, a
man of great ability, a town slowly grew up at the
foot and on the slopes of the hill which was in later
times crowned by a noble citadel, above which has
always floated the flag of Great Britain.   Then followed the erection of a fort at Chignecto, known as
Fort Lawrence in honour of the English officer who

built it—afterwards governor of Nova Scotia—and
intended to be a protection to the province, constantly threatened by the French and Indians, who
were always numerous at the French posts and settlements on the isthmus. The French constructed
on the northern bank of the Missiquash a fort of five
bastions known as Beauséjour, and a smaller one at
Bay Verte, with the object, as previously stated, of
keeping up communication with Louisbourg, which
they were strengthening in some measure. At Fort
Beauséjour the treacherous priest Le Loutre continued to pursue his insidious designs of creating dissat-
isfaction among the French Acadians and pressing
on them the necessity of driving the English from
the former possessions of France.

Though war was not formally proclaimed between
France and England until many months later, the
year 1755 was distinguished in America by conflicts
between the English and French—a prelude to the
great struggle that was only to end in the fall of
New France. The French frigates *Alcide* and *Lys*
were captured on the coast of Newfoundland by vessels of a fleet under Admiral Boscawen, who had
been sent by the English Government to intercept a
French fleet which had left France under Admiral
de la Mothe, having on board troops under Baron
Dieskau and the Marquis de Vaudreuil, the successor of Duquesne in the government of Canada.

In Acadia, in the valley of the Ohio, and at Lake
George, the opposing forces of England and France
also met in conflict. In the spring an English force
of regular and colonial troops, chiefly the latter,

under the command of Colonel Monckton, who has given his name to a prosperous city on the isthmus of Chignecto, and of Colonels Winslow and Scott, captured the two French forts and took a good many prisoners, among whom were a considerable number of French Acadians, forced by the French to assist in the defence of Beauséjour. Le Loutre succeeded during the confusion on the surrender of the fort, in evading capture, but only to find himself eventually taken prisoner by an English ship while on his way to France, and sent to the island of Jersey, where he was kept in confinement until the end of the war, and from that time disappears from American history.

In the same year General Braddock, an arrogant though experienced soldier, was sent in command of a large force of regular and colonial troops into the valley of the Ohio to attack Fort Duquesne and drive the French from that region, but chiefly through his want of caution and his ignorance of Indian methods of warfare in the American wilderness, he was surprised on the Monongahela by a small force of Indians and French under the Canadian Beaujeu, who were concealed in ravines, from which they were able in perfect security to prevent the advance of the English, and literally riddle them with bullets until they fled in dismay and confusion, leaving behind them a great store of munitions and provisions besides a large sum of money in specie. Braddock died from the wounds he received, and the remnant of his beaten regiments retired precipitately beyond the Alleghanies. This unhappy disaster was followed by a succession of Indian raids along hundreds of miles of frontier, and the *petite guerre* of the Abenakis and French in Acadia and New England, with all its horrors, was repeated by the Indians of the West. The southern colonies were paralysed for the moment, and the authorities of Pennsylvania gave evidences of indifference, if not of cowardice, that are discreditable features of its early history.

General Johnson, of the Mohawk country, at the head of a large colonial force, defeated Baron Dieskau at the foot of Lake George, which then received its present name in honour of the King of England, and the French general himself was taken prisoner. It was for his services on this occasion that Johnson was made a baronet, though he had not succeeded in the original object of his expedition, the capture of Crown Point. General Shirley, however, was not so fortunate as Johnson, for he abandoned the project of attacking Fort Niagara when he heard that it had received reinforcements.

The most memorable event of this time, which has been the subject of warm controversy between French and English historians and the theme of a most affecting poem, was the expulsion of the Acadian French from Nova Scotia. When Halifax was founded it was decided, as a matter of necessity, to bring the Acadians more entirely under the control of the English authorities. They had probably increased since the Treaty of Utrecht to at least twelve thousand souls, living for the most part in the Annapolis valley, by the Gaspereaux and Avon rivers, at Grand Pré, at Mines, and at Chignecto. When they were asked to take the oath of allegiance by Governor Lawrence, they refused to do so unless it was qualified by the condition that they should not be obliged at any time to take up arms. Many years before a considerable number, if not the majority, of the same people had taken this qualified oath, although it is also claimed that no one had legal authority to make such a condition with them. Under the treaty of 1713 the Acadian French had a year to choose between leaving the country or giving their submission to the British Government and becoming its subjects. It was natural that they should have hesitated to leave the humble though comfortable homes which their own industry had made on the most fertile lands of Nova Scotia, but it is also quite certain that every obstacle was thrown in the way of their removal by the English governors. Had the British authorities adopted from the very commencement a firm and decided policy towards them, they might have given an unreserved allegiance to the British Crown and eventually become peaceable and contented inhabitants. As it was, the British Government systematically neglected the country, and left the little garrison at Annapolis for many years practically at the mercy of the Acadians, who could have often half starved them, and even captured the only English post of the least importance in the province, had they been led at any time by a man of courage and determination. It was only the watchfulness of the government of Massachusetts, who fully recognised the importance of Nova Scotia in relation to New England, that retained the province in English hands during the time when English statesmen like Newcastle were even ignorant of the existence or situation of Annapolis. If French emissaries were often able to make these credulous and ignorant people believe that France would soon regain her dominion in Acadia, it was largely owing to the fact that the English showed such weakness in all their relations with the Acadians, and made no earnest or sustained effort to assert their sovereignty. At last when England decided to settle and strengthen Nova Scotia, a feeling of uneasiness was naturally created by the presence of a large and increasing population who were naturally in sympathy with the French, and had assumed an attitude quite irreconcilable with the security of English interests on the Atlantic coast of eastern America. It must be admitted that the position of the Acadians was one deserving of sympathy, tossed about as they were for many years between French and English. They were considered by the French of Canada and Cape Breton as mere tools to carry out the designs of French ambition. England, however, had at some time or other to assert her sovereignty in Nova Scotia, and to assure its security, seemingly threatened by the presence of people who would not formally declare themselves British subjects. The position of Nova Scotia between Cape Breton and Canada gave reason for constant alarm, and when Halifax was founded some decisive step was felt to be necessary by Cornwallis and his successors.

No doubt the feeling that had been created against the Acadians, by their refusal to take an unconditional oath of allegiance to Great Britain—the only oath that could be possibly offered to them by a self-respecting and strong government—was intensified by the notorious fact that a number of them had been actually captured at Fort Beauséjour with arms in their hands, though in this case they appear to have been really the mere tools of Le Loutre and French emissaries who grossly misled them. The people of New England were much prejudiced against them and asserted that they could never enjoy any security while the Acadians continued to maintain their attitude of neutrality. They had always supplied Louisbourg with provisions and helped to build the French forts on the isthmus, and it was difficult for Lawrence and his officers to obtain any assistance from them in the same way. When the Indians harassed the English settlers in Nova Scotia, the government of that province recalled the raids of the Abenakis and French Canadians, and believed with some reason there was to be the same condition of things in the peninsula. The war between the French and English had never really ceased in America, and it was well known that the hollow truce in Europe would be broken at any moment; and in the presence of the great danger that threatened the English colonies, they had some ground for fearing the presence of a large body of people who claimed to be neutrals in a country which was England's by conquest and treaty, and where they could and did enjoy an

amount of political and religious liberty which no
Protestant enjoyed in Catholic Europe. Then came
the defeat of Braddock in the Ohio country, and the
knowledge that France was preparing for a determined effort to strengthen and even increase her
dominions in America.

It was under these circumstances that Governor
Lawrence of Nova Scotia—a determined and harsh
military man—no doubt at the instigation of Shirley
and the authorities of New England, determined to
secure the peace and safety of the province by the
most cruel of all possible measures, the expulsion of
the whole body of French Acadians. It must be
admitted, however, that all the circumstances, when
reviewed in these later times, do not seem sufficient
to justify the stern action of the men who took the
leading part in this sad tragedy. The responsibility
must mainly rest on Governor Lawrence, and not
on the imperial government, who never formally
authorised the expatriation. Be that as it may,
the Acadians were driven from their settlements,
and the noble qualities of Lawrence, Monckton,
and Winslow, who carried out the measures of
expulsion, will be always obscured in the minds
of that great majority of people who think only
of the deed and its consequences, and are influenced by the dictates of the heart. It is a matter
for deep regret that the men who represented England in those days had not run a risk on the side
of humanity, rather than have driven thousands
of men, women, and children from their pleasant
homes by the sides of the beautiful bays and rivers

of Nova Scotia, and scattered them far and wide among the English colonies, where their treatment was rarely generous. Even those who reached Quebec were coldly received and were grudgingly supplied with miserable food. Poetry and sentiment have not exaggerated the sorrow and misery of these hapless exiles, so ill-fitted to go out into the bitter world of hardship and destitution.

XVII.

THE STRUGGLE FOR DOMINION IN THE GREAT VALLEYS OF NORTH AMERICA: ENGLISH REVERSES AND FRENCH VICTORIES—FALL OF LOUISBOURG AND FORT DUQUESNE.

(1756–1758.)

IN 1756 England was fully engaged in that famous war with France which was to end in driving her hereditary rival from the eastern and western hemispheres, and in the establishment of the German Empire by the military genius of Frederick the Great. For a while, however, the conflict in America was chiefly remarkable for the incapacity of English commanders on land and sea. Earl Loudoun, the sluggish commander-in-chief, of whom it was said, " he is like St. George on the signs; always on horseback, but never rides on," arranged a campaign against the French on Lake Champlain and against Louisbourg which ended only in disaster and humiliation for England. The forts at Oswego, always regarded as a menace by the French who occupied

Fort Frontenac on the opposite side of Lake Ontario, were successfully attacked and destroyed by
Montcalm,* who was sent to Canada in 1756 to
make a supreme effort for France.   The energetic
French general then proceeded a year later to storm
Fort William Henry, and largely owing to the incapacity or timidity of General Webb, who could
have marched to the assistance of the besieged from
Fort Edward, the brave Scotch officer, Lieutenant-
Colonel Monro, then in command of this important
defence of the northeastern frontier, was obliged to
surrender.   After the capitulation of this fort a large
number of helpless men, women, and children were
barbarously murdered by the body of Indians that
accompanied the French—one of the saddest episodes in American history, which must always dim
the lustre of Montcalm's victory, though it is now
generally admitted that the French general himself
was not responsible for the treachery of his Indian
allies, but used his most earnest efforts—even at the
risk of his own life—to save the English when the
savages were mad with lust for the blood of their
enemies.

At sea the results were equally discouraging for
the English.   Fifteen ships-of-the-line and three
frigates, under the orders of Admiral Holbourne, and
twelve thousand troops under the command of Earl
Loudoun himself, assembled in the harbour of Halifax in the July of 1757; but, owing to the absence

* His full name was Louis-Joseph, Marquis de Montcalm-Gozon de
Saint-Véran, whose family seat was Candiac, near Nismes, in the
south of France.

Montcalm. ÆT. 29.

230

of energy and celerity of movement from the very
day the project was decided upon in England until
after the arrival of the fleet in America, the French
were able to get reinforcements of ships and men
into Louisbourg, and the English admiral and
general came to the resolve—so strange for Englishmen in time of war—to run no risk in attacking the
fortress.   Loudoun returned to New York, but too
late to retrieve the injury he had done to the northern colonies by withdrawing so large a force from
the frontier at a critical period, when Montcalm was
marching on Fort William Henry with such unfortunate results for English interests.   Holbourne sailed
with his fleet for Louisbourg, and after a half-hearted
attempt to draw the French fleet, then safely moored
under the guns of the town, into an engagement,
even the elements combined against him, and when
he had lost a number of his vessels on the rocky
Cape Breton coast, he returned to England to tell
the story of his failure.

It was at this critical period, when England so
sadly needed a bold and wise statesman at the head
of her government in the place of weak and incompetent men like Newcastle, that the great Pitt, better known as Chatham at a later day, was called to
office by the unanimous opinion of the English
people outside, perhaps, of a small selfish clique of
the aristocracy.   It was his good fortune to be successful far beyond the hopes of the majority of
statesmen suddenly called upon to retrieve national
disaster.   It was mainly through his inspiration—
through the confidence with which he inspired all

those who served the country at this momentous epoch—that England became the centre of a vast colonial empire such as the world never saw, even in the days when Rome was mistress.

When Pitt was recalled to office in July, 1757, it was too late to prevent the humiliation of England through the incompetency of Holbourne, Loudoun, and Webb, and the year 1757 closed with Montcalm triumphant in America. But while France neglected to give adequate support to her brave sons in Canada, England rallied to the support of Pitt, and the whole nation felt a confidence in the future which it had never had during the administration of his predecessors. On the continent of Europe, Pitt contented himself with giving the largest possible subsidies of money to his great ally Frederick, and by entrusting the command of the English and Hanoverian forces to the best of his generals, Ferdinand, Prince of Brunswick, in place of the incompetent Duke of Cumberland. The victories of Rossbach, Leuthen, and Minden were the answers that Frederick gave to the English minister for the confidence he reposed in his ability to cope with the four great Powers then combined with Saxony to destroy Prussia and bring England to the feet of France, by invading her territory and marching into her very capital. Hanover was saved by the memorable victory on the Weser, and England was spared the humiliation and perils of an invasion by the destruction of a French fleet by Admiral Hawke in Quiberon Bay.

While the military genius of Frederick and the

16

inspiring statesmanship of Pitt were successfully
thwarting the ambitious plans of France and her
allies in Europe, the English minister had decided
on a vigorous campaign in America. With that
intuitive sagacity which he possessed above most
men for recognising ability in others for the purpose
in view, he chose General Amherst, Admiral Boscawen, and Brigadier-General Wolfe, not because of
their aristocratic or political influence, but because
of their military capacity, the want of which in Loudoun and Holbourne had brought disaster upon the
English arms. Unhappily he was forced, for the
time being, by strong influences around him to
retain General Abercromby at the head of one of
the expeditions in America, but he hoped that the
co-operation of Lord Howe would keep up the courage of the army, and prevent any blunders on the
part of the slow and obtuse soldier in command.
The plan of the campaign which opened in 1758 was
to send three expeditions simultaneously against the
three all-important French positions held by the
French in the Ohio valley, on Lake Champlain, and
at the entrance of the Gulf of St. Lawrence. General Forbes, a resolute Scotch veteran, was to march
on Fort Duquesne, General Abercromby was to lay
siege to Crown Point and Ticonderoga, and General
Amherst, with Admiral Boscawen, was to attack the
fortress of Louisbourg, which was acknowledged as
the key of the St. Lawrence.

The English fleet anchored in Gabarus Bay, to
the southward of Louisbourg, on the 2nd of June,
1758. It was composed of over fifty ships, twenty-

two of which were " liners," and carried eighteen hundred guns altogether. The army comprised between eleven and twelve thousand men, including a small force of provincial rangers. The fortress, which had been considerably strengthened since 1745, was defended by over three thousand regular troops, and a small number of Indians and inhabitants. A fleet of fourteen men-of-war, with a crew of nearly three thousand men, and five hundred and sixty-two guns, were in the harbour. Chevalier Drucour was governor of the island, and conducted the defences with skill and resolution, and had Admiral Desgouttes been as brave and capable as the former, Louisbourg would hardly have fallen so easily. On the morning of the 27th July, the English took possession of the West gate, and the cross of St. George was hoisted on the citadel of a fortress which was destined from that time to disappear from the pages of the world's history. In 1763 the fortress was levelled to the ground, and now a few mounds of turf alone represent the ambitions of France a century and a half ago. Nature has resumed dominion over the site of the once famous fortress, and the restless ocean, which stretches away beyond to the eastward without a break to Europe, brings no message of the fleets that came once, richly freighted, to this historic fort. Louisbourg is now only a place of memories—of associations which connect Cape Breton with most glorious episodes of England's history, with times when the genius of Pitt triumphed over France.

After the taking of Louisbourg, the English occu-

pied the island of St. John, now Prince Edward,
where there were several prosperous settlements at
Port La Joye (Charlottetown), St. Pierre, and other
places on the bays of the low-lying coast.   The
population was composed chiefly of Acadians, who
had commenced to cross from Nova Scotia after the
Treaty of Utrecht, and probably numbered in 1758
four thousand souls, engaged in fishing and farming.
These people were able to supply Louisbourg with
provisions, as no agricultural operations of importance were carried on in Cape Breton.

LOUISBOURG MEDALS OF 1758.

Wolfe destroyed the French settlements around
the bays of Gaspé, Miramichi, and Chaleurs, while
Colonel Monckton performed the same painful duty
in the valley of the St. John River.   Acadia, according to its " ancient limits," was at last completely
in the possession of England.

The news of the capture of Louisbourg was received in America and Europe with many rejoicings,
and the eleven stands of colours won at this gateway
of Canada were deposited in St. Paul's Cathedral

amid the roar of cannon. This victory came at an
opportune moment, since Abercromby had suffered
a humiliating repulse on the banks of Lake Champlain. With a splendid force of regular and provincial troops, from fourteen to fifteen thousand
altogether, but entirely destitute of artillery,—an
evidence of extraordinary incapacity, or of culpable
negligence,—he had thrown himself upon most formidable entrenchments of fallen trees, with their
sharp ends pointing outwards, that the French had
ingeniously constructed in front of Carillon, which
was still incomplete, and defended by less than three
thousand men under Montcalm and Lévis. The
most unhappy incident of this disaster was the death
of Lord Howe, described by Wolfe, who knew him
well, " as the noblest Englishman that has appeared
in my time, and the best soldier in the British
army." Abercromby hurriedly retired to the head
of Lake George, and was soon afterwards superseded
by the cautious Amherst. Montcalm was greatly
encouraged by the spirit of his soldiers throughout
the attack, and erected a cross on the battle ground
with the following inscriptions of his own—the latter
his paraphrase of the first:

Quid dux? Quid miles? Quid strata ingentia ligna?
En signum ! en victor ! Deus hîc, Deus ipse triumphat.

" Chrétien ! ce ne fut point Montcalm et la prudence,
  Ces arbres renversés, ces héros, ces exploits,
  Qui des Anglais confus ont brisé l'espérance,
  C'est le bras de ton Dieu, vainqueur sur cette croix." *

* Parkman gives the following paraphrase of the Latin inscription:
" Soldier and chief and ramparts' strength are nought ;
  Behold the conquering cross ! 'T is God the triumph wrought."

An important event of the year was the taking of Fort Frontenac by Colonel Bradstreet, who had assisted in the first siege of Louisbourg. The capture of this fort was regarded with every reason by the French as " of greater injury to the colony than the loss of a battle." Fort Duquesne, which was the key to the Ohio country, was abandoned by Ligneris on the approach of Brigadier Forbes, a very capable Scotch officer, but not until the French had beaten with considerable loss an advance of the main forces commanded by Major Grant. Ligneris withdrew his troops to Fort Machault (Venango), where he remained until the following year. Fort Duquesne was renamed in honour of Pitt, and a great manufacturing city has grown up on its site in the beautiful valley which, in 1758, passed away forever from the French who had only held possession of it for six short years.

XVIII.

THE STRUGGLE FOR DOMINION IN THE VALLEY OF THE ST. LAWRENCE—CANADA IS WON BY WOLFE ON THE PLAINS OF ABRAHAM.

(1759–1763.)

WHEN the campaign opened in 1759 the French had probably under arms in Canada not far from twenty thousand men, regulars, militia, and Indians —one-fifth only being French regiments. At Detroit there was a very insignificant garrison, as it was of minor importance compared with Niagara, which was the key to the Lakes and West. Here Pouchot, an able officer, who has given us an interesting memoir of the war, was stationed, with authority to call to his assistance the French forces at Presqu'ile, Le Bœuf, and Venango—some three thousand men altogether, made up mostly of colonial forces and Indian auxiliaries. At Fort Rouillé (Toronto) there was no force worth mentioning, as it was a mere dependency of Niagara. Fort Frontenac had been destroyed by the English, and the French had no posts from that point as far as Montreal except at

Point-au-Baril (near Ogdensburgh), and Île Galops, by the side of the well-known rapids of that name. The security of Montreal depended mainly on the French continuing to hold control of Lake Champlain, and Île-aux-Noix which they now set to work to fortify. Bourlamaque, an able officer, was in command at the French forts of the lake with a force of over two thousand men, of whom one-half were Canadian, and had orders to abandon Carillon and Crown Point, if necessary, and advance to Île-aux-Noix. At Quebec, probably fourteen thousand men, of whom four thousand were the pick of the French regiments in Canada, were under command of Montcalm, Lévis, and Vaudreuil, and were entrenched on a height of land stretching for nearly six miles from the St. Charles River, to the southeast of the fortress, as far as Montmorency River, where its current rushes wildly forward for its tremendous leap of over two hundred and fifty feet into a deep and rocky abyss, and forms that glistening sheet of billowy foam which, seen from a distance, resembles a snowdrift suspended in air. The fortifications of Quebec had been strengthened for some years back, and its defences were entrusted to Ramesay, who had led a force to Nova Scotia in the year of the Duke d'Anville's disastrous expedition. The city was ill-provided with provisions for any sustained siege, despite the opportune arrival of some relief from France in the spring. The whole country had been impoverished by the continuous drain on the agricultural and labouring population during the war, and the Canadians themselves began to lose courage, and assembled at the call of the authorities with less spirit than they had hitherto shown. Canada was literally on the brink of ruin, after so many years of war and privation. Corruption had eaten into the very body of Canadian

MAJOR–GENERAL JAMES WOLFE.

life and government. The Intendant Bigot had been for years amassing riches at the expense of the country, and had, in imitation of his lord and master at Versailles, his fair Canadian Pompadour to bedeck with jewels and favours from the proceeds of his ill-gotten gains.   The names of Péan, Varin, Cadet, Estèbe, and Clavery are the most conspicuous amongst those officials who became rich on Canadian misery and misfortune, and are dishonourably associated with the darkest hours of Canadian history.   " What a country," said Montcalm, " where all the knaves grow rich, and honest men are ruined."   Not the least discouraging feature of matters in Canada at this critical time, when unity and harmony were so necessary, was the jealousy that Governor de Vaudreuil, a weak, vain man, but honest and attached to his native province, entertained of Montcalm, who was himself imbued by the loftiest spirit that could animate a brave soldier and loyal Frenchman.

It was decided that the army under General Wolfe, less than nine thousand men, and the fleet under Admiral Saunders, should attack Quebec; that the Commander-in-Chief, Amherst, should advance against Montreal by way of Lake Champlain, and that Brigadier Prideaux and Sir William Johnson should lead a considerable force against Niagara. The English fleet arrived before Quebec on the 20th June, and no time was lost in commencing operations against the fortress.   Wolfe was well supported by such able soldiers as Monckton, Murray, and Carleton, the latter of whom became famous in later Canadian history as Lord Dorchester.   Brigadier Townsend, however capable, was irritable and egotistic.   The soldiers admired Wolfe for his soldierly qualities, and loved him for his thoughtfulness for everyone above or below him.   Admiral Saunders

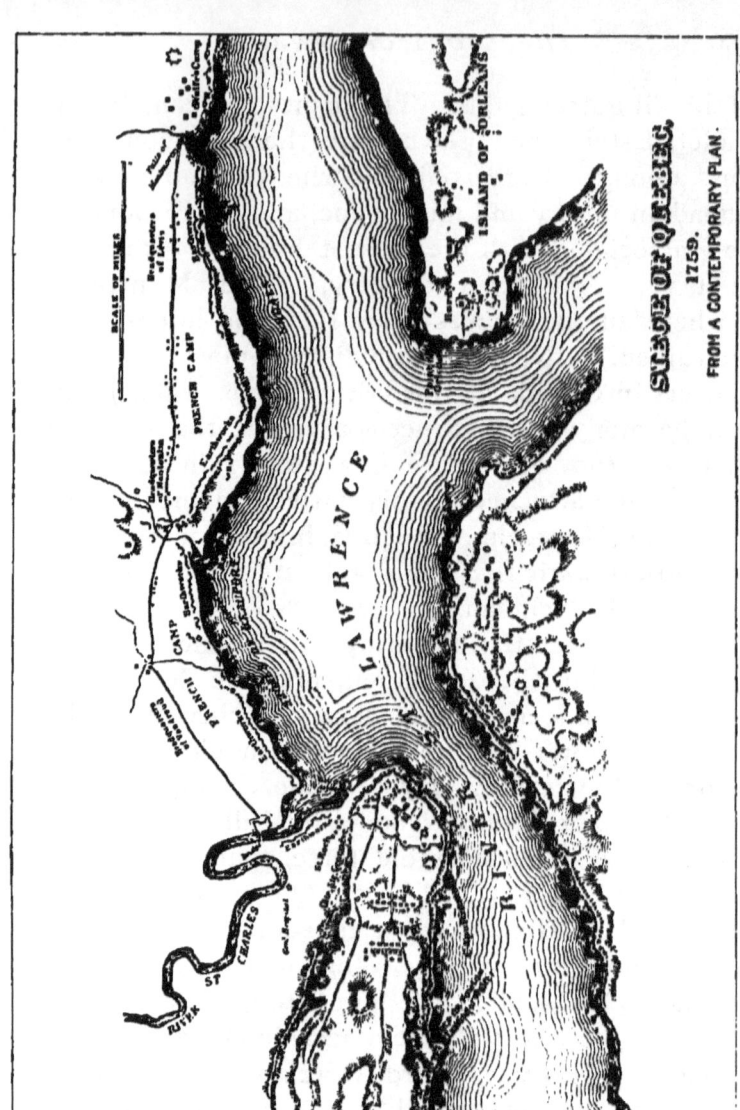

SIEGE OF QUEBEC.
1759.
FROM A CONTEMPORARY PLAN.

was well aided by Holmes and Durell, and gave a loyal and ready response to the plans of Wolfe. The regiments had seen service at Louisbourg, and were fully animated by the courage and spirit of their general. The siege lasted for eleven weeks, and was then only ended by an act of boldness on the part of Wolfe, which took the French entirely by surprise.

The principal events between the 26th June and the 12th September, when the last act in this great international drama was played, can be described in a few pages. One of the most important incidents was the occupation by the English of the heights of Lévis, whence the fortress was bombarded with an effectiveness that surprised the French, who, under the advice of Vaudreuil, and in opposition to that of Montcalm, had not taken adequate measures for the protection of so valuable a position. So destructive was the bombardment that, when the English took possession of Quebec, they found all the churches and buildings of importance in ruins, and the Ursuline Convent alone was saved from complete destruction.

The English sustained a severe repulse near the Montmorency end of the French lines. They had made an attack on an outwork at that point, and the grenadiers had been carried away by excitement and dashed up the slope of the heights, where from twelve to fourteen thousand French soldiers were strongly intrenched. A furious storm of bullets assailed the reckless and brave grenadiers, who could not even gain a firm footing on the slippery slope, while the rain came down in torrents, and their blood reddened the rivulets of water. This was, however, the only serious disaster that the English suffered throughout the siege. The fire ships of the French had been ill-managed, and failed to do any damage as they were sent down against the fleet. Montcalm, sure of his impregnable position, refused to be drawn from his intrenchments and to offer battle to Wolfe. He knew that delay was everything to him, for the autumn was drawing near. In a few weeks storm and frost would drive the Englishmen from the river. Wherever Montcalm looked, his position seemed unassailable. The high cliffs that stretched for miles above Quebec offered a guaranty of security in that direction, and to prevent any doubt, Bougainville, a capable officer—in later years famous as a navigator—was on the alert with a force of upwards of two thousand soldiers. He had double work to do, to guard these apparently impregnable cliffs, and to assure the arrival of provisions from the country by river and land. It was the expected arrival of a convoy of provisions that proved an important factor in the successful accomplishment of a plan that Wolfe had devised for the capture of the city.

While the siege was in progress, the news from the west and from Lake Champlain was discouraging for the French. Niagara had been surrendered by Pouchot to Sir William Johnson, who had taken command on the death of Prideaux—killed at the beginning of operations—and a large force that was brought up by Ligneris from the Ohio valley to succour the post had been severely defeated. Crown Point and Ticonderoga had been abandoned by Bourlamaque, and there was for a time some expectation of the advance of Amherst to the St. Lawrence. Montcalm was obliged to weaken his army by sending his ablest general, Lévis, with a force of fifteen hundred men, to look after the defences of Montreal, but the sluggish English general wasted his time on the banks of Lake Champlain.

It was quite clear to Wolfe and Saunders that Amherst was not to give them any assistance in the difficult work before them. It was on the night of the 12th of September that Wolfe carried out the project which had been for some time forming in his mind. He had managed to concentrate a force of four thousand men above the fortress without awakening the suspicions of the French, who were confident that Bougainville was fully able to prevent any force from attempting so impossible and foolhardy an exploit as the ascent of the high cliffs. The visitor to the historic places around Quebec will be deeply interested in a cove, just above Sillery, now known as Wolfe's Cove, but in old times as the *Anse-au-Foulon*. A zig-zag and difficult path led from this cove to the top of the height, and Wolfe conceived the hope that it was possible to gain access in this way to the table-land where he could best give battle to Montcalm. He saw that the cliff at this point was defended by only a small guard, under the command, as it afterwards appeared, of Vergor, who had been tried and acquitted for his questionable surrender of Beauséjour. When the

English boats dropped down the river with the tide at midnight, on the 12th of September, there was no moon, and the stars alone gave a faint light. Montcalm had no conception of the importance of the movement of troops which, it had been reported to him, was going on for some days above Quebec, and his attention was diverted by the constant bombardment on the town from Lévis, and a fierce cannonading that was kept up against Beauport by Saunders. Wolfe's thoughts on that memorable night as his boat passed under the shadow of the dark cliff, we can imagine from an incident that is related by one who was present. Hardly a dip of an oar was heard from the flotilla as it was borne down the river, but from Beauport and Lévis came the constant roar of cannon. Every moment was carrying him to fame and death, and perhaps it was some foreboding of his fate that led him to repeat the words of Gray's Elegy, which from that hour has become more famous in English literature :

> " The boast of heraldy, the pomp of power,
>   And all that beauty, all that wealth e'er gave,
> Await alike th' inevitable hour ;
>   The paths of glory lead but to the grave."

As the boats came close to a point on the bank a sentinel challenged," *Qui vive ?* " " *La France !* " replied an officer of Fraser's Highlanders who spoke French well. "*À quel régiment?*" again challenged the suspicious soldier. " *De la Reine,*" answered the same officer, who happily remembered that some companies of this regiment were with Bougainville.

Fate that eventful night was on the side of the bold Englishman. The French were expecting a convoy of provisions, and the sentinel called out, "*Passe!*" Another sentry, more suspicious, ran down to the water's edge, and asked, "*Pourquoi est-ce que vous ne parlez plus haut?*" The captain replied with wonderful coolness, "*Tais-toi, nous serons entendus!*"—an answer which satisfied the guard. In this way the English boats were able to steal into the cove without being stopped. A few minutes later the heights were gained, the guard was overpowered, and the British regiments were climbing to the level land without hindrance. By six o'clock Wolfe was able to form his army of nearly four thousand men in line of battle on the Plains of Abraham.* "This is a serious business," exclaimed Montcalm, as he saw the red line of the English regiments on the table-land behind Quebec. He appears to have almost immediately come to the conclusion that it was necessary to fight the English before they received any accessions of strength, and not to wait for Bougain-ville, who would probably come up in time with his force of two thousand men. By ten o'clock the two armies—that of Montcalm outnumbering the English probably by fifteen hundred—were advancing on each other. The French as they drew near poured a volley into the ranks of the British regiments, but the latter reserved their fire until they were within forty yards of their enemy, when they discharged their guns with most deadly effect. The

* Named after Abraham Martin, a royal pilot, who, in early times, owned this now historic tract.

French fell in heaps, and as the bullets crashed amongst their faltering ranks, they broke and retreated. The battle was literally won in a few minutes. Wolfe, who had been wounded in the wrist at the beginning of the fight, was leading a charge of the grenadiers, who had shown such fateful precipitancy at Montmorency, when he was fatally wounded. He was removed to a redoubt in the rear and laid on the ground, where he remained for a few minutes in a swoon or stupour. "They run! See how they run!" exclaimed one of the men watching their wounded chief. "Who run?" he called, as he attempted to rise for an instant. "The enemy, sir; 'egad, they give place everywhere!" "Go, one of you, my lads," ordered the dying General, whose brain was still clear and active, "with all speed to Colonel Burton, and tell him to march Webb's regiment down to the St. Charles River, and cut off the fugitives to the bridge." He turned on his side and said: "God be praised, I now die in peace." Then, in a moment later, he passed into the great silent land. Montcalm also received his death blow while he was endeavouring to give some order to his beaten army. He was borne along by the crowd of retreating soldiers through the St. Louis gate into the town. A few hours later, on the 14th September, he breathed his last. His last words were in commendation of Chevalier de Lévis—a soldier in no way inferior to himself in military genius.

Monckton, who was next to Wolfe in rank, had been also severely wounded in the battle, and con-

17

sequently by a strange irony of fate, Townshend, who had been unfriendly to Wolfe, and had doubted his military capacity, was called upon to take command. Lévis was absent at Montreal, unfortunately for French interests at this very critical juncture, and Vaudreuil's opinion prevailed for a retreat to Jacques Cartier. When Lévis arrived and Vaudreuil consented to march to the support of Quebec it was too late. Ramesay had decided to capitulate, in view of the ruined condition of the city and walls, the scarcity of rations, and the unwillingness of the Canadian troops and citizens to continue the defence, when they found that the English were about to resume the attack. When the French army was moving towards Quebec, the English were in possession, and the *fleur-de-lis* had given place to the red cross of England on the old fort of St. Louis. By the terms of capitulation the troops were to be allowed to march out with the honours of war, and to be landed in France; the inhabitants were not to be disturbed; the free exercise of the Roman Catholic religion was allowed, and safeguards granted to houses of clergy and communities. All conditions were provisional until a treaty was arranged between the Powers.

The body of Montcalm was buried beneath the floor of the Ursuline Convent, in a grave which had been already partly hollowed out by a bursting shell. Many years later an English governor-general, Lord Aylmer, placed in the chapel of the convent a plain marble slab, with the following graceful tribute to the memory of a great soldier of whom English and French Canadians are equally proud.

HONNEUR
À
MONTCALM

———

LE DESTIN EN LUI DÉROBANT
LA VICTOIRE
L'A RÉCOMPENSÉ PAR
UNE MORT GLORIEUSE !

Wolfe's remains were taken to England, where they were received with every demonstration of respect that a grateful nation could give. In Europe and America the news of this victory had made the people wild with joy. " With a handful of men," said Pitt, in the House of Commons, " he has added an empire to English rule." A monument in that Walhalla of great Englishmen, Westminster Abbey, records that he " was slain in a moment of victory." On the heights of Quebec, in the rear of its noble terrace, still stands the stately obelisk which was erected in 1828 under the inspiration of the Earl of Dalhousie in honour of Montcalm and Wolfe, and above all others attracts the interest of the historical student since it pays a just tribute to the virtue and valour of the two great commanders in the following simple but well conceived language:

MORTEM. VIRTUS. COMMUNEM.
FAMAM. HISTORIA.
MONUMENTUM. POSTERITAS.
DEDIT.

Wolfe was only in his thirty-third year when he died on the field of Abraham. Montcalm was still in the prime of life, having just passed forty-seven years. Both were equally animated by the purest dictates of honour and truth, by a love for the noble profession of arms, and by an ardent desire to add to the glory of their respective countries. Montcalm was a member of the French nobility, and a man of high culture. His love for his mother, wife, and children is shown in his published letters, written while in Canada, and he was ever looking forward to the time when he could rejoin them in his beloved château of Candiac, and resume the studies he liked so well. Some Canadian writers have endeavoured to belittle Montcalm, that they may more easily explain away the failings of Vaudreuil, a native Canadian, who thwarted constantly the plans of a greater man; but an impartial historian can never place these two men on the same high level. Wolfe's family was of respectable origin, and he inherited his military tastes from his father, who became a general in the English army. He had few advantages of education in his youth, though in later life he became studious, and had much love for mathematics. A soldier's life was his ambition, and fame was his dominating impulse. His indomitable spirit governed his physical weakness. The natural kindness of his nature rose superior to the irritability sometimes caused by his ill-health, and made him always sympathise with the joys, sorrows, and feelings of all classes among whom he lived. He had that magnetic power of

MONTCALM AND WOLFE MONUMENT AT QUEBEC.

261

inspiring his soldiers and companions with his own confidence and courage which must sooner or later give them victory. He was a good son and made a confidant of his mother. He was fond of female companionship, and was looking forward hopefully to a woman's love, and to a home of his own, when Fate ruthlessly struck him down before the walls of Quebec at the moment of victory.

It is impossible within the limited space of this story to dwell at any length on the events that followed from the taking of the Canadian capital until the cession of Canada three years later. General Murray, who was afterwards the first governor-general of Canada, had charge of the fortress during the winter of 1759-60, when the garrison and people suffered much from cold and disease—firewood being scarce, and the greater number of the buildings in ruins.

Lévis had decided to attack the town in the spring, as soon as the French ships were able to come down from near Sorel, where they had been laid up all the winter. Towards the last of April, Murray marched out of the fortress and gave battle at St. Foy to the French army, which largely outnumbered his force. His object was to attack the French before they were able to place themselves thoroughly in position before Quebec, but he suffered a considerable loss, and was obliged to retire hurriedly within the walls of the town, which was then regularly invested by Lévis and the French ships. The opportune arrival of the English fleet dashed the rising hopes of the French to the ground,

VIEW OF QUEBEC IN 1760.

263

and Lévis was obliged to retreat to Montreal. In
the month of September of the same year General
Amherst descended the St. Lawrence, after having
captured the fort at Île Galops—afterwards Fort
William Augustus. Brigadier Haviland left Lake
Champlain, captured Île-aux-Noix, and then marched
on Montreal; Brigadier Murray came up from Quebec. All these forces concentrated on the same day
on the island of Montreal, and Vaudreuil had no
alternative except to capitulate. By the terms of
capitulation, which were drawn up, like those of
Quebec, in French, Great Britain bound herself to
allow the French Canadians the free exercise of
their religion, and certain specified fraternities, and
all communities of *religieuses* were guaranteed the
possession of their goods, constitutions, and privileges, but a similar favour was denied to the Jesuits,
the Franciscans, or Recollets, and the Sulpicians,
until the King should be consulted on the subject.
The same reservation was made with respect to the
parochial clergy's tithes. On the 10th of February,
1763, by the Treaty of Paris, France ceded to Great
Britain Canada, with all its dependencies, the island
of Cape Breton, and the Laurentian Isles. By this
treaty the King pledged himself " to give the most
effectual orders, that his new Roman Catholic subjects may profess the worship of their religion, according to the rites of the Roman Catholic Church,
as far as the laws of Great Britain permit." All the
pretensions of France to Acadia were at last formally
renounced. England also received all the country
east of the River Mississippi, except the city of New

VIEW OF MONTREAL IN 1760.

205

Orleans and the neighbouring district, as well as Florida from Spain in return for Havana. Subsequently France gave up New Orleans to Spain, as well as the great region of Louisiana westward of the Mississippi. France was allowed to retain the barren islands of St. Pierre and Miquelon, and certain fishing rights on the coasts of Newfoundland, which she had previously given by the Treaty of Utrecht. George II. had died during 1760, and George III. was now King of England. Pitt was forced to resign, and the King's favourite, the incapable Bute, who became premier, made peace without delay. Pitt opposed the fishery concessions to France, but Bute attached relatively little importance to them, and they have ever since remained to torment the people of Newfoundland, and create complications in case that island consents to enter the Canadian Dominion. Still, despite these concessions, England gained great advantages from the peace, and became the greatest colonial and maritime power of the world.

Freedom won on the Plains of Abraham, and a great Frenchman and a great Englishman consecrated by their deaths on the same battlefield the future political union of two races on the northern half of the continent, now known as the Dominion of Canada.

XIX.

A PERIOD OF TRANSITION—PONTIAC'S WAR—
THE QUEBEC ACT.

(1760-1774.)

THE Canadian people, long harassed and impoverished by war, had at last a period of rest. They
were allowed the ministrations of their religion without hindrance, and all that was required of the parochial clergy was that they should not take part in
civil affairs, but should attend exclusively to their
clerical duties. The seigniors and priests, no doubt,
did not give up for some time the hope that Canada
would be restored to France, but they, too, soon
bowed to the necessity of things, and saw that their
material and spiritual interests were quite secure
under the new government. None of the *habitants*
ever left Canada after the war. A few members of
the seigniorial nobility, the officials and some merchants—perhaps three hundred in all—may have
gone back to France. Men like Bigot and Varin
on their return were severely punished, and forced
to give up as much as possible of their ill-gotten

gains. Governor de Vaudreuil himself was cast into the Bastile, but it was ascertained after investigation that he had no connection with the crimes of the worthless parasites that had so long fattened on the necessities of the unhappy province. He died soon after his imprisonment; the iron of humiliation had probably eaten into the heart of a man who, whatever his faults, had many estimable qualities, and loved his native country.

For several years Canada was under what has been generally called the military régime; that is to say, the province was divided into the three districts of Quebec, Three Rivers, and Montreal, of which the government was administered by military chiefs; in the first place by General Murray, Colonel Burton, and General Gage respectively. These military authorities—notably General Murray—endeavoured to win the confidence of the people by an impartial and considerate conduct of affairs. Civil matters in the parishes were left practically under the control of the captains of militia, who had to receive new commissions from the British Crown. Appeal could be always made to the military chief at the headquarters of the district, but, as a matter of fact, the people generally managed their affairs among themselves, in accordance with their old usages and laws. Military councils tried criminal cases according to English law.

While the French Canadians were in the enjoyment of rest on the banks of the St. Lawrence and its tributary rivers, the Western Indians, who had been the allies of France during the war, suddenly arose and seized nearly all the forts and posts which had been formerly built by the French on the Great Lakes, in the valley of the Ohio, and in the Illinois country. After the taking of Montreal, Captain Robert Rogers, the famous commander of the Colonial Rangers, whose name occurs frequently in the records of the war, was sent by General Amherst to take possession of the forts at Presqu'ile, Detroit, Michillimackinac, Green Bay, and other places in the West. In the course of a few months there were in all these western posts small garrisons of English soldiers. In the neighbourhood of Detroit and Michillimackinac there were French Canadian villages, conspicuous for their white cottages with overhanging bark roofs and little gardens, orchards, and meadows. Forts Chartres and Vincennes were still in the possession of the French, and there was a population of nearly two thousand French Canadians or Louisiana French living in the Illinois country, chiefly at Cahokia and Kaskaskia on the Mississippi. The Indian tribes that took part in the rising of 1763 were the Ottawas, Pottawattomies, Ojibways (Chippeways), Wyandots (Hurons), and Kickapoos, who lived in the vicinity of the upper lakes; the Delawares (Loups or Lenapes) and the Shawanoes, who had their villages on the Ohio and its tributary rivers, especially on the Muskingkum and the Scioto; the Sauks or Saks, who encamped on the Wisconsin; the Senecas, who lived not far from the Niagara. All these Indians, except the Wyandots and Senecas, were members of the Algonquin family. The Senecas were the only tribe of the Six Nations that took part in the alliance against

England; the other tribes were, happily for English interests, under the influence of Sir William Johnson.

French emissaries from the settlements on the Mississippi made the Indians believe that they would be soon driven by the English from their forest homes and hunting grounds, and that their only hope was in assisting France to restore her power in America. Many of these Indian tribes, as well as French settlers, believed until the proclamation of the treaty of Paris that Canada would be restored to the French. Indian sympathy for France was intensified by the contumely and neglect with which they were treated by the English traders and authorities. The French, who thoroughly understood the Indian character, had never failed to administer to their vanity and pride—to treat them as allies and friends and not as a conquered and subject race. By the judicious distribution of those gifts, on which the tribes had begun to depend and receive as a matter of right, the French cemented the attachment of the Indians. The English, on the other hand, soon ceased to make these presents, and neglected the Indians in other ways, which excited their indignation and wounded their pride.

Among the Western chiefs was Pontiac, whose name is as prominent in the history of the past as the names of the Onondaga Garangula, the Huron Kondiaronk (Rat), the Mohawk Thayendenagea (Brant), and the Shawanoese Tecumseh. He was the son of an Ottawa chief and an Ojibway mother, and had a high reputation and large influence among the tribes of the upper lakes. He showed in his career all the strength and weaknesses of the Indian character—great courage, treachery, vanity, and generosity, according to the impulses of the moment. The war in which he took so prominent a part is generally called by his name; his is the central figure in the striking drama which was enacted in the Western and Ohio country for two years and a half before peace generally reigned and Canada could be considered secure from Indian attacks.

At Detroit, where Major Gladwin was in command, Pontiac hoped to seize the fort by a stratagem. The Ottawas and other Indians under that chief were to meet the English officers in council within the fort at an appointed time. They had filed off the tops of the barrels of their muskets so as to conceal them easily under their garments. While in council Pontiac was to give a signal which would tell the assembled warriors that the time had come for falling on the garrison and taking possession of the fort.* Some writers give credence to the story that an Indian maiden, the mistress of Gladwin, warned him of the scheme of the Indian chief, who came to the council, in accordance with his intention, and found the garrison in arms and ready for any treacherous movement on his part. He left the fort in anger, and soon afterwards attacked it with all his force, though to no purpose, as Gladwin was able to hold it for many months, until aid reached him from

---

* The siege of Detroit by Pontiac inspired one of the best historic novels ever written by a Canadian—*Wacousta, or the Prophecy*, by Major Richardson, who was the author of several other books.

the east. As one Indian woman's devotion saved
Detroit, so the treachery of a Delaware girl gave
Fort Miami and its little garrison to the Indians
encamped on the Maumee. Holmes, the commandant, was her lover, and believed her when she
told him that a squaw, who was seriously ill in one
of the wigwams, wished to see him. He proceeded
on his charitable mission, and was shot dead while
about entering the place of his destination. At
Michillimackinac Captain Etherington was surprised
by a clever piece of strategy on the part of a body
of Sacs and Ojibways, who invited him to witness a
contest between them at their favourite sport of La-
crosse, which in these modern times has been made
the national game of Canadians. While the game
was going on, the gate was left open while the officers and soldiers stood in groups outside, close to
the palisades, watching the Indians as they tossed
the ball to and fro between the goals on the level
ground opposite the fort. The squaws, wrapped in
their blankets, passed in and out the fort, without
attracting any attention from the interested spectators. Suddenly, when the game was most hotly
contested, the ball was violently driven in the direction of the pickets of the fort. A crowd of the savage players tumultuously followed the ball, and in a
moment were inside the fort where they snatched
weapons from the squaws. One officer and several
soldiers were instantly killed, but Etherington and
the remainder of the garrison were taken prisoners.
Etherington and a well-known trader of the West,
Alexander Henry, eventually escaped, after having

been on several occasions on the point of death. In six weeks' time from the first attack on Detroit, on the 9th of May, 1763, all the forts in the Western and Ohio country had been seized and destroyed by the Indians, except Fort Pitt at the forks of the Ohio, the one at Green Bay which was abandoned, and another at Ligonier. The garrisons were massacred or made prisoners, and in many cases tortured and even eaten. The frontiers of Virginia and Pennsylvania were laid waste by hordes of savages, who burned the homes of the settlers, murdered a large number, and carried off many prisoners, men, women, and children, to their savage fastnesses in the western wilderness. The war never ended until Virginia and Pennsylvania—where the Quaker element still prevailed—were aroused from their apathy and gave the requisite aid to an expedition under the command of an able officer, Colonel Bouquet, who had been one of Brigadier Forbes's officers during the campaign of 1759 in the Ohio valley. He rescued Fort Pitt, after administering to the Indians a severe defeat at Bushy Run. A year later he succeeded in taking a large force into the very heart of a country where the Indians thought themselves safe from any attack of their white enemy. His unexpected appearance on the banks of the Muskingum awed the Delawares, Shawanoes, and Mingoes, who gladly agreed to terms of peace, especially as they knew that Colonel Bradstreet was in their rear on the banks of Lake Erie. The prisoners, whom the Indians had taken during their raids on the frontier settlements of Virginia and Pennsyl-

18

vania, were restored to their friends and relatives who had, in the majority of cases, never hoped to see them again.   The annals of those days tell us strange stories of the infatuation which some young women felt for the savage warriors whom they had wedded in Indian fashion.   Some children had forgotten their mothers, and Parkman relates in his graphic narrative of those memorable times that one girl only recalled her childhood when she heard her distracted mother sing a song with which she had often lulled her daughter to sleep in happier days.

Peace again reigned in the West.   Detroit, after repulsing Pontiac so successfully, was at last relieved, and the red cross of England floated above the forts of Chartres and Vincennes, which were given up by the French.

By the end of the autumn of 1765 France possessed only a few acres of rock, constantly enveloped in fog, on the southern coast of Newfoundland, of all the great dominion she once claimed in North America.   Pontiac now disappears from history, and is believed to have been killed by an Indian warrior of the Illinois nation, after a drunken bout at the village of Cahokia—an ignominious ending to the career of a great chief whose name was for so many months a menace to English authority in that wilderness region, which was declared in later years by an imperial statute, the Quebec Act, to be a part of Canada's illimitable domain.

While this Indian war was going on, George III., in the autumn of 1763, issued a proclamation establishing four new governments in North America:

Quebec, East Florida, West Florida, and Grenada. The governors were empowered to summon general assemblies, and to make laws and ordinances for good government with the consent of the councils and the representatives of the people, and to establish courts of justice. Members elected to the proposed assemblies had to take the oaths of allegiance and supremacy, and the declaration against transubstantiation. No assembly, however, ever met, as the French Canadian population were unwilling to take the test oath, and the government of the province was carried on solely by the Governor-General—General Murray—with the assistance of an executive council, composed of certain officials and leading residents in the colony. From 1763 to 1774 the province remained in a very unsettled state, chiefly on account of the uncertainty that prevailed as to the laws actually in force. The "new subjects," or French Canadians, contended that justice, so far as they were concerned, should be administered in accordance with their ancient customs and usages. On the other hand, "the old," or English subjects, argued from the proclamation of 1763, that it was His Majesty's intention at once to abolish the old jurisprudence of the country, and to establish English law in its place.

Not the least important part of the proclamation of 1763 was that relating to the Indians, who were not to be disturbed in the possession of their hunting grounds. Lands could be alienated by the Indians only at some public meeting or assembly called for that special purpose by the Governor or commander-in-chief where such lands were situated. This was the commencement of that just and honest policy towards the Indians which has ever since been followed by the government of Canada. One hundred and ten years later, an interesting spectacle was witnessed in the great Northwest Territory of Canada. The lieutenant-governor of the new province of Manitoba, constituted in 1870 out of the prairie lands of that rich region, met in council the representatives of the Indian tribes, and solemnly entered into treaties with them for the transfer to Canada of immense tracts of prairie lands where we now see wide stretches of fields of nodding grain.

Governor Murray conducted his government on principles of justice and forbearance towards the French Canadians, and refused to listen to the unwise and arbitrary counsel of the four or five hundred "old subjects," who wished to rule the province. He succeeded in inspiring the old inhabitants of the province, or "new subjects," with confidence in his intentions. The majority of the "old subjects," who were desirous of ruling Canada, are described by the Governor in a letter to Lord Shelburne, as "men of mean education, traders, mechanics, publicans, followers of the army,"—a somewhat prejudiced statement. As a rule, however, the judges, magistrates, and officials at that time were men of little or no knowledge.

In 1774, Parliament intervened for the first time in Canadian affairs, and passed the Quebec Act, which greatly extended the boundaries of the province of Quebec, as defined by the proclamation of

1763. On one side, the province now extended to the frontiers of New England, Pennsylvania, New York province, the Ohio, and the left bank of the Mississippi; on the other, to the Hudson's Bay Territory. Labrador, Anticosti, and the Magdalen islands, annexed to Newfoundland by the proclamation of 1763, were made part of the province of Quebec.

The Quebec Act created much debate in the House of Commons. The Earl of Chatham, in the House of Lords, described it as " a most cruel, and odious measure." The opposition in the province was among the British inhabitants, who sent over a petition for its repeal or amendment. Their principal grievance was that it substituted the laws and usages of Canada for English law. The Act of 1774 was exceedingly unpopular in the English-speaking colonies, then at the commencement of the revolution on account of the extension of the limits of the province so as to include the country long known as the old Northwest in American history, and the consequent confinement of the Thirteen Colonies between the Atlantic coast and the Alleghany Mountains, beyond which the hardy and bold frontiersmen of Virginia and Pennsylvania were already passing into the great valley of the Ohio. Parliament, however, appears to have been influenced by a desire to adjust the government of the province so as to conciliate the majority of the Canadian people at this critical time.

The advice of Sir Guy Carleton, afterwards Lord Dorchester, who succeeded General Murray as Gov-

ernor-General, had much to do with the liberality
of the Quebec Act towards the French Canadians.
After a careful study of the country he came to the
conclusion that the French civil law ought to be
retained, although he was met by the earnest advice
to the contrary of two able lawyers, Chief-Justice
Hay and Attorney-General Masères, who believed
a code adopted from English and French principles
was preferable.   Masères, who was of Huguenot
descent and much prejudiced against Roman Catholics, was also an advocate of a legislative assembly
to be exclusively Protestant—in other words, of
giving all power practically into the hands of a small
British minority.   When the subject of a new Canadian constitution came to be discussed in England,
Carleton crossed the Atlantic in 1769 and remained
absent from Canada for four years.   He returned to
carry out the Quebec Act, which was the foundation of the large political and religious liberties which
French Canada has ever since enjoyed.

The new constitution came into force in October,
1774.   It provided that Roman Catholics should be
no longer obliged to take the test oath, but only the
oath of allegiance.   The government of the province was entrusted to a governor and a legislative
council, appointed by the Crown, inasmuch as it was
"inexpedient to call an assembly."   This council
had the power, with the consent of the Governor, to
make ordinances for the good government of the
province.   In all matters of controversy, relative to
property and civil rights, recourse should be had to
the French civil procedure, whilst the law of Eng-

land should obtain in criminal cases. Roman Catholics were permitted to observe their religion with perfect freedom, and their clergy were to enjoy their " accustomed dues and rights," with respect to such persons as professed that creed.

Sir Guy Carleton nominated a legislative council of twenty-three members, of whom eight were Roman Catholics. This body sat, as a rule, with closed doors; both languages were employed in the debates, and the ordinances agreed to were drawn up in English and French. In 1776 the Governor-General called to his assistance an advisory privy council of five members.

When Canada came under the operation of the Quebec Act, the Thirteen Colonies were on the eve of that revolution which ended in the establishment of a federal republic, and had also most important influence on the fortunes of the country through which the St. Lawrence flows.

XX.

THE AMERICAN REVOLUTION—INVASION OF CANADA—DEATH OF MONTGOMERY—PEACE.

(1774 1783.)

THE Canadian people had now entered on one of the most important periods of their history. Their country was invaded, and for a time seemed on the point of passing under the control of the congress of the old Thirteen Colonies, now in rebellion against England. The genius of an able English governor-general, however, saved the valley of the St. Lawrence for the English Crown, and the close of the war for American independence led to radical changes in the governments of British North America. A large population, imbued with the loftiest principles of patriotism and self-sacrifice, came in and founded new provinces, and laid the basis of the present Dominion of Canada.

During the revolution emphatic appeals were made to the Canadian French to join the English colonies in their rebellion against England. With a curious ignorance of the conditions of a people, who could not read and rarely saw a printed book, and never owned a printing-press * during the French régime, references were made by the congress that assembled at Philadelphia in September in 1774, to the writings of Beccaria and the spirit of the " immortal Montesquieu." The delegates attacked the Quebec Act as an exhibition of Roman Catholic tyranny at the very time they were asking the aid and sympathy of French Canadians in the struggle for independence. A few weeks later the same congress ignored the ill-advised address and appealed to the Canadians to join them on the broad grounds of continental freedom. The time, however, was too short to convince the clergy and leading men of the province that there was a change in the feeling of the majority in the congress with respect to the Roman Catholic religion. The mass of the French Canadians, especially in the rural districts, no doubt looked with great indifference on the progress of the conflict between the King of England and his former subjects, but in Quebec and Montreal, principally in the latter town, there were found English, as well as French-speaking persons quite ready to welcome and assist the forces of congress when they invaded Canada. On the other hand, the influences of the Quebec Act and of the judicious administrations of Murray and Carleton were obvious from the outset, and the bishop, Monseigneur Briand—who had been chosen with the silent acquiescence of the English Government—the

* The first paper printed in French Canada was the *Quebec Gazette*, which appeared in 1764.

clergy of the Roman Catholic Church, and the leading seigniors combined to maintain Canada under the dominion of a generous Power which had already given such undoubted guaranties for the preservation of the civil and religious rights of the " new subjects." In fact, the enemies of England were to be found chiefly among the " old subjects," who had attempted to obtain an assembly in which the French Canadians would be ignored, and had been, and were still bitterly antagonistic to the Quebec Act, with its concessions to the French Canadian majority. Many of these disaffected persons were mere adventurers who were carrying on a secret correspondence with the leaders of the American Revolution, and even went so far as to attempt to create discontent among the French Canadians by making them believe that their liberties were in jeopardy, and that they would have to submit to forced military service, and all those exactions which had so grievously burdened them in the days of the French dominion. The *habitants*, ignorant and credulous, however, remained generally inert during the events which threatened the security of Canada. It was left to a few enlightened men, chiefly priests and officers of the old French service, to understand the exact nature of the emergency, and to show their appreciation of what England had done for them since the cession.

When the first Continental Congress met at Philadelphia, on September 5, 1774, the colonies were on the eve of independence as a result of the coercive measures forced on Parliament by the King's pliable ministers, led by Lord North. The " declaration," however, was not finally proclaimed until nearly two years later—on July 4, 1776,—when the Thirteen Colonies declared themselves " free and independent States," absolved of their allegiance to the British Crown. But many months before this great epoch-making event, war had actually commenced on Lake Champlain. On an April day, in the now memorable year, 1775, the " embattled farmers " had fired at Concord and Lexington, the shots " heard round the world," and a few weeks later the forts of Crown Point and Ticonderoga, then defended by very feeble garrisons, were in the possession of Colonial troops led by Ethan Allen and Seth Warner, two of the " Green Mountain Boys," who organised this expedition. Canada was at this time in a very defenceless condition. Only eight hundred regular troops altogether were in the colony, very many of the English residents of Montreal and Quebec were of doubtful loyalty, the majority of the French Canadians were indifferent, and could not be induced to rally in any numbers to the defence of the province. Happily for the best interests of Canada at this crisis there was at the head of the administration one of the ablest men who have ever been sent to Canada—a governor-general who may well be compared with Frontenac as a soldier and Lord Elgin as a statesman—and that was Sir Guy Carleton, the friend of Wolfe, with whom he had served at Quebec. His conciliatory attitude towards the French Canadian population, and his influence in moulding the Quebec Act. gave him great weight with the bishop and clergy of the Roman Catholic faith and leading men of the majority. The British Government, with culpable neglect of his warnings and appeals, left him unsupported until the very last moment, when the fate of Canada was literally trembling in the balance. In the autumn of 1775 General Montgomery, at the head of a considerable force of congress troops, captured the forts of Chambly and St. Johns on the Richelieu, and a few days later occupied Montreal, which had been hastily evacuated by Carleton, who at once recognised the impracticability of defending it with any chance of success, since he had an insufficient force, and could not even depend on the fealty of the inhabitants. Quebec, at this juncture, was the key to Canada, and there he determined to make his fight. He passed in the night-time the batteries which the congress troops had built at Sorel and the adjacent islands. The oars of his boat were muffled, and when in close proximity to the enemy the men used the palms of their hands. He reached Quebec safely, and at once inspired the garrison and loyal residents with his courageous spirit. He arrived not a moment too soon. General Benedict Arnold —a name discredited in history—had succeeded in reaching Quebec by the route of the Kennebec and Chaudière rivers—a route which in early times had been followed by the Abenakis, those firm allies of the Canadians. Arnold was not able to commence any active operations against Quebec until the arrival of Montgomery from Montreal, with a force of fifteen hundred men, of whom a very small number were French Canadians. At this time there were in

Quebec only some eighteen hundred regular and militia troops, of whom over five hundred were French Canadians, under Colonel Voyer. No doubt the American commanders confidently expected to find in Quebec many active sympathisers who would sooner or later contrive to give the town into their hands, when these learned that all Canada except the capital was in the possession of the invading forces.

Many of their men were sick, and the artillery was insufficient for the siege of the fortress. It was decided then to attempt to seize the town by a piece of strategy, which was very simple though it had some chance of success. Arnold was well acquainted with the locality and entered heartily into the plan which was devised by Montgomery for a combined attack on Lower Town. Late at night on the 31st December, during a heavy snowstorm, Montgomery marched from Anse-au-Foulon along a rough and narrow road between the foot of Cape Diamond and the St. Lawrence, as far as Près-de-ville, or what is now Little Champlain Street. Arnold at the same time advanced from the direction of the St. Charles. It was arranged that the two parties should meet at the lower end of Mountain Street and force Prescott Gate, then only a rough structure of pickets. While the two bodies were carrying out this plan, attacks were made on the western side of the fortress to distract the attention of the defenders. Carleton, however, was not taken by surprise as he had had an intimation of what was likely to happen. Consequently the garrison was on the alert and Mont-

gomery's force was swept by a sudden discharge of
cannon and musketry as they came to Près-de-ville
—a defile with a precipice towards the river on one
side, and the scarped rock above him on the other
—where all further approach to the lower town was
intercepted by a battery. Montgomery, his two
aides, and a considerable number of his soldiers were
instantly killed. In the meantime Arnold had led
his party from the St. Charles to the Sault-au-Matelot, where he captured the first barrier defended by
two guns. Arnold was wounded in the knee, and
his force was obliged to proceed without him under
the command of Captain Morgan, to the attack of
the second battery near the eastern end of the narrow street, known as Sault-au-Matelot from the
most early times. They succeeded in obtaining
possession of some houses in the street, but it was
not long before they were surrounded by Carleton's
men and forced to surrender to the number of
several hundreds. Arnold remained, during the
winter, in command of the congress troops, who
suffered severely from small-pox, the cold, and even
want of sufficient provisions. In the spring he was
superseded by General Wooster who brought with
him a reinforcement, but the arrival of English frigates with troops and supplies, forced him to raise
the siege and retire hastily to Montreal. A few
weeks later General Burgoyne, with seven regiments, including a large German contingent under
General Frederick Riedesel, arrived at Quebec, and
arrangements were made for an active campaign
against the rebellious colonists. Arnold found it

prudent immediately to leave Montreal which was again occupied by English troops. The forts on the Richelieu were regained by the English, Carleton destroyed the congress fleet under the command of Arnold on Lake Champlain, and Crown Point was partly destroyed and abandoned by the retreating Americans. Soon after these occurrences in 1775, Carleton found to his chagrin that the command of the forces was given to Burgoyne, a much inferior man, who had influence with Lord Germain, better known in English history as that Lord George Sackville who had disgraced himself on the battlefield of Minden, but had subsequently found favour with the King, who made him one of his ministers, and gave him virtually the direction of the campaign in America. Carleton, however, remained Governor-General until 1778, when he was replaced at his own request by General Haldimand, a very energetic and capable man, to whom Canadian historians have, as a rule, never rendered adequate justice. During these years Carleton had his difficulties arising out of the unsettled condition of things in the province, the prospects of invasion, and the antagonism of Chief-Justice Livius, who replaced a far better man, Hey, and was himself superseded by the Governor-General on account of his efforts to weaken the authority of the government at a time when faction and rivalry should have ceased among those who wished to strengthen British interests in America. Livius appealed to the home authorities, and through the influence of Lord George Germain was reinstated, though he did not find even in this quarter an approval in words of his own conduct, and never returned to fill his former position in Canada.

It is not necessary to dwell here on the events of a war whose history is so familiar to every one. Burgoyne was defeated at Saratoga, and his army, from which so much was expected, made prisoners of war. This great misfortune of the British cause was followed by the alliance of France with the States. French money, men, and ships eventually assured the independence of the republic whose fortunes were very low at times, despite the victory at Saratoga. England was not well served in this American war. She had no Washington to direct her campaign. Gage, Burgoyne, and Cornwallis were not equal to the responsibilities thrown upon them. Cornwallis's defeat at Yorktown on the 19th October, 1781, was the death-blow to the hopes of England in North America. This disaster led to the resignation of Lord North, whose heart was never in the war, and to the acknowledgment by England, a few months later, of the independence of her old colonies. Before this decisive victory in the south, the Ohio valley and the Illinois country were in the possession of the troops of congress. George Rogers Clark, the bold backwoodsman of Kentucky, captured Kaskaskia, Cahokia, and Vincennes, and gave the new States that valid claim to the west which was fully recognised in the treaty of peace.

The definitive treaty of peace, which was signed in 1783, acknowledged the independence of the old English colonies, and fixed the boundaries of the new republic and of Canada, and laid the foundation of fruitful controversies in later times.

The United States now controlled the territory extending in the east from Nova Scotia (which then included New Brunswick) to the head of the Lake of the Woods and to the Mississippi River in the west, and in the north from Canada to the Floridas in the south, the latter having again become Spanish possessions. The boundary between Nova Scotia and the Republic was so ill-defined that it took half a century to fix the St. Croix and the Highlands which were by the treaty to divide the two countries. In the far west the line of division was to be drawn through the Lake of the Woods " to the most northwestern point thereof, and from thence on a due west course to the River Mississippi "—a physical impossibility, since the head of the Mississippi, as was afterwards found, was a hundred miles or so to the south. In later times this geographical error was corrected, and the curious distortion of the boundary line that now appears on the maps was necessary at the Lake of the Woods in order to strike the forty-ninth parallel of north latitude, which was subsequently arranged as the boundary line as far as the Rocky Mountains. Of the difficulties that arose from the eastern boundary line I shall speak later.

From 1778 until 1783 the government of Canada was under the direction of General Haldimand, who possessed that decision of character absolutely essential at so critical a period of Canadian history. The Congress of the States had never despaired of obtaining the assistance of the French Canadians, and of

19

bringing the country into the new republic.   Haldimand had to arrest Du Calvet, Mesplet, and Jotard, as leaders in a seditious movement against England. Fleury Mesplet put up in Montreal the first printing-press, which gave him and his friends superior facilities for circulating dangerous appeals to the restless element of the population.   Du Calvet was a French Protestant, in active sympathy with Congress, and had a violent controversy with Haldimand, who was, at last, forced to take severe measures against him. While on his way to England he was drowned, and the country spared more of his dangerous influence. Jotard, a French attorney, was a contributor to a paper owned by Mesplet, and a warm sympathiser with the efforts of Admiral D'Estaing and General Lafayette to win back the allegiance of the French Canadians.   The appeals of these two distinguished men to the memories of the old subjects of France had no immediate effect except upon a very small class, although it might have been different had French troops made their appearance on the St. Lawrence.   One Canadian priest, La Valinière, who was connected with the seminary of St. Sulpice in Montreal, was sent to England with the approval of the bishop, for his openly expressed sympathy with France.   Happily Monseigneur Briand and the great majority of the clergy stood always firm on the side of England.

XXI.

COMING OF THE LOYALISTS.

(1783–1791.)

It was during Governor Haldimand's administration that one of the most important events in the history of Canada occurred as a result of the American war for independence. This event was the coming to the provinces of many thousand people, known as United Empire Loyalists, who, during the progress of the war, but chiefly at its close, left their old homes in the thirteen colonies. When the Treaty of 1783 was under consideration, the British representatives made an effort to obtain some practical consideration from the new nation for the claims of this unfortunate people who had been subject to so much loss and obloquy during the war. All that the English envoys could obtain was the insertion of a clause in the treaty to the effect that Congress would recommend to the legislatures of the several States measures of restitution—a provision which turned out, as Franklin intimated at the time, a perfect nullity. The English Government subsequently indemnified these people in a measure for their self-sacrifice, and among other things gave a large number of them valuable tracts of land in the provinces of British North America.   Many of them settled in Nova Scotia, others founded New Brunswick and Upper Canada, now Ontario.   Their influence on the political fortunes of Canada has been necessarily very considerable.   For years they and their children were animated by a feeling of bitter animosity against the United States, the effects of which could be traced in later times when questions of difference arose between England and her former colonies. They have proved with the French Canadians a barrier to the growth of any annexation party, and as powerful an influence in national and social life as the Puritan element itself in the Eastern and Western States.

Among the sad stories of the past the one which tells of the exile of the Loyalists from their homes, of their trials and struggles in the valley of the St. Lawrence, then a wilderness, demands our deepest sympathy.   In the history of this continent it can be only compared with the melancholy chapter which relates the removal of the French population from their beloved Acadia.   During the Revolution they comprised a very large, intelligent, and important body of people, in all the old colonies, especially in New York and at the South, where they were in the majority until the peace. They were generally known as Tories, whilst their opponents, who supported independence, were called Whigs.   Neighbour was arrayed against neighbour, families were divided, the greatest cruelties were inflicted as the war went on upon men and women who believed it was their duty to be faithful to king and country. As soon as the contest was ended, their property was confiscated in several States. Many persons were banished and prohibited from returning to their homes. An American writer, Sabine, tells us that previous to the evacuation of New York, in the month of September, 1783, " upwards of twelve thousand men, women, and children embarked at the city, at Long and Staten Islands, for Nova Scotia and the Bahamas." Very wrong impressions were held in those days of the climate and resources of the provinces to which these people fled. Time was to prove that the lot of many of the loyalists had actually fallen in pleasant places, in Nova Scotia, New Brunswick, and Upper Canada; that the country, where most of them settled, was superior in many respects to the New England States, and equal to the State of New York from which so many of them came.

It is estimated that between forty and fifty thousand people reached British North America by 1786. They commenced to leave their old homes soon after the breaking out of the war, but the great migration took place in 1783–84. Many sought the shores of Nova Scotia, and founded the town of Shelburne, which at one time held a population of ten or twelve thousand souls, the majority of whom were entirely unsuited to the conditions of the rough country around them, and soon sought homes elsewhere. Not a few settled in more favourable parts of Nova Scotia, and even in Cape Breton. Considerable numbers found rest in the beautiful valley of the St. John River, and founded the province of New Brunswick. As many more laid the beginnings of Upper Canada, in the present county of Glengarry, in the neighbourhood of Kingston and the Bay of Quinté, on the Niagara River, and near the French settlements on the Detroit. A few also settled in the country now known as the Eastern Townships of French Canada. A great proportion of the men were officers and soldiers of the regiments which were formed in several colonies out of the large loyal population. Among them were also men who had occupied positions of influence and responsibility in their respective communities, divines, judges, officials, and landed proprietors, whose names were among the best in the old colonies, as they are certainly in Canada. Many among them gave up valuable estates which had been acquired by the energy of their ancestors. Unlike the Puritans who founded New England, they did not take away with them their valuable property in the shape of money and securities, or household goods. A rude log hut by the side of a river or lake, where poverty and wretchedness were their lot for months, and even years in some cases, was the refuge of thousands, all of whom had enjoyed every comfort in well-built houses, and not a few even luxury in stately mansions, some of which have withstood the ravages of time and can still be pointed out in New England. Many of the loyalists were quite unfitted for the rude experiences of a pioneer life, and years passed before they and their children conquered the wilderness and made a livelihood. The British Government was extremely liberal in its grants of lands to this class of persons in all the provinces.

The government supplied these pioneers in the majority of cases with food, clothing, and necessary farming implements. For some years they suffered many privations; one was called " the year of famine," when hundreds in Upper Canada had to live on roots, and even the buds of trees, or anything that might sustain life. Fortunately some lived in favoured localities, where pigeons and other birds, and fish of all kinds, were plentiful. In the summer and fall there were quantities of wild fruit and nuts. Maple sugar was a great luxury, when the people once learned to make it from the noble tree, whose symmetrical leaf may well be made the Canadian national emblem. It took the people a long while to accustom themselves to the conditions of their primitive pioneer life, but now the results of the labours of these early settlers and their descendants can be seen far and wide in smiling fields, richly laden orchards, and gardens of old-fashioned flowers throughout the country which they first made to blossom like the rose. The rivers and lakes were the only means of communication in those early times, roads were unknown, and the wayfarer could find his way through the illimitable forests only by the help of the " blazed " trees and the course of streams. Social intercourse was infrequent except in autumn and winter, when the young managed to assemble as they always will. Love and courtship went on even in this wilderness, though marriage was uncertain, as the visits of clergymen were very rare in many places, and magistrates could alone tie the nuptial knot—a very unsatisfactory performance to the cooler lovers who loved their church, its ceremonies and traditions, as dearly as they loved their sovereign. The story of those days of trial has not yet been adequately written; perhaps it never will be, for few of those pioneers have left records behind them. As we wander among the old burying grounds of those founders of Western Canada and New Brunswick, and stand by the gray, moss-covered tablets, with names effaced by the ravages of years, the thought will come to us, what interesting stories could be told by those who are laid beneath the sod, of sorrows and struggles, of hearts sick with hope deferred, of expectations never realised, of memories of misfortune and disaster in another land where they bore so much for a stubborn and unwise king. Yet these grass-covered mounds are not simply memorials of suffering and privation; each could tell a story of fidelity to principle, of forgetfulness of self-interest, of devotion and self-sacrifice—the grandest story that human annals can tell—a story that should be ever held up to the admiration and emulation of the young men and women of the present times, who enjoy the fruits of the labours of those loyal pioneers.

Although no noble monument has yet been raised to the memory of these founders of new provinces—of English-speaking Canada; although the majority lie forgotten in old graveyards where the grass has grown rank, and common flowers alone nod over their resting-places, yet the names of all are written in imperishable letters in provincial annals. Those loyalists, including the children of both sexes, who joined the cause of Great Britain before the Treaty of Peace in 1783, were allowed the distinction of having after their name the letters U. E. to preserve the memory of their fidelity to a United Empire. A Canadian of these modern days, who traces his descent from such a source, is as proud of his lineage as if he were a Derby or a Talbot of Malahide, or inheritor of other noble names famous in the annals of the English peerage.

The records of all the provinces show the great influence exercised on their material, political, and intellectual development by this devoted body of immigrants. For more than a century they and their descendants have been distinguished for the useful and important part they have taken in every matter deeply associated with the best interests of the country. In New Brunswick we find among those who did good service in their day and generation the names of Wilmot, Allen, Robinson, Jarvis, Hazen, Burpee, Chandler, Tilley, Fisher, Bliss, Odell, Botsford; in Nova Scotia, Inglis (the first Anglican bishop in the colonies), Wentworth, Brenton, Blowers (Chief Justice), Cunard, Cutler, Howe, Creighton, Chipman, Marshall, Halliburton, Wilkins, Huntingdon, Jones; in Ontario, Cartwright, Robinson, Hagerman, Stuart (the first Anglican clergyman), Gamble, Van Alstine, Fisher, Grass, Butler, Macaulay, Wallbridge, Chrysler, Bethune,

Merritt, McNab, Crawford, Kirby, Tisdale, and
Ryerson. Among these names stand out prominently those of Wilmot, Howe, and Huntingdon,
who were among the fathers of responsible government; those of Tilley, Tupper, Chandler, and Fisher,
who were among the fathers of confederation; of
Ryerson, who exercised a most important influence
on the system of free education which Ontario now
enjoys. Among the eminent living descendants of
U. E. Loyalists are Sir Charles Tupper, long a
prominent figure in politics; Christopher Robinson, a distinguished lawyer, who was counsel for
Canada at the Bering Sea arbitration; Sir Richard
Cartwright, a liberal leader remarkable for his keen,
incisive style of debate, and his knowledge of financial questions ; Honourable George E. Foster, a
former finance minister of Canada. We might extend the list indefinitely did space permit. In all
walks of life we see the descendants of the loyalists,
exercising a decided influence over the fortunes of
the Dominion.

Conspicuous among the people who remained
faithful to England during the American revolution,
we see the famous Iroquois chief, Joseph Brant,
best known by his Mohawk name of Thayendanegea, who took part in the war, and was for many
years wrongly accused of having participated in the
massacre and destruction of Wyoming, that beauteous vale of the Susquehanna. It was he whom the
poet Campbell would have consigned to eternal
infamy in the verse:

Jos. Brant
Thayendanegea

" The mammoth comes—the foe, the monster, Brandt—
   With all his howling, desolating band ;
These eyes have seen their blade and burning pine
   Awake at once, and silence half your land.
Red is the cup they drink, but not with wine—
   Awake and watch to-night, or see no morning shine."

Posterity has, however, recognised the fact that Joseph Brant was not present at this sad episode of the American war, and the poet in a note to a later edition admitted that the Indian chief in his poem was " a pure and declared character of fiction." He was a sincere friend of English interests, a man of large and statesmanlike views, who might have taken an important part in colonial affairs had he been educated in these later times. When the war was ended, he and his tribe moved into the valley of the St. Lawrence, and received from the government fine reserves of land on the Bay of Quinté, and on the Grand River in the western part of the province of Upper Canada, where the prosperous city and county of Brantford, and the township of Tyendi-naga—a corruption of Thayendanegea—illustrate the fame he has won in Canadian annals. The de-scendants of his nation live in comfortable homes, till fine farms in a beautiful section of Western Canada, and enjoy all the franchises of white men. It is an interesting fact that the first church built in Ontario was that of the Mohawks, who still preserve the communion service presented to the tribe in 1710 by Queen Anne of England.

General Haldimand's administration will always be noted in Canadian history for the coming of the loyalists, and for the sympathetic interest he took in settling these people on the lands of Canada, and in alleviating their difficulties by all the means in the power of his government. In these and other matters of Canadian interest he proved conclusively that he was not the mere military martinet that some Canadian writers with inadequate information would make him. When he left Canada he was succeeded by Sir Guy Carleton, then elevated to the peerage as Lord Dorchester, who was called upon to take part in great changes in the constitution of Canada which must be left for review in the following chapter.

XXII.

FOUNDATION OF NEW PROVINCES—ESTABLISH-MENT OF REPRESENTATIVE INSTITUTIONS.

(1792–1812.)

THE history of the Dominion of Canada as a self-governing community commences with the conces-sion of representative institutions to the old provinces now comprised within its limits. By 1792 there were provincial governments established in Upper and Lower Canada, Nova Scotia, New Brunswick, and Prince Edward Island. From 1713 to 1758 the gov-ernment of Nova Scotia consisted of a governor, or lieutenant-governor, a council possessing legislative, executive, and even judicial powers. In October, 1758, an assembly met for the first time in the town of Halifax, which had been the capital since 1749. New Brunswick had been separated from Nova Scotia in 1784, but a representative assembly did not assemble until 1786, when its form of govern-ment was identical with that of the older province. Prince Edward Island was a part of Nova Scotia until 1769 when it was created a distinct province,

with a lieutenant-governor, a combined executive
and legislative council, and also an assembly in 1773.
The island of Cape Breton had a lieutenant-governor
and executive council, and remained apart from
Nova Scotia until 1820 when it was included in its
government. In 1791 the province of Upper Canada was formally separated from the province of
Quebec by an act of the imperial parliament, and
was called Upper Canada, while the French section
received the name of Lower Canada. At that time
the total population of British North America did
not exceed a quarter of a million of souls, of whom
at least a hundred and forty thousand lived on the
banks of the St. Lawrence and its tributary streams,
and almost entirely represented the language, institutions, and history of the French régime. In the
French province there was also a small British population, consisting of officials, commercial men, and
loyalists who settled for the most part in the Eastern Townships. The population of Upper Canada,
about twenty-five thousand, was almost exclusively
of loyalist stock—a considerable number having
migrated thither from the maritime provinces.
Beyond the Detroit River, the limit of English settlement, extended a vast region of wilderness which
was trodden only by trappers and Indians.

The Constitutional Act of 1791, which created the
two provinces of Upper and Lower Canada, caused
much discussion in the British Parliament and in
Canada, where the principal opposition came from
the English inhabitants of the French province.
These opponents of the act even sent Mr. Adam

Lymburner, a Quebec merchant of high standing, to express their opinions at the bar of the English House of Commons. The advocates of the new scheme of government, however, believed that the division of 'Canada into two provinces would have the effect of creating harmony, since the French would be left in the majority in one section, and the British in the other. The Quebec Act, it was generally admitted, had not promoted the prosperity or happiness of the people at large. Great uncertainty still existed as to the laws actually in force under the act. In not a few cases the judges were confessedly ignorant—Chief Justice Livius, for instance —of French Canadian jurisprudence. The increase of the English population was a strong argument for a grant of representative institutions. Accordingly the constitutional act provided for an assembly, elected by the people on a limited franchise, in each province, and for a legislative council, appointed by the Crown. The sovereign might annex hereditary letters of honour to the right of summons to the legislative council, but no attempt was ever made to create a Canadian aristocracy, or distinct class, under the authority of this section of the act. The British Government reserved the right of imposing, levying, and collecting duties of customs, and of appointing or directing their payment, though it left the exclusive apportionment of all moneys levied in this way to legislature. The free exercise of the Roman Catholic religion was permanently guaranteed. A seventh part of all uncleared Crown lands was reserved for the use of the Protestant clergy—a provision that caused much trouble in the future. The civil law of French Canada was to regulate property and civil rights in that province. English criminal law was to prevail in both the Canadas. The Governor-General of Quebec and Lieutenant-Governor of Upper Canada were each assisted by an executive council chosen by those functionaries, and having a right to sit also in the legislative council. Lord Dorchester was the first governor-general, not only of Canada, but likewise of the other provinces by virtue of separate commissions to that effect. The heads of the executive in all the provinces except Quebec were called lieutenant-governors, but they became only directly subordinate to the governor-general when he was present in a province in his official capacity.

The city where the first assembly of Lower Canada met in 1792 was one of great historic interest. The very buildings in which the government transacted its business had echoed to the tread of statesmen, warriors, and priests of the old régime. The civil and military branches of the government then occupied apartments in the old Château St. Louis, elevated on the brink of an inaccessible precipice. On a rocky eminence, in the vicinity of a battery close to Prescott Gate, erected in 1797, was an old stone building, generally known as the Bishop's Palace. Like all the ancient structures of Quebec, this building had no claims to elegance of form, although much labour and expense had been bestowed on its construction. The chapel of this building, situated near the communication with the lower

20

town, was converted into a chamber, in which were held the first meetings of the representatives of Lower Canada.

On the 17th of December, the two houses assembled in their respective chambers in the old palace, in obedience to the proclamation of Major-General Alured Clarke, who acted as lieutenant-governor in the absence of the governor-general, Lord Dorchester. Among the officers who surrounded the throne on that occasion, was probably his Royal Highness the Duke of Kent, who was in command of the 7th Royal Fusiliers, then stationed in the old capital. On so momentous an occasion, the assemblage was large, and comprised all the notabilities of English and French society. In the legislature were not a few men whose families had long been associated with the fortunes of the colony. Chaussegros de Léry, St. Ours, Longueuil, Lanaudière, Rouville, Boucherville, Salaberry, and Lotbinière, were among the names that told of the old régime, and gave a guaranty to the French Canadians that their race and institutions were at last protected in the legislative halls of their country. M. Panet, a distinguished French Canadian, was unanimously elected the speaker of the first assembly of French Canada.

Now let us leave the Bishop's Palace, among the rocks of old Quebec, and visit the humble village of Newark, where Lieutenant-Governor Simcoe opened his first legislature under the new constitution in the autumn of 1792. Across the rapid river was the territory of the Republic, which was engaged in a grand experiment of government. The roar of the

PRESCOTT GATE AND BISHOP'S PALACE AT QUEBEC IN 1830.

307

mighty cataract of Niagara could be heard in calm
summer days. On the banks of this picturesque
river was the residence of the lieutenant-governor,
known as Navy Hall, where the legislators of Upper
Canada probably met. This was but a mean parliament house, compared with the massive pile
which was chosen for a similar purpose in Quebec;
and yet each was appropriate in its way. The
Bishop's Palace illustrated an old community, which
had aimed at the conquest of the larger part of
America, and had actually laid the foundations of
an empire; the legislative cabin of Newark was a fit
type of the ruggedness and newness of western
colonial life. The axe was whirring amid the forests, and only here and there, through a vast wilderness, could be seen the humble clearings of the
pioneers.

The session was opened with the usual speech,
which was duly reported to the house of assembly
by the speaker, Mr. McDonnell of Glengarry, and
immediately taken into consideration by the representatives of the yeomanry of the western province.
It is said that on more than one occasion, the representatives were forced to leave their confined chamber and finish their work under the trees before the
door. If the attendance was small on this occasion,
it must be remembered that there were many difficulties to overcome before the two Houses could
assemble in obedience to the governor's proclamation. The seven legislative councillors and sixteen
members who represented a population of only
25,000 souls, were scattered at very remote points,

and could only find their way at times in canoes and slow sailing craft. Nor must it be forgotten that in those early days of colonisation men had the stern necessities of existence to consider before all things else. However urgent the call to public duty, the harvest must be gathered in before laws could be made.

Such were the circumstances under which the legislatures were opened in the two provinces, representing the two distinct races of the population. Humble as were the beginnings in the little parliament house of Newark, yet we can see from their proceedings that the men, then called to do the public business, were of practical habits and fully alive to the value of time in a new country, as they sat for only five weeks and passed the same number of bills that it took seven months at Quebec to pass.

The history of Canada, during the twenty years that elapsed between the inauguration of the constitution of 1792 and the war of 1812, does not require any extended space in this work. Lieutenant-Governor Simcoe, who had distinguished himself during the war for independence as a commander of the Queen's Rangers, was a skilful and able administrator, who did his best to develop the country. It was during his régime that Toronto, under the name of York, was chosen, by the influence of Lord Dorchester, as the capital in place of Newark, which was too close to the American frontier, although the Lieutenant-Governor would have preferred the site of the present city of London, on the River

Thames, then known as La Tranche. Mainly through his efforts a considerable immigration was attracted from the United States. Many of the new settlers were loyal and favourable to British institutions, but in the course of time there came into the country not a few discontented, restless persons, having radical and republican tendencies. Among the important measures of his administration was an act preventing the future introduction of slaves, and providing for the freedom of children of slaves then in the province. Governor Simcoe devoted his energy not only to the peopling of the province, but to the opening up of arteries of communication, of which Yonge and Dundas Streets— still well-known names—were the most noted. The founder of an important settlement in the west, an eccentric Irishman of noble ancestry, Colonel Thomas Talbot, was a member of the Lieutenant-Governor's staff, and eventually made his home in the western part of the province, where he became a useful and influential pioneer. Among the most desirable immigrants were the Scotch Highlanders, who settled and named the county of Glengarry, and came to the country by the advice of the energetic and able priest, Macdonell, afterwards the first Roman Catholic bishop of Upper Canada. In Nova Scotia a number of Scotch settled in Pictou county as early as 1773, and were followed in later years by many others who found homes in the same district, in Antigonishe and Cape Breton, where their descendants are still greatly in the majority. In Prince Edward Island, Lord Selkirk, the founder of the

Red River settlement, to whose history I shall refer in a later chapter, established a colony of thrifty Scotch in one of the deserted settlements of the

LIEUTENANT-GENERAL SIMCOE.

French. Charlottetown was founded in those days on the bay first known as Port La Joye, and is now a pleasing example of the placid dignity and rural tranquillity that a capital may attain even in these restless modern times. In this island, the seeds of discontent were planted at a very early time by the transfer of nearly all its lands in one day by ballot to a few English landlords, whose absenteeism long retarded its advancement, and whose claims of proprietorship were not settled until after the confederation of the provinces.

The political condition of the provinces from the beginning of the nineteenth century began to assume considerable importance according as the assemblies became discontented with their relatively small share in the government of the country. In all the provinces there was a persistent contest between the popular assemblies and prerogative, as represented by the governors, and upper houses appointed by the same authority. Charles the First, with all his arrogance, never treated his parliament with greater superciliousness than did Sir James Craig, when governor-general, on more than one occasion when the assembly had crossed his wishes. In the absence of a ministry responsible to the assembly, a conflict was always going on between that body and the representative of the Crown. The assembly began now to claim full control over the taxes and revenues which belonged to the people of the provinces. The presence of judges in the legislature was a just cause for public discontent for years, and although these high functionaries were eventually removed from the assembly they continued to sit in the upper house until 1840. The constant interference of the Imperial Government in matters of purely local concern also led to many unfortunate misunderstandings.

In Lower Canada, where the population was the largest, and the racial distinctions strongly accentuated, the political conflict was, from the outset, more bitter than in other sections. The official class, a little oligarchy composed exclusively of persons brought from the British Isles, treated the French Canadians with a studied superciliousness, and arrogated to themselves all the important functions of government. This element dominated the executive and legislative councils, and practically the governors, who, generally speaking, had extreme views of their prerogative, and were cognisant of the fact that the colonial office in England had no desire to entrust the Canadian Government with much larger powers than those possessed by a municipal organisation. In the assembly the French Canadians were largely in the majority—the English element had frequently not more than one-fifth of the total representation of fifty members. The assembly too often exhibited a very domineering spirit, and attempted to punish all those who ventured to criticise, however moderately, their proceedings. The editor of the *Quebec Mercury*, an organ of the British minority, was arrested on this ground. *Le Canadien* was established as an organ of the French Canadian majority with the motto, *Nos institutions, notre langue, et nos lois.* By its constant attacks on the government and the English governing class it did much harm by creating and perpetuating racial antagonisms and by eventually precipitating civil strife. As a result of its attacks on the government, the paper was seized, and the printer, as well as M.

Bedard and several other members of the assembly who were understood to be contributors to its pages, or to control its opinions, were summarily arrested by the orders of Sir James Craig. Though some of these persons obtained their release by an expression of regret for their conduct, M. Bedard would not yield, and was not released until the Governor-General himself gave up the fight and retired to England where he died soon afterwards, with the consciousness that his conduct with respect to Bedard, and other members of the assembly, had not met with the approval of the Imperial authorities, although he had placed the whole case before them by the able agency of Mr. Ryland, who had been secretary for years to successive governors-general, and represented the opinions of the ruling official class.

In Upper Canada there were no national or racial antipathies and rivalries to stimulate political differences. In the course of time, however, antagonisms grew up between the Tories, chiefly old U. E. Loyalists, the official class, and the restless, radical element, which had more recently come into the country, and now desired to exercise political influence. Lieutenant-governors, like Sir Francis Gore, sympathised with the official class, and often with reason, as the so-called radical leaders were not always deserving of the sympathy of reasonable men. One of these leaders was Joseph Willcocks, for some time sheriff of the Home district—one of the four judicial divisions of the province—and also the proprietor and editor of the *Upper Canada Guar-*

dian, the second paper printed in Upper Canada—the first having been the *Upper Canada Gazette*, or the *American Oracle*, which appeared at Newark on the 18th April, 1793. He was a dangerous agitator, not worthy of public confidence, but he was able to evoke some sympathy, and pose as a political martyr, on account of the ill-advised conduct of the majority of the assembly ordering his arrest for expressing some unfavourable opinion of their proceedings in his paper.

In the maritime provinces the conflict between the executive and the assemblies was less aggravated than in the St. Lawrence country, although Sir John Wentworth, the Lieutenant-Governor of Nova Scotia, who had been a governor of New Hampshire before the revolution, had a very exalted idea of the prerogative, and succeeded in having an acrimonious controversy with Mr. Cottnam Tonge, the leader of the popular party, and the predecessor of a far greater man, Joseph Howe, the father of responsible government.

Such, briefly, was the political condition of the several provinces of British North America when events occurred to stifle discontent and develop a broader patriotism on all sides. The War of 1812 was to prove the fidelity of the Canadian people to the British Crown and stimulate a new spirit of self-reliance among French as well as English Canadians, who were to win victories which are among the most brilliant episodes of Canadian history.

XXIII.

THE WAR OF 1812–1815—PATRIOTISM OF THE CANADIANS.

AT the outbreak of the unfortunate War of 1812 the United States embraced an immense territory extending from the St. Lawrence valley to Mexico, excepting Florida—which remained in the possession of Spain until 1819—and from the Atlantic indefinitely westward to the Spanish possessions on the Pacific coast, afterwards acquired by the United States. The total population of the Union was upwards of eight million souls, of whom a million and a half were negro slaves in the south. Large wastes of wild land lay between the Canadian settlements and the thickly populated sections of New England, New York, and Ohio. It was only with great difficulty and expense that men, munitions of war, and provisions could be brought to the frontier during the contest.

The principal causes of the war are quite intelligible to the historical student. Great Britain was engaged in a great conflict not only for her own national security but also for the integrity of Europe, then dominated by the insatiable ambition of Bonaparte. It was on the sea that her strength mainly lay. To ensure her maritime supremacy, she found it necessary, in the course of events, to seize and condemn neutral American vessels whenever there was conclusive evidence that their cargoes were not the produce of the United States, but had been actually bought in an enemy's colony and were on their way to the mother country. But such an interruption of a commerce, which had been carried on for years at a great profit by American merchants, was by no means so serious an affair as the stoppage of American vessels on the high seas, and the forcible abduction and impressment, by British naval officers, of sailors who were claimed as British subjects, even when they had been naturalised in the United States. To such an extent did Great Britain assert her pretensions, that one of her frigates, the *Leopard*, actually fired into the American cruiser *Chesapeake*, off the coast of the bay of the same name, and made prisoners of several men who were claimed as deserters from an English man-of-war—a national outrage for which Great Britain subsequently made an apology and gave a measure of reparation. Then came the British orders in council which forbade American trade with any country from which the British flag was excluded, allowed direct trade from the United States to Sweden only in American products, and permitted American trade with other parts of Europe only on condition of touching at English ports and paying duties. Napoleon retaliated with decrees which were practically futile while England was victorious on the ocean, but which nevertheless threw additional difficulties in the way of the commerce of a country like the United States, which possessed such exceptional facilities for its development from its position as a neutral nation, and its great maritime and mercantile enterprise. The British measures meant the ruin of an American commerce which had become very profitable, and the Washington government attempted to retaliate by declaring an embargo in their own ports, which had only the result of still further embarrassing American trade. In place of this injudicious measure a system of non-intercourse with both England and France was substituted as long as either should continue its restrictive measures against the United States. The Democratic governing party practically fell under the influence of France, and believed, or at least professed to believe, that Napoleon had abandoned his repressive system, when, as a matter of fact, as the English ministry declared, it still existed to all intents and purposes. The Democratic leaders, anxious to keep in power, fanned the flame against England, whose naval superiority enabled her to inflict an injury on American commercial interests, which France was entirely powerless to do. The Democrats looked to the South and West for their principal support in holding power. In these sections the interests were exclusively agricultural, while in New England, where the Federalists—the peace party—were in the majority—and the war was very unpopular—the commercial and maritime element largely prevailed. In the West there had been for years an intense feeling against England on account of the fact that after the definitive treaty of peace in 1783, the English Government continued to occupy the Western posts and dependent terri- tory for thirteen years, nominally on the ground of the harsh treatment meted out to the loyalists in violation of its terms, and of the non-payment of debts due to English creditors, but probably also with the view of keeping control of the fur trade. The feeling prevailed among the western frontiers- men that the English secretly instigated Indian attacks on the new settlements, a belief proved by recent investigations to be groundless. Even after the victories of Mayne in 1794, and of Harrison in 1811, when the Indian power was effectively broken, this bitter sentiment still existed in the West against English and Canadians, and had much influence with the politicians who favoured the war.

The Southern leaders, Clay of Kentucky and Cal- houn of South Carolina, were most inimical to Eng- land, and succeeded in forcing Madison to agree to a declaration of war, as a condition to his re-election to the presidency. The consequence of this suc- cessful bargain was the passage of a war measure by Congress as soon as Madison issued his message, and the formal declaration of hostilities on the 18th of June, 1812. On the previous day, England had actually repealed the obnoxious orders in council, but it was too late to induce the war party in the United States to recede and stop the progress of the forces, which were already near the western

Canadian frontier when the governor-general of Canada, Sir George Prevost, a military man, heard the news of the actual declaration of hostilities.

With the causes of the War of 1812 the Canadian people had nothing whatever to do; it was quite sufficient for them to know that it was their duty to assist England with all their might and submit to any sacrifices which the fortunes of war might necessarily bring to a country which became the principal scene of conflict. Ontario, then Upper Canada, with a population of about eighty thousand souls, was the only province that really suffered from the war. From the beginning to the end its soil was the scene of the principal battles, and a great amount of valuable property destroyed by the invading forces. " On to Canada " had been the cry of the war party in the United States for years; and there was a general feeling that the upper province could be easily taken and held until the close of the struggle, when it could be used as a lever to bring England to satisfactory terms or else be united to the Federal Union. The result of the war showed, however, that the people of the United States had entirely mistaken the spirit of Canadians, and that the small population scattered over a large region— not more than four hundred thousand souls from Sydney to Sandwich—was animated by a stern determination to remain faithful to England.

No doubt the American Government had been led to believe from the utterances of Willcocks in the *Guardian*, as the representative of the discontented element in Upper Canada, that they would find not

only sympathy but probably some active co-operation in the western country as soon as the armies of
the Republic appeared on Canadian soil and won, as
they confidently expected, an easy victory over the
small force which could be brought to check invasion and defend the province. General Hull's proclamation, when he crossed the Detroit River at the
commencement of hostilities, was so much evidence
of the belief that was entertained in the United
States with regard to the fealty of the Canadians.
Willcocks proved himself a disloyal man, for he
eventually joined the American forces and fell fighting against the country which he and a very small
disaffected class would willingly have handed to
a foreign invader. The forces at the disposal of
the Canadian authorities certainly appeared to be
inadequate for the defence of a country with so long
and exposed a frontier. In the provinces of Canada
there were, in 1812, only four thousand five hundred
regular troops, and of these hardly one-third were
stationed above Montreal. The Canadian militia,
however, rallied with extraordinary readiness to the
call of the authorities. The majority of the loyal
population that had come into the country had been
engaged in military services, and even the old settlers, who were exempted from active duty, volun-
tarily came forward, and exercised, as General
Sheaffe, said, "a happy influence on the youth of
the militia ranks." The legislative bodies of all the
provinces responded liberally to the call of the executive and placed at the disposal of the government
all their resources. Army bills were issued to a

21

large amount, and found a most valuable currency throughout the war.

During the first year of the war, there was a continuous record of success for Canada. The key to the upper lakes, Michillimackinac, was captured and held by a small force of English regulars and Canadian voyageurs. The immediate consequence of this victory was to win the confidence and alliance of the western Indians, then led by Tecumseh, the famous Shawanoese chief, who had been driven from Tippecanoe by General Harrison. Then followed the capitulation of General Hull and his army, who had invaded Canada and were afterwards forced to retreat to Detroit, where they surrendered to General Brock with a much inferior force. By this capitulation, which led to the disgrace and nearly to the execution of Hull on his return to his own country, the whole territory of Michigan, over two thousand five hundred troops, and a large quantity of munitions of war and provisions fell into the possession of the British. The next important event of this memorable year was the defeat of the attempt of Van Rensselaer to occupy Queenston Heights, with the object of establishing there a base of future operations against Upper Canada. The Americans were routed with great loss and many of the men threw themselves down the precipice and were drowned in the deep and rapid river. At the beginning of the battle, General Brock was unhappily slain while leading his men up the heights, and the same fate befell his chivalrous aide-de-camp, Colonel McDonell, the attorney-general of the province. It

MAJOR-GENERAL BROCK.

was left for General Sheaffe to complete the victory, which gave many prisoners to the English force, and drove the remainder of the beaten American army across the beautiful river. General Smyth, a most incompetent man, who succeeded to the command of the American army on the resignation of Van Rensselaer, subsequently attempted to storm and carry Fort Erie, but Colonel Bisshopp successfully held this important post, which controlled the outlet of Lake Erie into the Niagara River. When the campaign closed, in 1812, Canada was free from the invader, chiefly through the energy and sagacity with which the gallant General Brock had made his preparations to repel invasion.

In 1813 the campaign commenced with a signal victory by General Procter, who was in command at Detroit, over a considerable American force at Frenchtown, on the Raisin River, under the command of Brigadier Winchester. Then came a successful attack by Colonel McDonnell on Ogdensburgh (La Présentation of the French régime), in retaliation for raids on Gananoque and Elizabethtown, subsequently named Brockville—now a beautiful city near the Thousand Isles—in honour of the gallant soldier who perished on the heights of Queenston. Commodore Chauncey, in command of a small American fleet organised at Sackett's Harbour, an important base of naval and military operations for the Americans, attacked the little capital of York, now Toronto, which was evacuated by General Sheaffe, then administrator of the government, who retired to Kingston, the strongest position to the west of Montreal. The invaders burnt the legislative and other public buildings. The small library and public records were not even spared by the pillaging troops. No precautions had been taken by Sheaffe to improve defences which at the best were of little strength. During the summer, the American army was so much superior to the English forces that they were able to occupy the whole Niagara frontier from Fort Erie to Fort George, both of which were captured by General Dearborn. Major-General Vincent, the English commander, was compelled to retire to Burlington Heights, overlooking the present city of Hamilton. Sir George Prevost, who proved himself a most irresolute and incapable commander-in-chief, retreated ignominiously from Sackett's Harbour, although Commodore Chauncey and his fleet were absent and the post was defended by only a small garrison. This discreditable failure, which cannot be in any way excused, was soon forgotten when the news came of the success of Colonel Harvey, afterwards a lieutenant-governor of the maritime provinces, at Stoney Creek, quite close to Burlington Bay. With an insignificant detachment from Vincent's main body, Harvey succeeded in surprising at night a large American force, commanded by Brigadiers Chandler and Winder, both of whom, as well as one hundred officers and men, were taken prisoners. This serious disaster and the approach of Admiral Yeo's fleet from the eastward forced the invading army to retire to Fort George, where they concentrated their strength, after abandoning Fort

Erie and other posts on the frontier. It was during the campaign of this year that Laura Secord, the courageous daughter of a sturdy loyalist stock which has given the name of Ingersoll to a Canadian town, afforded a memorable example of the devotion which animated Canadian women in these years of trial. General Dearborn had ordered Colonel Boerstler to surprise and attack the Canadian outposts at Twelve Mile Creek, now St. Catharine's, and at De Ceu's farm, close to the present town of Thorold. Lieutenant Fitzgibbon, with a picket of thirty men, was stationed at De Ceu's. A Canadian militiaman, James Secord, who lived at Queenston, heard of the proposed attack, but as he had been severely wounded in the attack on Queenston Heights in the previous October, he was unable to warn Fitzgibbon. His wife, a woman of nearly forty years, volunteered for the hazardous duty, and started at dawn for a journey of twenty miles, through dense woods, where the paths were few and had to be avoided for fear of meeting American marauders or suspicious Indians who might take her for a spy. It took her all day to reach her destination, where she first disturbed an encampment of Indians who received her with yells, which dismayed her for the moment. However, she was taken to the commanding officer, who made his arrangements immediately to surprise Boerstler, who soon made his appearance with five hundred men at least. The Americans were forced to surrender to what they believed was a vastly superior force, so cleverly had Fitzgibbon succeeded in deceiving them. In fact, he had only at first thirty soldiers, and two hundred and forty Indians, and when a captain and twenty troopers of the Chippewa cavalry came up Boerstler was quite ready to surrender.

All the successes in the west, however, were now rendered worthless by the unfortunate defeat at Put-in-Bay on Lake Erie of the English flotilla under Captain Barclay, by Commodore Perry, who had command of a large number of vessels, with a superior armament and equipment. The result of this victory was to give the control of Lake Erie and of the State of Michigan to the Americans. Procter retreated from Detroit, and was defeated near Moraviantown, an Indian village, about sixty miles from Sandwich, by General Harrison, who had defeated Tecumseh in the northwest, and now added to his growing fame by his victory over the English army, who were badly generalled on this occasion. Tecumseh, the faithful ally of the Canadians, fell in the battle, and his body was treated with every indignity, his skin, according to report, having been carried off to Kentucky as a trophy. Procter fell into disgrace, and was subsequently replaced by Colonel de Rottenburg. On his return to England, Procter was tried by court-martial, suspended from his rank for six months, and censured by the commander-in-chief.

Passing by such relatively unimportant affairs as a successful attack on Black Rock, near Buffalo, by Colonel Bisshopp, and a second attack on York by Chauncey, who took some prisoners and a quantity of stores, we have now to state other facts in the

history of the campaign of 1813 which compensated
Canada for Procter's disasters in the west.   The
Americans had decided to make an attack on Montreal by two forces—one coming by the St. Lawrence and the other by Lake Champlain—which
were to form a junction at Chateauguay on Lake
St. Louis.   General Wilkinson, with eight thousand
men, descended the river from Sackett's Harbour,
landed below Prescott, and then proceeded towards
Cornwall.   Some two thousand five hundred men,
under Colonel Boyd, protected the rear of the main
body, and was compelled to fight a much inferior
force, under Colonel Morrison, on Chrystler's farm,
near what is now known as Cook's Point on the
north bank of the St. Lawrence.   The Americans
gave way in all directions, and sustained a heavy
loss.   Boyd rejoined Wilkinson at the foot of the
Long Sault rapids, in the neighbourhood of the
present town of Cornwall, and here the news arrived
that General Hampton had received a serious
repulse.   Hampton, leading an army of probably
seven thousand men, had been routed near the
junction of the Chateauguay and Outarde rivers by
an insignificant force of Canadian Fencibles and
Voltigeurs under Colonel de Salaberry, a French
Canadian in the English military service, with the
aid of Colonel McDonnell, in command of seven companies of Lower Canadian militia.   These combined
forces did not exceed nine hundred men, all French
Canadians, with the exception of Colonel McDonnell
and several other officers.   Three hundred French
Canadian Voltigeurs and Fencibles formed the front

of the line, and when the former gave way to the onslaught of the four thousand men who advanced against them Salaberry held his ground with a

COLONEL DE SALABERRY.

bugler, a mere lad, and made him sound lustily. Colonel McDonnell, with a remarkably keen under-standing of the situation, immediately ordered his buglers to play, and to continue doing so while they scattered in the woods. As the woods echoed

to the call of the bugles, to the shouts of the soldiers, and to the yells of the Indians, the American
force halted as if they were paralysed. Then, believing from the noises that filled the forest in every
direction that they were to be attacked in front
and rear by an overwhelming force, they broke and
fled tumultuously. Salaberry and the Canadians had
won a victory that has only a few parallels in warlike
annals. Hampton retreated as rapidly as possible
to Plattsburg, while Wilkinson found his way to
Salmon River. These two victories of Chrystler's
farm and Chateauguay were won almost entirely by
Canadian prowess and skill, and must be always
mentioned among the glorious episodes of Canadian
history.

Before the end of the year, General McClure, in
command of the American troops on the Niagara
frontier, evacuated Fort George, when he heard of
the advance of the English forces under General
Murray. McClure committed the cowardly outrage
of destroying the town of Newark. All the houses
except one were burned, and no pity was shown
even to the weak and helpless women, all of whom
were driven from their comfortable houses and
forced to stand on the snow-clad earth, while they
saw the flames ascend from their homes and household treasures. As an act of retribution the British
troops destroyed all the posts and settlements from
Fort Niagara to Buffalo. When the campaign of
1813 closed, Lake Erie was still in the possession of
the Americans, but the Niagara district on both
sides of the river had been freed from the American

forces, and not an inch of Canadian territory except Amherstburg was in possession of the enemy.

In the following year the campaign commenced by the advance of a large force of American troops under General Wilkinson into Lower Canada, but they did not get beyond Lacolle Mill, not far from Isle aux Noix on the Richelieu, where they met with a most determined resistance from the little garrison under Colonel Handcock. Wilkinson retreated to Plattsburg, and did not again venture upon Canadian territory. Sir Gordon Drummond took Oswego, and succeeded in destroying a large amount of public property, including the barracks. The greatest success of the year was won in the Niagara country, where the English troops under Drummond and Riall had been concentrated with the view of opposing the advance of an American army into Upper Canada. The Americans occupied Fort Erie, and Riall sustained a repulse at Street's Creek—now known as Usher's—near Chippewa, although General Brown, who was in command of a much superior force, did not attempt to follow up his advantage, but allowed the English to retreat to Fort George. Then followed, on the 25th of July, the famous battle of Lundy's Lane, where the English regulars and Canadian militia, led by General Drummond, fought from six in the evening until midnight, a formidable force of American troops, commanded by General Brown and Brigadiers Ripley, Porter, and Scott—the latter the future hero of the Mexican war. The darkness through this hotly contested engagement was intense, and the English more than once seemed on the point of yielding to sheer exhaustion as they contested every foot of ground against overpowering numbers of well handled troops. The undaunted courage and persistence of the British and Canadian soldiery won the battle, as the Americans retired from the field, though with a remarkable perversion of the facts this memorable event is even claimed by some American writers as a success on their side. This was the last great fight of the war, and will be always cited by Canadians as illustrating the mettle of their own militia in old times.

Drummond did not win other successes, and even failed to capture Fort Erie. The American army, however, did not make another advance into the country while he kept it so well guarded. Erie was eventually evacuated, while the Americans concentrated their strength at Buffalo. Prairie du Chien on the Mississippi was captured in this same summer by the English, and the Americans were repulsed in an attempt to seize the fort at Michillimackinac. In eastern Canada there was no such record of victory to show as Drummond and his officers had made in the west. Prevost again gave a signal proof of his incapacity. His fleet sustained a complete defeat on Lake Champlain, and so great was his dismay that he ordered the retreat to Montreal of a splendid force of over ten thousand troops, largely composed of peninsula veterans, though Plattsburg and its garrison must have fallen easily into his hands had he been possessed of the most ordinary resolution. This retreat was confessedly a disgrace to the Eng-

MONUMENT AT LUNDY'S LANE.

333

lish army, which Canadian and English writers must always record with a feeling of contempt for Prevost.

It is not necessary to dwell at any length on other features of this war. The American navy, small though it was, won several successes mainly through the superiority of their vessels in tonnage, crew, and armament. The memorable fight between the British frigate *Shannon*, under Captain Broke, and the United States frigate *Chesapeake*, under Captain Lawrence, off Massachusetts Bay, illustrates equally the courage of British and American sailors—of men belonging to the same great stock which has won so many victories on the sea. The two ships were equally matched, and after a sharp contest of a quarter of an hour the *Chesapeake* was beaten, but not until Captain Lawrence was fatally wounded and his victorious adversary also severely injured. During the war Nova Scotia and the other maritime provinces were somewhat harassed at times by American privateers, but the presence of a large fleet constantly on their coasts—Halifax being the rendezvous of the British navy in American waters —and the hostility of New England to the war saved these sections of British America from invasion. On the other hand, all the important positions on the coast of Maine from the Penobscot to the St. Croix, were attacked and occupied by the English. The whole American coast during the last year of the war was blockaded by the English fleet with the exception of New England ports, which were open to neutral vessels. The public buildings of Washington, the federal capital, were destroyed by an English army, in retaliation for the burning of York, Newark, and Moraviantown. The attempt to take Baltimore failed, and a bold man from Tennessee, Andrew Jackson—in later years President—drove Pakenham from New Orleans. The taking of Mobile by British ships was the closing incident of the war on the Atlantic coast. In fact peace was happily declared by the Treaty of Ghent on the 24th December, 1814, or a fortnight before the defeat of the English at New Orleans. The two nations gladly came to terms. It is questionable if the heart of either was ever deeply enlisted in this unhappy war which should never have been fought between peoples so closely connected by language and race. It was mainly a war of Western and Southern politicians, and when it ended New England, whose interests had been so seriously affected, was showing signs of serious restlessness which had broken out in the Hartford convention, and might have even threatened the integrity of the Union.

Although the war ended without any definite decision on the questions at issue between the United States and Great Britain, the privileges of neutrals were practically admitted, and the extreme pretensions of Great Britain as to the right of search can never again be asserted. One important result of the war, as respects the interests of Canada, was the re-opening of the question of the British American fisheries. Certain privileges extended by the Treaty of 1783 to American fishermen on the coasts of British North America were not again conceded, and the convention of 1818, which followed the peace of 1815, is the basis of the rights which Canadians have always maintained in disputes between themselves and the United States as to the fisheries on their coasts.   Looking, however, to its general results, the war gave no special advantages to the Canadian people.   When peace was proclaimed not an inch of Canadian territory, except the village of Amherstburg, was held by the American forces. On the other hand, Great Britain occupied the greater part of the sea-board of Maine, and her flag flew over Michillimackinac, the key to the North-west.   Had British statesmen seized this opportunity of settling finally the western boundary of New Brunswick, Canada would have obtained a territory most useful to the commercial development of the present Dominion.   England, however, was very desirous of ending the war—perhaps the humiliating affair at Plattsburg had some effect on the peace—and it was fortunate for the provinces that they were allowed in the end to control their most valuable fisheries.

The people of Canada will always hold in grateful recollection the names of those men who did such good service for their country during these momentous years from 1812 to 1815.   Brock, Tecumseh, Morrison, Salaberry, McDonnell, Fitzgibbon, and Drummond are among the most honourable names in Canadian history.   Englishmen, Scotchmen, Irishmen, Canadians, Indians, were equally conspicuous in brilliant achievement.   A stately monument overlooks the noble river of the Niagara, and recalls

the services of the gallant soldiers, Brock and Mc-
Donell, whose remains rest beneath. A beautiful
village, beyond which stretches historic Lundy's
Lane, recalls the name and deeds of Drummond.
As the steamers pass up and down the St. Lawrence
they see on the northern bank the obelisk which the
Canadian Government has raised on the site of the
battlefield where Morrison defeated Boyd. On the
meadows of Chateauguay, another monument has
been erected by the same national spirit in honour
of the victory won by a famous representative of the
French Canadian race, who proved how courage-
ously French Canadians could fight for the new
régime under which they were then, as now, so
happy and prosperous.

22

XXIV.

POLITICAL STRIFE AND REBELLION.

(1815 1840.)

THE history of the twenty-five years between the peace of 1815 and the union of the Canadas in 1840, illustrates the folly and misery of faction, when intensified by racial antagonisms. In Lower Canada the difficulties arising from a constant contest for the supremacy between the executive and legislative authorities were aggravated by the fact that the French Canadian majority dominated the popular house, and the English-speaking minority controlled the government. "I found," wrote Lord Durham, in 1839, "two nations warring in the bosom of a single state; I found a struggle not of principles but of races." It is true that some Englishmen were found fighting for popular liberties on the side of the French Canadian majority. Mr. John Neilson, who was for years editor of the *Quebec Gazette*, was a friend of the French Canadians, and in close sympathy with the movement for the extension of public rights, but he was never prepared to go beyond the legitimate limits of constitutional agitation and threaten British connexion. On the other hand, Dr. Wolfred Nelson, descended from a loyalist stock, was one of the leaders of the majority that controlled the assembly of Lower Canada, and did not hesitate to join in the rebellion to which his rash and impetuous chief, Louis Joseph Papineau, led him at last. But while undoubtedly there were many persons among the British people, who were disgusted with the arrogance of some of the governing class, and discontented with the methods of government, they were gradually alienated by the demagogism of the French Canadian majority, who did not hesitate to profess their desire to make French Canada exclusively a French dominion. The tyranny of the majority was exhibited in the assembly by the attempt to impeach Chief Justices Sewell and Monk, on charges which had no justification in law or justice. Mr. Robert Christie, the member for Gaspé, who subsequently wrote a useful history of Lower Canada, was expelled several times because he was believed to have procured the dismissal from the magistracy of some members of the assembly who were inimical to the executive government. On the other hand, Lord Dalhousie, the governor-general, in 1827, refused to approve of the election of Mr. Papineau as speaker of the assembly, because he had reflected in strong terms in a manifesto on the public conduct of the former. Mr. Louis J. Papineau, the future leader of the rebellion in 1837, was a man of fine presence, gifted with remarkable powers of rhetoric and persuasion, but

he was entirely wanting in discretion, and in the
qualities which make a great statesman. When the
assembly refused to reconsider its action and elect
another speaker, Lord Dalhousie prorogued the legislature, which did not again meet until he was
recalled and sent to India as commander-in-chief.
Like other governors, Lord Dalhousie attempted to
govern to the best of his ability, and what mistakes
he committed arose from the contradictory and per-
plexing instructions he received from the officials in
Downing Street, who were quite incapable at times
of understanding the real condition of affairs in the
province.

The disputes at last between the contending parties in Lower Canada prevented the working of the
constitution. The assembly fought for years for
the independence of Parliament and the exclusive
control of the civil list and supply. When at last
the assembly refused to vote a civil list and other
necessary expenditures, the government were obliged
to use the casual and territorial revenues—such as
the proceeds of the sales and leases of Crown lands
—and these funds were inadequate for the purpose.
So carelessly were these funds managed that one
receiver-general, engaged in business, became a
heavy defaulter. The governors dissolved the legislatures with a frequency unparalleled in political
history, and were personally drawn into the conflict.
Public officials, including the judges, were harassed
by impeachments. Bills were constantly rejected
by the legislative council on various pretexts—some
of them constitutionally correct—and the disputes

between the two branches of the legislature eventually made it impossible to pass even absolutely necessary measures. Appeals to the home government were very common, and concessions were made time

LOUIS J. PAPINEAU, ÆT. 70.

and again to the assembly. In fact, the contest as to the revenues and expenditures ought to have closed, in a great measure, with the abandonment, in 1832, by the government of every portion of the previously reserved revenue, but, as Lord Durham pointed out, the assembly, " even when it obtained entire control over the public revenues," refused the civil list because it was determined " not to give up its only means of subjecting the functionaries of government to any responsibility." The conflict was carried on to the bitter end. It does not appear, however, that the majority in the assembly at all understood the crucial difficulty. They devoted their whole strength to attacks on the legislative council, and to demands for an elective body. The famous ninety-two resolutions of 1834, in which Papineau's party set forth their real or fancied grievances, did not contain a single paragraph laying down the principles of parliamentary or responsible government as worked out in England, and ably supported by the moderate Upper Canadian Reformers like Robert Baldwin. The home government ought to have appreciated the gravity of the situation, but they were not yet prepared to introduce into these colonies the principles of parliamentary government. In 1835 they appointed a commission to inquire into the nature of the grievances and the best method of remedying them. The governor-general, Lord Gosford, was the head of this commission, but it failed because Papineau and his party were not now prepared to listen to moderate and conciliatory counsels. When in 1837 the assembly continued to refuse supply for the payment of public officials, and of the arrears, which up to that time amounted to nearly one hundred and fifty thousand pounds sterling, Lord John Russell carried in the English House of Commons a series of resolutions, rejecting the demand for an elective legislative council and other changes in the constitution, and empowering the executive government to defray the expenses of the public service out of the territorial and casual revenues. This action of the imperial government increased the public discontent, and gave an opportunity to Papineau and his followers to declare that no redress of grievances could be obtained except by a resort to arms. In this year the rebellion broke out, but before I refer to it, it is necessary to review briefly the condition of things in the other provinces.

In Nova Scotia and New Brunswick, the disputes between the executive and legislative authorities were characterised by much acrimony, but eventually the public revenues were conceded to the assemblies. In Prince Edward Island the political difficulties arose from the land monopoly, and the efforts of the lieutenant-governors to govern as much as possible without assemblies. In these provinces, as in Canada, we find—to cite Lord Durham—" representative government coupled with an irresponsible executive, the same abuse of the powers of the representative bodies, and the same constant interference of the imperial administration in matters which should be left wholly to the provincial governments." In the maritime provinces, however, no disturbance occurred, and the leaders of the popular party were among the first to assist the authorities in their efforts to preserve the public tranquillity, and to express themselves emphatically in favour of the British connection.

In Upper Canada an official class held within its control practically the government of the province. This class became known, in the parlance of those days, as the "family compact," not quite an accurate designation, since its members had hardly any family connection, but there was just enough ground for the term to tickle the taste of the people for an epigrammatic phrase. The bench, the pulpit, the banks, the public offices were all more or less under the influence of the "compact." The public lands were lavishly parcelled out among themselves and their followers. Successive governors, notably Sir Francis Gore, Sir Peregrine Maitland, and Sir Francis Bond Head, submitted first to its influence and allowed it to have the real direction of affairs. Among its most prominent members were John Beverly Robinson, for some years attorney-general, and eventually an able chief-justice, and the recipient of a baronetage; William Dummer Powell, a chief-justice; John Henry Boulton, once attorney-general; John Strachan, the first bishop of the Episcopal Church in Upper Canada; Jonas Jones, the Sherwoods, and other well-known names of residents of York, Niagara, Kingston, and Brockville.

It was not until 1820 that a strong opposition was organised in the assembly against the ruling bureaucracy. The cruel treatment of Robert Gourlay, an erratic Scotch land-agent, by the ruling class who feared his exposure of public abuses, had much to do with creating a reform party in the legislature. Gourlay was a mere adventurer, who found plenty of material in the political condition of the province for obtaining the notoriety that he coveted. In the course of some inquiries he made in connexion with a statistical work he published in later years, he touched on some points which exposed the land monopoly and other abuses. He was immediately declared by the " compact" to be a dangerous person, who must be curbed by some means or other. He was tried on two occasions for libelling the government, but acquitted. Then his enemies conspired to accuse him most unjustly of being a seditious and dangerous person, who came under the terms of an alien act passed in 1804. He was arrested and kept in prison for seven months. When he was at last tried at Niagara, the home of Toryism, he was a broken-down man, hardly in full possession of his senses. A severe judge and prejudiced jury had no pity, and he was forced to leave the province, to which he did not return until happier times. The injustice which was meted out to a man who had thrown some light on public corruption, stimulated the opponents of the " family compact" to united action against methods so dangerous to individual liberty and so antagonistic to the redress of public grievances.

The disputes between the reformers and the " family compact " were aggravated by the " clergy reserves " question, which was largely one between the Episcopalians and the dissenting bodies. This question grew out of the grant to the Protestant Church in Canada of large tracts of land by the imperial act of 1791, and created much bitterness of feeling for a quarter of a century and more. The

reformers found in this question abundant material
for exciting the jealousies of all the Protestant sects
who wished to see the Church of England and the
Church of Scotland deprived of the advantages
which they alone derived from this valuable source
of revenue. The British Government for years were
on the side of the "family compact," whose leading adherents belonged to the Church of England,
and who opposed every effort that was made to dis-
pose of these lands for the support of education and
other public purposes. The Methodists, who outnumbered the Church of England, had for years
an additional grievance in the fact that their ministers were not allowed to solemnise marriages, and it
was not until 1829 that this disability was removed
by the legislature.

Among the minds that dominated the "family
compact" was the eminent divine, John Strachan,
who was originally a Presbyterian, and came to the
country as a teacher at the request of the Honourable Richard Cartwright, a prominent U. E. Loyalist, but eventually joined the Episcopalian Church,
and became its bishop. Like his countryman, John
Knox, he had extraordinary tenacity of purpose and
desire for rule. He considered the interests of the
Church as paramount to all other considerations.
He became both an executive and a legislative
councillor, and largely moulded the opinions and
acts of the governing classes. It was chiefly through
his influence that Sir John Colborne established a
number of rectories out of the clergy reserves, and
thereby gave additional offence to those religious

bodies who had no share in these lands. He hoped to create a state church, and the establishment of King's College, afterwards secularised, was a part of his ecclesiastical system. Eventually when King's

BISHOP STRACHAN.

College became a provincial institution, open to all denominations—the foundation of Toronto University—he devoted all his energies to the establishment of Trinity College, which is the noblest monument of the zealous prelate.

Another Scotchman, who came to the country some years later than the bishop, was William Lyon Mackenzie, who was always remarkable for his impulsiveness and rashness, which led him at last into difficulties and wrecked his whole career. He had a deep sense of public wrongs, and placed himself immediately in the front rank of those who were fighting for a redress of undoubted grievances. He was thoroughly imbued with the ideas of English radicalism, and had an intense hatred of Toryism in every form. He possessed little of that strong common sense and power of acquisitiveness which make his countrymen, as a rule, so successful in every walk of life. When he felt he was being crushed by the intriguing and corrupting influences of the governing class, aided by the lieutenant-governor, he forgot all the dictates of reason and prudence, and was carried away by a current of passion which ended in rebellion. His journal, *The Colonial Advocate*, showed in its articles and its very make-up the erratic character of the man. He was a pungent writer, who attacked adversaries with great recklessness of epithet and accusation. So obnoxious did he become to the governing class that a number of young men, connected with the best families, wrecked his office, but the damages he recovered in a court of law enabled him to give it a new lease of existence. When the " family compact " had a majority in the assembly, elected in 1830, he was expelled five times for libellous reflections on the government and house, but he was re-elected by the people, who resented the wrongs to which he was

349

subject, and became the first mayor of Toronto, as York was now called. He carried his grievances to England, where he received much sympathy, even in conservative circles. In a new legislature, where the "compact" were in a minority, he obtained a committee to consider the condition of provincial affairs. The result was a famous report on grievances which set forth in a conclusive and able manner the constitutional difficulties under which the country laboured, and laid down clearly the necessity for responsible government. It would have been fortunate both for Upper Canada and Mackenzie himself at this juncture, had he and his followers confined themselves to a constitutional agitation on the lines set forth in this report. By this time Robert Baldwin and Egerton Ryerson, discreet and prominent reformers, had much influence, and were quite unwilling to follow Mackenzie in the extreme course on which he had clearly entered. He lost ground rapidly from the time of his indiscreet publication of a letter from Joseph Hume, the English radical, who had expressed the opinion that the improper proceedings of the legislature, especially in expelling Mackenzie, "must hasten the crisis that was fast approaching in the affairs of Canada, and which would terminate in independence and freedom from the baneful domination of the mother-country." Probably even Mackenzie and his friends might have been conciliated and satisfied at the last moment had the imperial government been served by an able and discreet lieutenant-governor. But never did the imperial authorities make a greater mistake than when they sent out Sir Francis Bond Head, who had no political experience whatever.

From the beginning to the end of his administration he did nothing but blunder. He alienated even the confidence of the moderate element of the Reformers, and literally threw himself into the arms of the " family compact," and assisted them at the elections of the spring of 1836, which rejected all the leading men of the extreme wing of the Reform party. Mackenzie was deeply mortified at the result, and determined from that moment to rebel against the government which, in his opinion, had no intention of remedying public grievances. At the same time Papineau, with whom he was in communication, had made up his mind to establish a republic, *une nation Canadienne*, on the banks of the St. Lawrence.

The disloyal intentions of Papineau and his followers were made very clear by the various meetings which were held in the Montreal and Richelieu districts, by the riots which followed public assemblages in the city of Montreal, by the names of " Sons of Liberty " and " Patriots " they adopted in all their proceedings, by the planting of " trees," and raising of " caps " of liberty. Happily for the best interests of Canada the number of French Canadians ready to revolt were relatively insignificant, and the British population were almost exclusively on the side of the government. Bishop Lartigue and the clergy of the Roman Catholic Church now asserted themselves very determinedly against the dangerous and seditious utterances of

the leaders of the " Patriots." Fortunately a resolute, able soldier, Sir John Colborne, was called from
Upper Canada to command the troops in the critical
situation of affairs, and crushed the rebellion in its
very inception.   A body of insurgents, led by Dr.
Wolfred Nelson, showed some courage at St. Denis,
but Papineau took the earliest opportunity to find
refuge across the frontier.   Thomas Storrow Brown,
an American by birth, also made a stand at St.
Charles, but both he and Nelson were easily beaten
by the regulars.   A most unfortunate episode was
the murder of Lieutenant Weir, who had been captured by Nelson while carrying despatches from
General Colborne, and was butchered by some in-
surgent *habitants*, in whose custody he had been
placed.   At St. Eustache the rebels were severely
punished by Colborne himself, and a number burned
to death in the steeple of a church where they had
made a stand.   Many prisoners were taken in the
course of the rebellious outbreak.   The village of St.
Benoit and isolated houses elsewhere were destroyed
by the angry loyalists, and much misery inflicted on
all actual or supposed sympathisers with Papineau
and Nelson.   Lord Gosford now left the country,
and Colborne was appointed administrator.   Although the insurrection practically ended at St.
Denis and St. Charles, bodies of rebels and American marauders harassed the frontier settlements for
some time, until at last the authorities of the United
States arrested some of the leaders and forced them
to surrender their arms and munitions of war.

In Upper Canada the folly of Sir Francis Head

would have led to serious consequences had Mackenzie and Rolph been capable of managing a rebellious movement. The Lieutenant-Governor allowed
all the troops to go to Lower Canada, and the capital was entirely at the mercy of the rebels, had they
acted with any spirit or energy. Dr. Rolph, a clever
intriguer—who was to be the president of the new
republic—was playing a fast and loose game, and
temporised until the loyal forces from Hamilton
were able to advance to the assistance of Head.
Had the rebels, who were concentrating at Montgomery's tavern on Yonge Street, marched immediately on the capital, it could have been easily
captured, in consequence of the neglect of Head to
take the most ordinary precautions against surprise.
Toronto was mainly saved by the men of the Gore
district, led by Allan MacNab, an ardent loyalist,
afterwards a baronet and premier of Canada. The
insurgents, who at no time exceeded eight hundred
in all, were routed at their headquarters. Rolph
had previously thought it prudent to fly, and Mackenzie soon followed. Several lives were lost during
this *émeute*, for it was hardly more, and a considerable number of prisoners taken. Among the latter
were Samuel Lount, an ardent reformer, the first to
arm for the rebellion, and Colonel Von Egmond,
one of Napoleon's soldiers, the leader of the "pa-
triot army." Marshall Spring Bidwell, an able and
moderate leader of the Reformers, for some years
speaker, does not appear to have taken any active
part in the rebellious movement, but he availed himself of a warning given him by Head, who wished

23

to get rid of him as quietly as possible, and hurried to the United States, where he remained for the remainder of his life. Mackenzie also fled to the Republic, and industriously set to work to violate the neutrality of the country by inciting bands of ruffians to invade Canada.

As in the case of the Fenian invasion many years later, the authorities of the United States were open to some censure for negligence in winking at these suspicious gatherings avowedly to attack a friendly country. The raiders seized an island just above Niagara Falls, on the Canadian side, as a base of operations, and a steamer, called the *Caroline*, was freely allowed to ply between the island and the mainland with supplies. It became necessary to stop this bold attempt to provide the freebooters on Navy Island with the munitions of war, and a Canadian expedition was accordingly sent, under the command of Colonel MacNab, to seize the *Caroline*. As it happened, however, she was found on the American side; but at such a time of excitement men were not likely to consider consequences from the point of view of international law. She was cut from her moorings on the American side, her crew taken prisoners, one man killed, and the vessel set on fire and sent over the Falls of Niagara.

Until the month of December, 1838, Upper Canada was disturbed from time to time by bands of marauders, instigated by Mackenzie and others, but they were easily beaten back by the bravery of loyal Canadian volunteers commanded by Colonels Prince, MacNab, Cameron, Fitzgibbon, and other patriotic defenders of the country. Whatever sympathy may have been felt for Mackenzie by some persons at the outset of the insurrection, was alienated from him by his conduct after he crossed the border. He suffered much misery himself while he remained in the United States, and was a prisoner for some months when the American Government awoke to the necessity of punishing a man who had so nearly embroiled them with England by his violation of the municipal law of a friendly territory, and of the obligations that rest upon political refugees. When Sir Francis Bond Head was very properly recalled from the province whose affairs he had so badly administered, he was succeeded by Sir George Arthur, who had been governor of Van Diemen's Land. Both Samuel Lount and Peter Matthews suffered death. Von Shoultz, and a number of Americans who had invaded the country in 1838, were also executed, and some persons in both provinces were transported to New Holland or sent to the penitentiary, but in the majority of cases the Crown showed clemency. The outbreak was an unfortunate episode in the history of Canada, but it caused the "family compact" to break up, and brought about a better system of government.

The immediate result of the rebellion in Lower Canada was the intervention of the imperial authorities by the suspension of the constitution of that province, and the formation of a special council for purposes of temporary government. Lord Durham, a nobleman of great ability, who had won distinction in imperial politics as a Reformer, was sent out to Canada as governor-general and high commissioner to inquire into and adjust provincial difficulties. This distinguished statesman remained at the head of affairs in the province from the last of May, 1838, until the 3d of November in the same year, when he returned to England, where his ordinance of the 28th of June, sentencing certain British subjects in custody to transportation without a form of trial, and subjecting them and others not in prison to death in case of their return to the country, without permission of the authorities, had been most severely censured in England as quite unwarranted by law. By this ordinance Wolfred Nelson, Bouchette, Viger, and five others, then in prison, were banished to Bermuda, while Papineau, Cartier, O'Callaghan, Robert Nelson, and others beyond Canadian jurisdiction, were threatened with death if they returned to the province. Lord Durham's action was certainly in conflict with the principles of English law, but it was an error of judgment on the side of clemency. He was unwilling to resort to a court-martial—the only tribunal open to the authorities. A trial in the courts of justice was impracticable under existing conditions, as it was shown later. Lord Durham left Canada in deep indignation at the manner in which his acts had been criticised in England, largely through the influence of Lord Brougham, his personal enemy. The most important result of his mission was a report which was probably written by Charles Buller, his secretary, and an exceptionally able man, although there is no doubt that it embodied Lord Durham's own opinions and conclusions.

Soon after the departure of Lord Durham, who died a few months later, Sir John Colborne became governor-general. He was called upon to put down another rebellious movement led by Robert Nelson, brother of Wolfred Nelson, then in exile. At Caughnawaga, Montarville Mountain, Beauharnois, and Odelltown the insurgents made a stand from time to time, but were soon scattered. Bands of marauders inflicted some injury upon loyal inhabitants near the frontier, but in a few months these criminal attempts to disturb the peace of the province ceased entirely. The government now decided to make an example of men who had not appreciated the clemency previously shown their friends. Twelve men were executed, but it was not possible to obtain a verdict from a jury against the murderers of Weir and Chartrand—the latter a French Canadian volunteer murdered under circumstances of great brutality while a prisoner.

The rebellion opened the eyes of the imperial government to the gravity of the situation in Canada, and the result of Lord Durham's report was the passage of an imperial act reuniting the provinces into one, with a legislature of two houses. The constitutional act of 1791, which had separated French and English, as far as possible, into two sections, was clearly a failure. An effort was now to be made to amalgamate, if possible, the two races. The two provinces were given an equal representation in one legislature, and the French language was placed in a position of inferiority, compared with English in parliamentary and official proceedings and documents. At the same time the British Government recognised the necessity of giving a larger expansion of local self-government.

During the period of which I am writing Canada had given evidences of material, social, and intellectual progress. With the close of the War of 1812, and the downfall of Napoleon, large bodies of immigrants came into the province and settled some of the finest districts of Upper and Lower Canada. Scotch from the highlands and islands of Scotland continued until 1820 to flock into Nova Scotia and other maritime provinces. Although the immigration had been naturally stopped by the troubles of 1836 and 1838, the population of Canada had increased to over a million of souls, of whom at least four hundred and fifty thousand were French Canadians. The Rideau, Lachine, and Welland Canals date from this period, and were the commencement of that noble system of artificial waterways that have, in the course of time, enabled large steamers to come all the way from Lake Superior to tidewater.* In 1833 the *Royal William*, entirely propelled by steam, crossed the ocean—the pioneer in ocean steam navigation. A few years later Samuel Cunard, a native Nova Scotian, established the line that has become so famous in the world's maritime history. In Lower Canada the higher education was confined to the Quebec Seminary, and a few colleges and institutions, under the direction of the

* Governor Haldimand first established several small canals between Lakes Saint Louis and Saint Francis, which were used for some years.

Roman Catholic clergy and communities. Among the *habitants* generally there were no schools, and the great majority could neither read nor write. In

JUDGE HALIBURTON (" SAM SLICK ").

Upper Canada high schools for the education of the upper classes were established at a very early day, and the Cornwall Grammar School, under the super- intendence of Dr. John Strahan, for some years was

the resort of the provincial aristocracy. Upper
Canada College dates from these early times. But
in 1838 there were only twenty-four thousand children at school out of a total population of four hundred thousand. In the maritime provinces things
were not much better, but in Nova Scotia the foundation of King's,—the oldest university in Canada—
Dalhousie, and Acadia Colleges, as well as Pictou
Academy, shows the deep interest that was taken in
higher education. In all the provinces there was an
active and even able newspaper press, although its
columns were too much disfigured by invective and
personalities. In 1836 there were at least forty
papers printed in Upper Canada alone. The names
of Cary, Neilson, Mackenzie, Parent, Howe, and
Young are among the names of eminent journalists.
It was only in the press, in the pulpit, at the bar,
and in the legislature that we can look for evidences
of intellectual development. The only original
literary works of importance were those of Judge
Haliburton, who had already given us the clever,
humorous creation of " Sam Slick," and also written an excellent history of Nova Scotia. In the
happy and more prosperous times that followed the
union of 1840, and the establishment of political
liberty, intellectual development kept pace with the
progress of the country in wealth and population.

XXV.

RESPONSIBLE GOVERNMENT AND ITS RESULTS—
FEDERAL UNION—RELATIONS BETWEEN
CANADA AND THE UNITED STATES.

(1839-1867.)

THE passage of the Union Act of 1840 was the commencement of a new era in the constitutional history of Canada as well as of the other provinces. The most valuable result was the admission of the all-important principle that the ministry advising the governor should possess the confidence of the representatives of the people assembled in parliament. Lord Durham, in his report, had pointed out most forcibly the injurious consequences of the very opposite system which had so long prevailed in the provinces. His views had such influence on the minds of the statesmen then at the head of imperial affairs, that Mr. Poulett Thomson, when appointed governor-general, received her Majesty's commands to administer the government of the united provinces " in accordance with the well-understood wishes and interests of the people," and to employ in the pub-

lic service only " those persons who, by their position and character, have obtained the general
confidence and esteem of the inhabitants of the
province." During the first session of the Canadian
legislature the assembly passed certain resolutions
which authoritatively expressed the views of the
supporters of responsible government.

Nevertheless, during the six years that elapsed
after the passage of this formal expression of the
views of the large majority of the legislature, " Responsible Government " did not always obtain in
the fullest sense of the phrase, and not a few misunderstandings arose between the governors and the
supporters of the principle as to the manner in which
it should be worked out. In Canada Lord Metcalfe,
who succeeded Baron Sydenham—the title of Mr.
Poulett Thomson—on his sudden death at Kingston
in 1841, brought about a political crisis in consequence of his contention for the privilege—utterly
inconsistent with the principles of responsible government—of making appointments to office without
the advice of his council. In Nova Scotia Sir Colin
Campbell, who was more suited to the military
camp than to the political arena, endeavoured to
throw obstacles in the way of the new system, but
he was soon recalled. His successor, Lord Falkland, a vain nobleman, was an unhappy choice of
the colonial office. He became the mere creature
of the Tory party, led by James W. Johnston, a
very able lawyer and eloquent speaker, and the
open enemy of the liberals led by Joseph Howe,
William Young, James Boyle Uniacke, and Herbert

Huntington. The imperial government recognised their mistake, and replaced Lord Falkland by Sir John Harvey, the hero of Stoney Creek in 1813, who had done much to establish parliamentary

JOSEPH HOWE IN 1865.

government in New Brunswick. In 1847 Lord Elgin—the son-in-law of Lord Durham—was appointed governor-general, and received positive instructions " to act generally upon the advice of his executive council, and to receive as members of that body those persons who might be pointed out to him as entitled to do so by their possessing the confidence of the assembly." No act of parliament was necessary to effect this important change; the insertion and alteration of a few paragraphs in the Governor's instructions were sufficient. By 1848 the provinces of Canada, Nova Scotia, and New Brunswick, and by 1851 Prince Edward Island, were in the full enjoyment of a system of self-government, which had been so long advocated by their ablest public men; and the results have proved, on the whole, despite the excesses and mistakes of party, eminently favourable to political as well as material development.

In the historic annals of the great contest that was fought for responsible government, some names stand out most prominently. Foremost is that of Joseph Howe, the eminent Liberal, whose eloquence charmed the people of Nova Scotia for many years. In his early life he was a printer and an editor, but he became a leader of his party soon after he entered the legislature, and died a lieutenant-governor of his native province. In New Brunswick, Lemuel A. Wilmot, afterwards a judge and lieutenant-governor, was a man of much energy, persuasive eloquence, and varied learning. Robert Baldwin, of Upper Canada, was a statesman of great discretion, who showed the people how their liberties could be best promoted by wise and constitutional agitation. Louis Hyppolite Lafontaine was one of the most distinguished and capable men that French Canada has ever given to the legislature and the bench. By his political alliance with Mr. Baldwin, the principles of responsible government were placed on a durable basis. In the parent state the names of Lord John

ROBERT BALDWIN.

Russell, Mr. Gladstone, and Earl Grey—colonial secretaries from 1839 to 1852—are especially associated with the concession of those great principles which have enlarged the sphere of self-government in the colonies of the English Crown.

During the quarter of a century that elapsed from 1842 to 1867—the crucial period of national development—an industrious population flowed steadily into the country, the original population became more self-reliant and pursued their vocations with renewed energy, and confidence increased on all sides in the ability of the provinces to hold their own against the competition of a wonderfully enterprising neighbour. Cities, towns, and villages were built up with a rapidity not exceeded even on the other side of the border. In those days Ontario became the noble province that she now is by virtue of the capacity of her people for self-government, the energy of her industrial classes, the fertility of her soil, and the superiority of her climate. The maritime industry of the lower provinces was developed most encouragingly, and Nova Scotia built up a commercial marine not equalled by that of any New England State. The total population of the provinces of British North America, now comprised within the confederation of 1867, had increased from a million and a half in 1840 to three millions and a quarter in 1861—the ratio of increase in those years having been greater than at any previous or later period of Canadian history. It was during this period that the Grand Trunk Railway, which has done so much to assist the material progress of the old province of Canada, was constructed. In 1850 there were only fifty miles of railway in operation throughout Canada, but by 1867 there were nearly three thousand miles, and that magnificent example of engineering skill, the Victoria Bridge, carried passengers across the St. Lawrence at Montreal, and connected Canada with the great railway system of the United States. With railway development must always be associated the name of Sir Francis Hincks, an able statesman of the Liberal party, who recognised the necessities of a new country.

So far from the act of 1840, which united the Canadas, acting unfavourably to the French Canadian people it gave them eventually a predominance in the councils of the country. French soon again became the official language by an amendment to the union act, and the claims providing for equality of representation proved a security when the upper province increased more largely in population than the French Canadian section. The particular measure which the French Canadians had pressed for so many years on the British Government, an elective legislative council, was conceded. When a few years had passed the Canadian legislature was given full control of taxation, supply, and expenditure, in accordance with English constitutional principles. The clergy reserves difficulty was settled and the land sold for public or municipal purposes, the interest of existing rectors and incumbents being guarded. The great land question of Canada, the seigniorial tenure of Lower Canada, was disposed of by buying off the claims of the seigniors, and the people of Lower Canada were freed from exactions which had become not so much onerous as vexatious. Municipal institutions of a liberal nature were established, and the people of the two Canadian provinces exercised that control of their local affairs in the

counties, townships, cities, and parishes which is
necessary to carry out public works indispensable to
the comfort, health, and convenience of the community, and to supplement the efforts made by the
legislature, from time to time, to provide for the
general education of the country. With the magnificent system of public schools now possessed by
Ontario must always be associated the name of Dr.
Egerton Ryerson, a famous Methodist, the opponent of Mackenzie's seditious action, and for many
years the superintendent of education. In Nova
Scotia it was chiefly through the foresight of Sir
Charles Tupper, when premier, that the foundations
were laid of the present admirable system. During
the same period the schools of New Brunswick and
Prince Edward Island were also placed on an excellent basis. In the maritime provinces no express
legal provision was made for separate or denominational schools, as in Upper and Lower Canada—
schools now protected by the terms of the federal
union of 1867. The civil service, which necessarily
plays so important a part in the administration of
government, was placed on a permanent basis.

The anxiety of the British Government to bury
in oblivion the unfortunate events of 1837–38 was
proved by an amnesty that was granted soon after
the union of 1841, to the banished offenders against
the public peace and the Crown. William Lyon Mackenzie, Louis Joseph Papineau, and Wolfred Nelson
came back and were elected to Parliament, though
the two first never exercised any influence in the
future.

Then occurred an event which had its origin in the rebellion, and in the racial antagonism which was still slumbering in the bosom of the State. In

SIR LOUIS H. LAFONTAINE.

the first session of the Union Parliament, compensation was granted to those loyalists of Upper Canada, whose property had been unnecessarily or wantonly

24

destroyed during the outbreak. The claim was then raised on behalf of persons similarly situated in Lower Canada. The Conservative Draper government of 1845 agreed to pay a small amount of rebellion losses as a sequence of a report made by commissioners appointed to inquire into the subject. At a later time, when Lord Elgin was governor-general, the Baldwin-Lafontaine ministry brought down a measure to indemnify all those persons who had not taken part in the rebellion, but were justly entitled to compensation for actual losses. The Tory opposition raised the cry," No pay to rebels," and some of them in their anger even issued a manifesto in favour of annexation. The parliament house at Montreal was burned down, a great number of books and records destroyed, and Lord Elgin grossly insulted for having assented to the bill. This very discreditable episode in the political history of Canada proved the extremes to which even men, professing extreme loyalty, can be carried at times of political passion and racial difficulty.

The union of 1841 did its work, and the political conditions of Canada again demanded another radical change commensurate with the material and political development of the country, and capable of removing the difficulties that had arisen in the operation of the act of 1840. The claims of Upper Canada to larger representation, equal to its increased population since 1840, owing to the great immigration which had naturally sought a rich and fertile province, were steadily resisted by the French Canadians as an unwarrantable interference with the security guaranteed to them under the act. This resistance gave rise to great irritation in Upper Can-

L. A. WILMOT.

ada, where a powerful party made representation by population their platform, and government at last became practically impossible on account of the

close political divisions for years in the assembly.
At the head of the party demanding increased representation was Mr. George Brown, an able man of
Scotch birth, who became the conductor of a most
influential organ of public opinion, *The Toronto
Globe*, and the leader of the " Grits," or extreme
wing of the Reformers or Liberals.   In opposition
to him were allied Mr. George Etienne Cartier, once
a follower of Papineau, but now a loyal leader of his
race, and Mr. John Alexander Macdonald, who had
occupied a prominent position for years as a Conservative leader.

The time had come for the accomplishment of a
great change foreshadowed by Lord Durham, Chief-
Justice Sewell, Mr. Howe, Sir Alexander Galt, and
other public men of Canada: the union of the provinces of British North America.   The leaders of the
different governments in Canada, and the maritime
provinces of Nova Scotia, New Brunswick, and
Prince Edward Island combined with the leaders of
the opposition with the object of carrying out this
great measure.   A convention of thirty-three representative men * was held in the autumn of 1864 in

---

* The delegates to the Quebec conference, held the following positions in their respective provinces :

Canada : Hon. Sir Etienne P. Taché, M.L.C., premier ; Hon.
John A. Macdonald, M.P.P., attorney-general of Upper Canada ;
Hon. George Etienne Cartier, M.P.P., attorney-general of Lower
Canada ; Hon. George Brown, M.P.P., president of the executive
council ; Hon. Alexander T. Galt, M.P.P., finance minister ; Hon.
Alexander Campbell, M.L.C., commissioner of crown lands ;
Hon. Jean C. Chapais, M.L.C., commissioner of public works ;
Hon. Thomas D'Arcy McGee, M.P.P., minister of agriculture ;
Hon Hector L. Langevin, M.P.P., solicitor-general for Lower

the historic city of Quebec, and after a deliberation of several weeks the result was the unanimous adoption of a set of seventy-two resolutions embodying the terms and conditions on which the provinces through their delegates agreed to a federal union. These resolutions had to be laid before the various legislatures and adopted in the shape of addresses to the Queen, whose sanction was necessary to embody the wishes of the provinces in an imperial statute.

The consent of the legislature was considered sufficient by the governments of all the provinces except one, though the question had never been discussed at the polls. In New Brunswick alone was the legislature dissolved on the issue, and it was only after a second general election that the legisla-

Canada ; Hon. William McDougall, M.P.P., provincial secretary ; Hon. James Cockburn, M.P.P., solicitor-general for Upper Canada ; Hon. Oliver Mowat, M.P.P., postmaster-general.

Nova Scotia : Hon. Charles Tupper, M.P.P., provincial secretary and premier ; Hon. William A. Henry, M.P.P., attorney-general ; Hon. Robert B. Dickey, M.L.C. ; Hon. Adams G. Archibald, M.P.P. ; Hon. Jonathan McCully, M.L.C.

New Brunswick : Hon. Samuel L. Tilley, M.P.P., provincial secretary and premier ; Hon. Peter Mitchell, M.L.C. ; Hon. Charles Fisher, M.P.P. ; Hon. William H. Steeves, M.L.C. ; Hon. John Hamilton Gray, M.P.P. ; Hon. Edward B. Chandler, M.L.C. ; Hon. John M. Johnson, M.P.P., attorney-general.

Prince Edward Island : Hon. John Hamilton Gray, M.P.P., premier ; Hon. George Coles, M.P.P. ; Hon. Thomas Heath Haviland, M.P.P. ; Hon. Edward Palmer, M.P.P., attorney-general ; Hon. Andrew Archibald Macdonald, M.L.C. ; Hon. Edward Whelan, M.L.C. ; Hon. William H. Pope, M.P.P., provincial secretary.

Newfoundland : Hon. Frederick B. T. Carter, M.P.P., speaker of the House of Assembly ; Hon. Ambrose Shea, M.P.P.

ture agreed to the union. In Nova Scotia, after
much discussion and feeling, the legislature passed
a resolution in favour of the measure, though a popular sentiment continued to exist against the union
for several years. In the December of 1866 a second conference of delegates from the governments
of Canada, Nova Scotia, and New Brunswick, was
held at the Westminster Palace Hotel in London,
and some modifications were made in the Quebec
resolutions, chiefly with a view of meeting objections from the maritime provinces. In the early
part of 1867 the imperial parliament, without a
division, passed the statute known as the " British
North America Act, 1867," which united in the first
instance the province of Canada, now divided into
Ontario and Quebec, with Nova Scotia and New
Brunswick, and made provisions for the coming in
of the other provinces of Prince Edward Island,
Newfoundland, British Columbia, and the admission
of Rupert's Land and the great Northwest.

From 1840 to 1867 the relations of Canada and
the United States became much closer, and more
than once assumed a dangerous phase. In 1840
the authorities of New York arrested one Macleod on the charge of having murdered a man employed in the *Caroline*, when she was seized by the
loyalists during the outbreak of 1837. The matter
gave rise to much correspondence between the governments of Great Britain and the United States,
and to a great deal of irritation in Canada, but happily for the peace of the two countries the courts
acquitted Macleod, as the evidence was clear he had

nothing to do with the seizure of the vessel. In 1842 the question of the boundary between Maine and New Brunswick was settled by what is generally known in Canada as " the Ashburton Capitulation." As a result of the settlement made by Mr. Daniel Webster on the part of the United States, and of Mr. Alexander Baring, afterwards Lord Ashburton, on behalf of Great Britain, the State of Maine now presses like a huge wedge into the provinces of New Brunswick and Quebec, and a Canadian railway is obliged to pass over American territory, which many Canadians still believe ought to be a part of the Canadian Dominion. In 1846 Great Britain yielded to the persistency of American statesmen, and agreed to accept the line 49° to the Pacific coast, and the whole of Vancouver Island, which, for a while, seemed on the point of following the fate of Oregon, and becoming exclusively American territory. But the question of boundary was not even then settled, as the Island of San Juan, which lies in the channel between Vancouver and the mainland, and is mainly valuable as a base of offensive and defensive operations in times of war, was, in later years, handed over to the Republic as a result of its successful diplomacy.

During this period the fishery question again assumed considerable importance. American vessels were shut out from the waters of certain colonial bays, in accordance with the convention of 1818, and a number of them captured from time to time for the infringement of the law. The United States Government attempted to raise issues which would limit Canadian rights, but all these questions were placed in abeyance for twelve years by the Reciprocity Treaty of 1854, which opened up the provincial fisheries to the people of the United States, on condition of free trade between the provinces and that country in certain natural products of the mines, fisheries, and farms of the two peoples. This measure was in itself an acknowledgment of the growing importance of the provinces, and of the larger measure of self-government now accorded them. The treaty only became law with the consent of the provincial legislatures; and, although the Canadian governments were not directly represented by any of their members, the governor-general, Lord Elgin, who personally conducted the negotiations on the part of England at Washington, in this, as in all other matters touching colonial interests, was assisted by the advice of his responsible ministers. The treaty lasted until 1866, when it was repealed by the action of the United States in accordance with the provision bringing it to a conclusion after one year's notice from one of the parties interested.

The commercial classes in the Eastern and Western States were, on the whole, favourable to an enlargement of the treaty, so as to bring in British Columbia and Vancouver Island, now colonies of the Crown, and to include certain other articles the produce of both countries, but the real cause of its repeal was the prejudice in the North against the provinces for their supposed sympathy for the Confederate States during the War of the Rebellion. A

large body of men in the North had brought themselves foolishly to believe that the repeal of the
treaty would, sooner or later, force the provinces
into annexation. A raid made by a few rash Con-
federates who had found refuge in Canada, on the
St. Albans Bank, in the State of Vermont, deeply
incensed the people of the North, though at no
time could it be proved that the Canadian authorities had the least suspicion of the proposed expedition. On the contrary, they brought the culprits
to trial, placed companies of volunteers along the
frontier, and even paid a large sum of money in
acknowledgment of an alleged responsibility when
some of the stolen money was returned to the rob-
bers on their release by a Montreal magistrate.
When we review the history of those times and
consider the difficult position in which Canada was
necessarily placed, it is remarkable how honourably
her government discharged its duties of a neutral
between the belligerents.

No doubt the position of Canada was made more
difficult at that critical time by the fact that she was
a colony of Great Britain, against whom both North
and South entertained bitter feelings by the close of
the war; the former mainly on account of the
escape of Confederate cruisers from English ports,
and the latter because she did not receive active
support from England. The North had also been
much excited by the promptness with which Lord
Palmerston had sent troops to Canada when Mason
and Slidell were seized on an English packet on the
high seas, and the bold tone held by some Canadian

papers when it was doubtful if the prisoners would be released.

Contemporaneously with the repeal of the Reciprocity Treaty came the raids of the Fenians—bands of men who did dishonour to the cause of Ireland, under the pretence of striking a blow at England through Canada, where their countrymen have always found happy homes, free government, and honourable positions. For months before the invasion American newspapers were full of accounts of the assembling and arming of these bands on the frontiers of Canada. They invaded the Dominion in 1866, property was destroyed, and a number of Canadian youth lost their lives near Ridgeway, in the Niagara district, but one O'Neil and his collection of disbanded soldiers and fugitives from justice were forced back by the Canadian forces to the country whose neutrality they had outraged. The United States authorities had calmly looked on while all the preparations for these raids were in progress. Proclamations were at last issued by the government when the damage had been done, and a few raiders were arrested; but the House of Representatives immediately sent a resolution to the President, requesting him " to cause the prosecutions, instituted in the United States courts against the Fenians, to be discontinued if compatible with the public interest "—a request which was complied with. In 1870 another raid * was attempted on the

* In the autumn of 1871, a body of Fenians were prevented from raiding the new province of Manitoba by the prompt action of the troops of the United States stationed on the frontier.

Lower Canadian frontier, but it was easily repulsed, and the authorities of the United States did their duty with promptitude. For all the losses, however, that Canada sustained through these invasions of her territory, she has never received any compensation whatever.

Out of the very circumstances which were apparently calculated to do much injury to Canada, her people learned lessons of wisdom and self-reliance, and were stimulated to go vigorously to work to carry out that scheme of national development which had its commencement in the Quebec conference of 1864, and was constitutionally inaugurated in 1867 when the provinces entered on the new era of federal union.

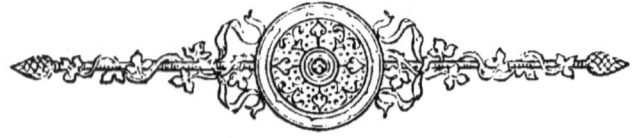

XXVI.

END OF THE RULE OF FUR-TRADERS—ACQUISI-
TION OF THE NORTHWEST—FORMATION OF
MANITOBA—RIEL'S REBELLIONS—
THE INDIANS.

(1670-1885.)

IN 1867 the Dominion of Canada comprised only
the four provinces, formerly contained in the ancient
historical divisions of Acadia and Canada, and it
became the immediate duty of its public men to
complete the union by the admission of Prince Edward Island and British Columbia, and by the
acquisition of the vast region which had been so
long under the rule of a company of fur-traders.
In the language of the eloquent Irishman, Lord
Dufferin, when governor-general, "the historical
territories of the Canadas—the eastern sea-boards
of New Brunswick, Nova Scotia, and Labrador—
the Laurentian lakes and valleys, corn lands and
pastures, though themselves more extensive than
half a dozen European kingdoms, were but the ves-
tibules and antechambers to that, till then, undreamt

of dominion whose illimitable dimensions alike confound the arithmetic of the surveyor and the verification of the explorer.''

The history of this northwest, whose rolling prairies now constitute so large a proportion of the wealth of Canada was, until 1867, entirely the history of the fur trade. Two centuries and a half ago a company of traders, known as the '' honourable company of adventurers from England trading into Hudson's Bay,'' received from Charles II. a royal licence in what was long known as Rupert's Land, and first raised its forts on the inhospitable shores of the great bay, only accessible to European vessels during the summer months. Among the prominent members of this company was the cousin of the King, Prince Rupert, that gallant cavalier. The French in the valley of the St. Lawrence looked with jealousy on these efforts of the English to establish themselves at the north, and Le Moyne d'Iberville, that daring Canadian, had destroyed their trading-posts. Still the Hudson's Bay Company persevered in their enterprise, and rebuilt their forts where they carried on a very lucrative trade with the Indians who came from all parts of that northern region to barter their rich furs for the excellent goods which the company always supplied to the natives. In the meantime, while the English were established at the north, French adventurers, the Sieur de La Vérendrye, a native of Three Rivers, and his two sons, reached the interior of the northwest by the way of Lake Superior and that chain of lakes and rivers which extends from Thunder Bay

to Lake Winnipeg.   These adventurous Frenchmen
raised rude posts by the lakes and rivers of this
region, and Vérendrye's sons are said to have extended their explorations in January, 1743, to what
was probably the Bighorn Range, an outlying but-
tress of the Rocky Mountains, running athwart the
sources of the Yellowstone.   The wars between
France and England, however, stopped French trade
in that northwestern region, and the Hudson's Bay
Company's posts at the north were the only signs of
European occupation when Wolfe and Montcalm
fell on the Plains of Abraham, and the fleur-de-lis
was struck on the old fort of the Canadian capital.

Towards the latter part of the eighteenth century,
the merchants of Canada, who were individually
dealing in furs, formed an association which, under
the title of the Northwest Company, was long the
rival of the Hudson's Bay adventurers.   Both these
companies were composed of Englishmen and
Scotchmen, but they were nevertheless bitter enemies, engaged as they were in the same business in
the wilderness.   The employés of the Hudson's Bay
Company were chiefly Scotch, while the Canadian
Company found in the French Canadian population
that class of men whom it believed to be most suitable to a forest life.   The differences in the nationality and religion of the servants of the companies
only tended to intensify the bitterness of the competition, and at last led to scenes of tumult and
bloodshed.   The Northwest Company found their
way to the interior of Rupert's Land by the Ottawa
River and the Great Lakes.   Their posts were seen

by the Assiniboine and Red rivers, even in the
Saskatchewan and Athabascan districts, and in the
valley of the Columbia among the mountains of the
great province which bears the name of that noble
stream. The Mackenzie River was discovered and
followed to the Arctic Sea by one of the members
of the Northwest Company, whose name it has
always borne. At a later time a trader, Simon
Fraser, first ventured on the river whose name now
recalls his famous journey, and David Thompson, a
surveyor of the Northwest Company, discovered the
river of the same name. Previous, however, to these
perilous voyages, the Hudson's Bay Company had
been forced by the enterprise of its rival to reach
the interior and compete for the fur traffic which
was being so largely controlled by the Canadian
Company. In 1771, Samuel Hearne, one of the
Hudson's Bay Company's employés, discovered the
Coppermine River, and three years later established
a fort on the Saskatchewan, still known as Cumberland House. In later years, Sir John Franklin,
George Back, and Thomas Simpson added largely
to the geographical knowledge of the northern parts
of the great region watered by the Coppermine, the
Great Fish—also called the Back,—and other streams
which fall into the Arctic Seas. As we glance at
the map of this vast region, we still see the names
of the numerous posts where the servants of the fur
companies passed their solitary lives, only relieved
by the periodical visits of Indian trappers, and the
arrival of the " trains " of dogs with supplies from
Hudson's Bay. Forts Enterprise, Providence, Good

Hope, and Resolution are among the names of posts which tell in eloquent terms the story of the courage, endurance, and hope that first planted them throughout that solitary land.

It was on the banks of Red River, where it forms a junction with the Assiniboine, that civilisation made the first effort to establish itself in the illimitable domain of fur-traders, always jealous of settlement which might interfere with their lucrative gains. The first person to erect a post on the Red River was the elder Vérendrye, who built Fort Rouge about 1735 on the site of the present city of Winnipeg. The same adventurer also built Fort La Reine at Portage La Prairie. In 1811 an enterprising Scotch nobleman, the Earl of Selkirk, who had previously made a settlement in Prince Edward Island, became a large proprietor of Hudson's Bay stock, and purchased from the company over a hundred thousand square miles of territory, which he named Assiniboia. In 1812 he made on the banks of the Red River a settlement of Highland Scotch and a few Irishmen. The Northwest Company looked with suspicion on this movement of Lord Selkirk, especially as he had such large influence in the rival company. In 1816, the employés of the former, chiefly half-breeds, destroyed Fort Douglas and murdered Governor Semple, who was in charge of the new Scotch settlement. As soon as the news of this outrage reached Lord Selkirk, he hastened to the succour of his settlement, and by the aid of some disbanded soldiers, whom he hired in Canada, he restored order. Subsequently he succeeded in bringing to a trial at York several partners and persons in the service of the Northwest Company on the charges of " high treason, murder, robbery, and conspiracy," but in all cases the accused were acquitted. The Northwest Company had great influence at this time throughout Canada, and by their instigation actions were brought against Lord Selkirk for false imprisonment, and for conspiring to ruin the trade of the company, and he was mulcted in heavy damages. Two years later Lord Selkirk died in France, and then the two companies, which had received great injury through their rivalry, were amalgamated, and the old Hudson's Bay Company reigned supreme in this region until 1870. The Red River settlement became the headquarters of the company, who established in 1835 a system of local government—a president and council and a court of law—and built Fort Garry on the site of a fort also bearing the same name—that of a director of the company. The new fort was a stone structure, having walls from ten to twelve feet high, and flanked by bastions defended by cannon and musketry. In 1867 the houses of the settlers occupied the banks of the Red River at short intervals for twenty-four miles. Many evidences of prosperity and thrift were seen throughout the settlement; the churches and school-houses proved that religion and education were highly valued by the people. The most conspicuous structure was the Roman Catholic Church of St. Boniface, whose bells at matins and vespers were so often a welcome sound to the wanderers on the plains.

25

" Is it the clang of wild-geese,
        Is it the Indians' yell
    That lends to the voice of the North wind
        The tone of a far-off bell ?

" The voyageur smiles as he listens
        To the sound that grows apace :
    Well he knows the vesper ringing
        Of the bells of Saint Boniface.

" The bells of the Roman mission
        That call from their turrets twain,
    To the boatmen on the river,
        To the hunters on the plain."

On all sides there were evidences of comfort in
this little oasis of civilisation amid the prairies.
The descendants of the two nationalities dwelt apart
in French and British parishes, each of which had
their separate schools and churches. The houses
and plantations of the British settlers, and of a few
French Canadians, indicated thrift, but the majority
of the French half-breeds, or *Métis*, the descendants
of French Canadian fathers and Indian mothers,
continued to live almost entirely on the fur trade,
as voyageurs, trappers, and hunters. They exhibited all the characteristics of those hardy and adventurous men who were the pioneers of the west.
Skilful hunters but poor cultivators of the soil, fond
of amusement, rash and passionate, spending their
gains as soon as made, too often in dissipation,
many of them were true representatives of the *coureurs de bois* of the days of Frontenac. This class
was numerous in 1869 when the government of Canada first presented itself to claim the territory of the

Northwest as a part of the Dominion. After years of negotiation the Hudson's Bay Company had recognised the necessity of allowing the army of civilisation to advance into the region which it had so long kept as a fur preserve. The British Government obtained favourable terms for the Dominion, and the whole country from line 49° to the Arctic region, and from Lake Superior to the Rocky Mountains became a portion of the Canadian domain, with the exception of small tracts of land in the vicinity of the company's posts, which they still continue to maintain wherever the fur trade can be profitably carried on. In 1869 the Canadian ministry, of which Sir John Macdonald was premier, took measures to assume possession of the country, where they proposed to establish a provisional government. Mr. William McDougall, a prominent Canadian Liberal, one of the founders of confederation, always an earnest advocate of the acquisition of the Northwest, was appointed to act as lieutenant-governor as soon as the formal transfer was made. This transfer, however, was not completed until a few months later than it was at first expected, and the government of Canada appears to have acted with some precipitancy in sending surveyors into the country, and in allowing Mr. McDougall to proceed at once to the scene of his proposed government. It would have been wise had the Canadian authorities taken measures to ascertain the wishes of the small but independent population with respect to the future government of their own country. The British as well as French settlers resented the

hasty action of the Canadian authorities. The half-
breeds, little acquainted with questions of government, saw in the appearance of surveying parties an
insidious attempt to dispossess them eventually of
their lands, to which many of them had not a sound
title. The British settlers, the best educated and
most intelligent portion of the population, believed
that a popular form of government should have
been immediately established in the old limits of
Assiniboia, as soon as it became a part of Canada.
Some of the Hudson's Bay Company's employés
were not in their hearts pleased at the transfer, and
the probable change in their position in a country
where they had been so long masters. Although
these men stood aloof from the insurrection, yet
their influence was not exercised at the commencement of the troubles, in favour of peace and order,
or in exposing the plans of the insurgents, of which
some of them must have had an idea. The appearance of Mr. McDougall on the frontier of the settlement, was the signal for an outbreak which has been
dignified by the name of rebellion. The insurgents
seized Fort Garry, and established a provisional
government with Mr. John Bruce, a Scotch settler,
as nominal president, and Mr. Louis Riel, the actual leader, as secretary of state. The latter was a
French half-breed, who had been superficially educated in French Canada. His temperament was
that of a race not inclined to steady occupation,
loving the life of the river and plain, ready to put
law at defiance when their rights and privileges were
in danger. This restless man and his half-breed

FORT GARRY AND A RED RIVER STEAMBOAT IN 1870.

associates soon found themselves at the head and
front of the whole rebellious movement, as the British settlers, while disapproving of the action of the
Canadian Government, were not prepared to support
the seditious designs of the French Canadian *Métis*.
Riel became president, and made prisoners of Dr.
Schultz, in later times a lieutenant-governor of the
new province, and of a number of other British settlers who were now anxious to restore order and
come to terms with the Canadian Government, who
were showing every disposition to arrange the difficulty. In the meantime Mr. McDougall issued a
proclamation which was a mere *brutum fulmen*, and
then went back to Ottawa, where he detailed his
grievances and soon afterwards disappeared from
public life. The Canadian authorities by this time
recognised their mistake and entered into negotiations with Red River delegates, representing both
the loyal and rebellious elements, and the result
was most favourable for the immediate settlement
of the difficulties. At this critical juncture the
Canadian Government had the advantage of the
sage counsels of Sir Donald Smith, then a prominent official of the Hudson's Bay Company, who at
a later time became a prominent figure in Canadian
public life. Chiefly through the instrumentality of
Archbishop Taché, whose services to the land and
race he loved can never be forgotten by its people,
an amnesty was promised to those who had taken
part in the insurrection, and the troubles would
have come to an end had not Riel, in a moment of
recklessness, characteristic of his real nature, tried

one Thomas Scott by the veriest mockery of a
court-martial on account of some severe words he
had uttered against the rebels' government, and
had him mercilessly shot outside the fort. As Scott
was a native of Ontario, and an Orangeman, his
murder aroused a widespread feeling of indignation
throughout his native province. The amnesty
which was promised to Archbishop Taché, it is now
quite clear, never contemplated the pardon of a
crime like this, which was committed subsequently.
The Canadian Government were then fully alive to
the sense of their responsibilities, and at once decided to act with resolution. In the spring of 1870
an expedition was organised, and sent to the Northwest under the command of Colonel Garnet Wol-
seley, now a peer, and commander-in-chief of the
British army. This expedition consisted of five
hundred regulars and seven hundred Canadian
volunteers, who reached Winnipeg after a most
wearisome journey of nearly three months, by the
old fur-traders' route from Thunder Bay, through
an entirely unsettled and rough country, where the
portages were very numerous and laborious. Towards the end of August the expedition reached
their destination, but found that Riel had fled to
the United States, and that they had won a blood-
less victory. Law and order henceforth prevailed in
the new territory, whose formal transfer to the
Canadian Government had been completed some
months before, and it was now formed into a new
province, called Manitoba, with a complete system
of local government, and including guaranties with

respect to education, as in the case of the old provinces. The first lieutenant-governor was Mr. Adams Archibald, a Nova Scotian lawyer, who was one of the members of the Quebec conference, and a statesman of much discretion. Representation was also given immediately in the two houses of the Dominion parliament. Subsequently the vast territory outside of the new prairie province was divided into six districts for purposes of government: Alberta, Assiniboia, Athabasca, Keewatin, and Saskatchewan. Keewatin is under the jurisdiction of the lieutenant-governor of Manitoba, but the other districts have an assembly and a lieutenant-governor whose seat of government is Regina, though the people do not yet enjoy responsible government. In 1896 four new provisional districts were marked out in the great northern unsettled district under the names of Franklin, Mackenzie, Yukon, and Ungava.

In the course of a few years a handsome, well-built city arose on the site of old Fort Garry, and with the construction of the Canadian Pacific Railway—a national highway built with a rapidity remarkable even in these days of extraordinary commercial enterprise—and the connection of the Atlantic sea-board with the Pacific shores, villages and towns have extended at distant intervals across the continent, from Port Arthur to Vancouver, the latter place an instance of western phenomenal growth. Stone and brick buildings of fine architectural proportions, streets paved and lit by electricity, huge elevators, busy mills, are the characteristics of some towns where only yesterday brooded silence, and the great flowery stretches of prairie were only crushed by the feet of wandering Indians and voyageurs.

Fourteen years after the formation of the province of Manitoba, whilst the Canadian Pacific Railway was in the course of construction, the peace of the territories was again disturbed by risings of half-breeds in the South Saskatchewan district, chiefly at Duck Lake, St. Laurent, and Batoche. Many of these men had migrated from Manitoba to a country where they could follow their occupation of hunting and fishing, and till little patches of ground in that shiftless manner characteristic of the *Métis*. The total number of half-breeds in the Saskatchewan country were probably four thousand, of whom the majority lived in the settlements just named. These people had certain land grievances, the exact nature of which it is not easy even now to ascertain; but there is no doubt that they laboured under the delusion that, because there was much red-tapeism and some indifference at Ottawa in dealing with their respective claims, there was a desire or intention to treat them with injustice. Conscious that they might be crowded out by the greater energy and enterprise of white settlers—that they could no longer depend on their means of livelihood in the past, when the buffalo and other game were plentiful, these restless, impulsive, illiterate people were easily led to believe that their only chance of redressing their real or fancied wrongs was such a rising as had taken place on the Red River in

1869. It is believed that English settlers in the
Prince Albert district secretly fomented the rising
with the hope that it might also result in the establishment of a province on the banks of the Saskatchewan, despite its small population. The agitators
among the half-breeds succeeded in bringing Riel
into the country to lead the insurrection. He had
been an exile ever since 1870, and was at the time
teaching school in Montana. After the rebellion he
had been induced to remain out of the Northwest
by the receipt of a considerable sum of money from
the secret service fund of the Dominion Government, then led by Sir John Macdonald. In 1874 he
had been elected to the House of Commons by the
new constituency of Provencher in Manitoba; but
as he had been proclaimed an outlaw, when a true
bill for murder was found against him in the Manitoba Court of Queen's Bench, and when he had
failed to appear for trial, he was expelled from the
house on the motion of Mr. Mackenzie Bowell, a
prominent Orangeman, and, later, premier of the
Canadian Government. Lepine, a member also of
the so-called provisional government of Red River,
had been tried and convicted for his share in the
murder of Scott, but Lord Dufferin, when governor-
general, exercised the prerogative of royal clemency,
as an imperial officer, and commuted the punish-
ment to two years' imprisonment. In this way
the Mackenzie government was relieved—but only
temporarily—of a serious responsibility which they
were anxious to avoid, at a time when they were
between the two fires: of the people of Ontario,

anxious to punish the murderers with every severity, and of the French Canadians, the great majority of whom showed a lively sympathy for all those who had taken part in the rebellion of 1869. The influence of French Canada was also seen in the later action of the Mackenzie government in obtaining a full amnesty for all concerned in the rebellion except Riel, Lepine, and O'Donohue, who were banished for five years. The popularity enjoyed by Riel and his associates in French Canada, as well as the clemency shown to them, were doubtless facts considered by the leaders in the second rising on the Saskatchewan as showing that they had little to fear from the consequences of their acts. Riel and Dumont—the latter a half-breed trader near Batoche—were the leaders of the revolt which broke out at Duck Lake in the March of 1885 with a successful attack on the Mounted Police and the Prince Albert Volunteers, who were defeated with a small loss of life. This success had much effect on the Indian tribes in the Saskatchewan district, among whom Riel and his associates had been intriguing for some time, and Poundmaker, Big Bear, and other chiefs of the Cree communities living on the Indian reserves, went on the warpath. Subsequently Battleford, then the capital of the Territories, was threatened by Indians and *Métis*, and a force under Big Bear massacred at Frog Lake two Oblat missionaries, and some other persons, besides taking several prisoners, among whom were Mrs. Delaney and Mrs. Gowanlock, widows of two of the murdered men, who were released at the close of the rising. Fort Pitt, on the North Saskatchewan, thirty miles from Frog Lake, was abandoned by Inspector Dickens—a son of the novelist—and his detachment of the Mounted Police, on the approach of a large body of Indians under Big Bear. When the news of these outrages reached Ottawa, the government acted with great promptitude. A French Canadian, now Sir Adolphe Caron, was then minister of militia in Sir John Macdonald's ministry, and showed himself fully able to cope with this, happily, unusual, experience in Canadian Government. From all parts of the Dominion—from French as well as English Canada—the volunteers patriotically rallied to the call of duty, and Major-General Middleton, a regular officer in command of the Canadian militia, led a fine force of over four thousand men into the Northwest. The Canadian Pacific Railway was now built, with the exception of a few breaks of about seventy-two miles in all, as far as Qu'Appelle, which is sixteen hundred and twenty miles from Ottawa and about two hundred and thirty-five miles to the south of Batoche. The Canadian troops, including a fine body of men from Winnipeg, reached Fish Creek, fifteen miles from Batoche, on the 24th of April, or less than a month after the orders were given at Ottawa to march from the east. Here the insurgents, led by Dumont, were concealed in rifle-pits, ingeniously constructed and placed in a deep ravine. They checked Middleton, who does not appear to have taken sufficient precautions to ascertain the position of the enemy—thoroughly trained marksmen who were able to shoot down a considerable number of the volunteers. Later, at Batoche, the Canadian troops, led with great bravery by Colonels Straubenzie, Williams, Mackeand, and Grassett, scattered the insurgents, who never made an attempt to rally. The gallantry of Colonel Williams of the Midlanders—an Ontario battalion—was especially conspicuous, but he never returned from the Northwest to receive the plaudits of his countrymen, as he died of fever soon after the victory he did so much to win at Batoche. Colonel Otter, a distinguished officer of Toronto, had an encounter with Poundmaker at Cut Knife Creek on Battle River, one of the tributaries of the North Saskatchewan, and prevented him from making any hostile demonstrations against Battleford and other places. Riel's defeat at Batoche cowed these Indians, who gave up their arms and prisoners to Otter. Elsewhere in the Territories all trouble was prevented by the prompt transport of troops under Colonel Strange to Fort Edmonton, Calgary, and other points of importance. The Blackfeet, the most formidable body of natives in the Territories, never broke the peace, although they were more than once very restless. Their good behaviour was chiefly owing to the influence of Chief Crowfoot, always a friend of the Canadians.

When the insurrection was over, an example was made of the leaders. Dumont succeeded in making his escape, but Riel, who had been captured after the fight at Batoche, was executed at Regina after a most impartial trial, in which he had the assistance of very able counsel brought from French Canada. Insanity was pleaded even, in his defence, not only

in the court but subsequently in the Commons at
Ottawa, when it was attempted to censure the Canadian Government for their stern resolution to
vindicate the cause of order in the Territories.
Poundmaker and Big Bear were sent for three years
to the penitentiary, and several other Indians suffered the extreme penalty of the law for the mur-
ders at Frog Lake.   Sir John Macdonald was at the
head of the Canadian Government, and every possible effort was made to force him to obtain the pardon of Riel, but he felt that he could not afford to
weaken the authority of law in the west, and his
French Canadian colleagues, Sir Hector Langevin,
then minister of public works, Sir Adolphe Chap-
leau, then secretary of state,—now lieutenant-governor of Quebec—Sir Adolphe Caron, then minister
of militia, exhibited commendable courage in resist-
ing the passionate and even menacing appeals of
their countrymen, who were carried away at this
crisis by a false sentiment, rather than by a true
sense of justice.   Happily, in the course of no long
time, the racial antagonisms raised by this unhappy
episode in the early history of confederation disappeared under the influence of wiser counsels, and
the peace of this immense region has never since
been threatened by Indians or half-breeds, who have
now few, if any, grievances on which to brood.   The
patriotism shown by the Canadian people in this
memorable contest of 1885 illustrated the desire of
all classes to consolidate the union, and make it
secure from external and internal dangers, and had
also an admirable influence in foreign countries

COLONEL WILLIAMS.

which could now appreciate the growing national strength of the Dominion. In the cities of Ottawa, Toronto, and Winnipeg, monuments have been raised to recall the services of the volunteers who fought and died at Fish Creek and Batoche. On the banks of the Saskatchewan a high cairn and cross point to the burial place of the men who fell before the deadly shot of the half-breed sharpshooters at Fish Creek:

" Not in the quiet churchyard, near those who loved them best;
  But by the wild Saskatchewan, they laid them to their rest.
  A simple soldier's funeral in that lonely spot was theirs,
  Made consecrate and holy by a nation's tears and prayers.
  Their requiem—the music of the river's surging tide ;
  Their funeral wreaths, the wild flowers that grow on every side ;
  Their monument—undying praise from each Canadian heart,
  That hears how, for their country's sake, they nobly bore their
    part."

One of the finest bodies of troops in the world, the Mounted Police of Canada, nearly one thousand strong, now maintains law and order throughout a district upwards of three hundred thousand square miles in area, and annually cover a million and a half miles in the discharge of their onerous duties. The half-breeds now form but a very small minority of the population, and are likely to disappear as a distinct class under the influence of civilisation. The Indians, who number about thirty thousand in Manitoba and the Northwest, find their interests carefully guarded by treaties and statutes of Canada, which recognise their rights as wards of the Canadian Government. They are placed on large reserves,

INDIAN CARVED POSTS IN BRITISH COLUMBIA

101

where they can carry on farming and other industrial occupations for which the Canadian Government, with commendable liberality, provide means
of instruction.   Many of the Indians have shown an
aptitude for agricultural pursuits which has surprised
those who have supposed they could not be induced
to make much progress in the arts of civilised life.
The average attendance of Indian children at the
industrial and other schools is remarkably large compared even with that of white children in the old
provinces.   The Indian population of Canada, even
in the Northwest territory, appear to have reached
the stationary stage, and hereafter a small increase
is confidently expected by those who closely watch
the improvement in their methods of life.   The high
standard which has been reached by the Iroquois
population on the Grand River of Ontario, is an
indication of what we may even expect in the course
of many years on the banks of the many rivers of
the Northwest.   The majority of the tribes in Manitoba and the Northwest—the Crees and Blackfeet—
belong to the Algonquin race, and the Assiniboines
or Stonies, to the Dacotahs or Sioux, now only
found on the other side of the frontier.   The Tinneh
or Athabaskan family occupy the Yukon and Mackenzie valleys, while in the Arctic region are the
Eskimo or Innuits.   In British Columbia * there are
at least eight distinct stocks; in the interior, Tinneh, Salish or Shuswap; on the coast, Haida, Ishim-
sian, Kwakiool (including Hailtzuk), Bilhoola, Aht,

* Dr. Geo. M. Dawson, F.R.S., has given me this division of
Indian tribes.

or Nootka, and Kawitshin, the latter including several names, probably of Salish affinity, living around the Gulf of Georgia. The several races that inhabit Canada, the Algonquins, the Huron-Iroquois, the Dacotah, the Tinneh, and the several stocks of British Columbia, have for some time formed an interesting study for scholars, who find in their languages and customs much valuable archæological and ethnological lore. The total number of Indians that now inhabit the whole Dominion is estimated at over one hundred thousand souls, of whom one-third live in the old provinces.

XXVII.

COMPLETION OF THE FEDERAL UNION—MAKERS OF THE DOMINION.

(1871–1891.)

WITHIN three years after the formation of the new province of Manitoba in the Northwest, Prince Edward Island and British Columbia came into the confederation, and gave completeness to the federal structure. Cook and Vancouver were among the adventurous sailors who carried the British flag to the Pacific province, whose lofty, snow-clad mountains, deep bays, and many islands give beauty, grandeur, and variety to the most glorious scenery of the continent. Daring fur-traders passed down its swift and deep rivers and gave them the names they bear. The Hudson's Bay Company held sway for many years within the limits of an empire. The British Government, as late as 1849, formed a Crown colony out of Vancouver, and in 1858, out of the mainland, previously known as New Caledonia. In 1866 the two provinces were united with a simple form of government, consisting of a lieutenant-gov-

John A. Macdonald

105

ernor, and a legislative council, partly appointed by the Crown and partly elected by the people; but in 1871, when it entered into the Canadian union, a complete system of responsible government was established as in the other provinces. Prince Edward Island was represented at the Quebec conference, but it remained out of confederation until 1873, when it came in as a distinct province; one of the conditions of admission was the advance of funds by the Dominion government for the purchase of the claims of the persons who had held the lands of the island for a century. The land question was always the disturbing element in the politics of the island, whose history otherwise is singularly uninteresting to those who have not had the good fortune to be among its residents and to take a natural interest in local politics. The ablest advocate of confederation was Mr. Edward Whelan, a journalist and politician who took part in the Quebec conference, but did not live to see it carried out by Mr. J. C. Pope, Mr. Laird, and others.

With the successful establishment of a federal union which stretches from the Gulf of St. Lawrence to the Pacific Ocean,—whose two extremes of east and west are linked together by the Intercolonial and Pacific Railways—the historical portion of this book properly closes. It is not proposed to enter into the conflicts of political parties, which have been too often carried to extremes in the Dominion, or to review those dominion and provincial questions which make up the politics of Canada. The history of Canadian politics since 1867 has

been mainly a record of conflict between Conserva-
tives and Liberals for the supremacy; of differences
of opinion with respect to the advantages of the
system of protection, established by the Conserva-

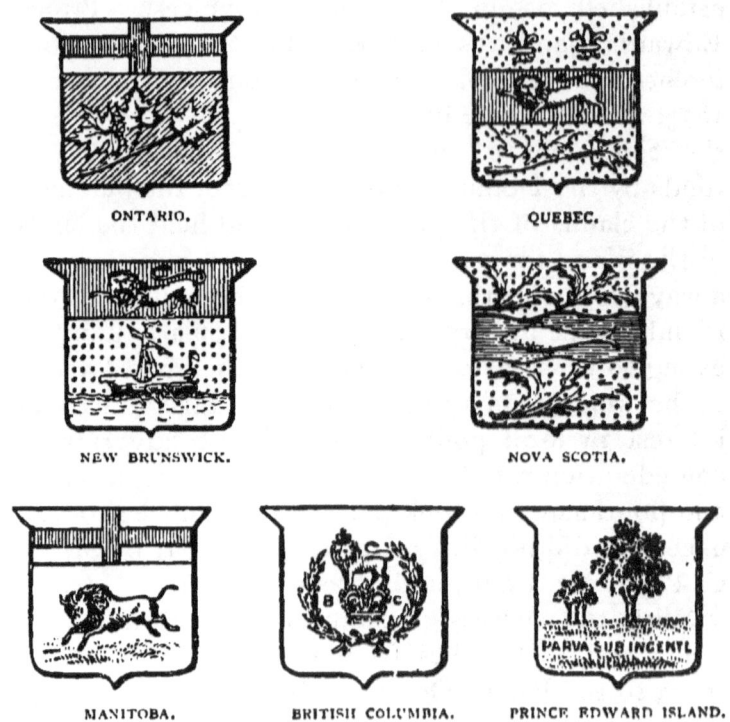

ONTARIO.   QUEBEC.

NEW BRUNSWICK.   NOVA SCOTIA.

MANITOBA.   BRITISH COLUMBIA.   PRINCE EDWARD ISLAND.

ARMS OF THE PROVINCES.

tive government in 1879, compared with a mere
revenue tariff; of questions arising out of the inter-
pretation of the federal constitution; of issues deeply
affecting the provincial, racial, or religious interests
of the various communities that compose the Do-

minion.   Such issues cannot form any part of a
story which has only to deal with those epoch-
making events which, for nearly three centuries,
have had most influence on the development of the
Canadian people as a nation.

Many names occur to the student as he reviews
the past history of confederation, but there are a
few who, beyond all others, deserve the meed of
praise for their readiness to rise above the narrow
claims of provincialism and recognise the necessity
of a broad and generous patriotism.   As I have
already shown, when confederation was forced on
the attention of Canadian statesmen from Halifax
to Toronto, the situation had become most critical
from the point of view of provincial government, as
well as from the point of view of national security.
The destinies of old Canada were virtually in the
hands of three men—the Honourable George Brown,
Sir George Cartier, and Sir John Macdonald, to give
the two latter the titles they received at a later time.
Mr. Brown was mainly responsible for the difficulties
that had made the conduct of government practically impossible, through his persistent and even
rude assertion of the claims of Upper Canada to
larger representation and more consideration in the
public administration.   No one will deny his con-
summate ability, his inflexibility of purpose, his
impetuous oratory, and his financial knowledge, but
his earnestness carried him frequently beyond the
limits of political prudence, and it was with reason
that he was called " a governmental impossibility,"
as long as French and English Canada continued

Geo. Brown

pitted against each other, previous to the union of
1867. The journal which he conducted with so
much force, attacked French Canada and its institutions with great violence, and the result was the
increase of racial antagonisms. Opposed to him
was Sir George Etienne Cartier, who had found in
the Liberal-Conservative party, and in the principles
of responsible government, the means of strengthening the French Canadian race and making it a
real power in the affairs of the country. Running
throughout his character there was a current of
sound sense and excellent judgment which came to
the surface at national crises. A solution of difficulties, he learned, was to be found not in the
violent assertion of national claims, but in the principles of compromise and conciliation. With him
was associated Sir John Macdonald, the most successful statesman that Canada has yet produced, on
account of his long tenure of office and of the importance of the measures that he was able to carry
in his remarkable career. He was premier of the
Dominion from 1867 until his death in 1891, with
the exception of the four years of the administration
of the Liberals (1873–1878), led by the late Mr.
Alexander Mackenzie, who had raised himself from
the humble position of stonemason to the highest
place in the councils of the country, by dint of his
Scotch shrewdness, his tenacity of purpose, his public honesty, and his thorough comprehension of
Canadian questions, though he was wanting in
breadth of statesmanship. Many generations must
pass away before the personal and political merits of

Geo. W. Cartin

411

Sir John Macdonald can be advantageously and im-
partially reviewed.   A lawyer by profession, but a
politician by choice, not remarkable for originality
of conception, but possessing an unusual capacity
for estimating the exact conditions of public sentiment, and for moulding his policy so as to satisfy
that opinion, having a perfect understanding of the
ambitions and weaknesses of human nature, believing that party success was often as desirable as the
triumph of any great principle, ready to forget his
friends and purchase his opponents when political
danger was imminent, possessing a fascinating manner, which he found very useful at times when he
had to pacify his friends and disarm his opponents,
fully comprehending the use of compromise in a
country of diverse nationalities, having a firm conviction that in the principles of the British constitution there was the best guaranty for sound political
progress, having a patriotic confidence in the ability
of Canada to hold her own on this continent, and
become, to use his own words, a " nation within a
nation,"—that is to say, within the British Empire
—Sir John Macdonald offers to the political student
an example of a remarkable combination of strength
and weakness, of qualities which make up a great
statesman and a mere party politician, according to
the governing circumstances.   Happily for the best
interests of Canada, in the case of confederation the
statesman prevailed.   But his ambition at this crisis
would have been futile had not Mr. Brown consented to unite with him and Cartier.   This triple
alliance made a confederation possible on terms

acceptable to both English and French Canadians. These three men were the representatives of the antagonistic elements that had to be reconciled and cemented. The readiness with which Sir Charles Tupper and Sir Leonard Tilley, the premiers of Nova Scotia and New Brunswick, co-operated with the statesmen of the upper provinces, was a most opportune feature of the movement, which ended in the successful formation of a confederation in 1867. Although the Liberal leaders in Nova Scotia, Mr., afterwards Sir, Adams Archibald, and Mr. Jonathan McCully, like Brown, Howland, Mowat, and McDougall in old Canada, supported the movement with great loyalty, the people of the province were aroused to a passionate opposition mainly through the vigorous action of the popular leader, Mr. Joseph Howe, who had been an eloquent advocate of colonial union before it assumed a practical shape, but now took the strong ground that the question should not be forced on the country by a legislature which had no mandate whatever to deal with it, that it should be determined only by the people at the polls, and that the terms arranged at Quebec were unfair to the maritime provinces. Mr. Howe subsequently obtained " better terms " for Nova Scotia by every available means of constitutional agitation—beyond which he was never willing to go, however great might be public grievances—and then he yielded to the inevitable logic of circumstances, and entered the Dominion government, where he remained until he became lieutenant-governor of his native province. The feelings, however, he aroused against confederation lasted with some intensity for years, although the cry for repeal died away, according as a new generation grew up in place of the one which remembered with bitterness the struggles of 1867.

Mr. George Brown died from the wound he received at the hands of a reckless printer, who had been in his employ, and Canadians have erected to his memory a noble monument in the beautiful Queen's Park of the city where he laboured so long and earnestly as a statesman and a journalist. Sir George Cartier died in 1873, but Sir John Macdonald survived his firm friend for eighteen years, and both received State funerals. Statues of Sir John Macdonald have been erected in the cities of Montreal, Toronto, Hamilton, and Kingston. In Ottawa on one side of the Parliament building we see also a statue of the same distinguished statesman, and on the other that of his great colleague, Sir George Cartier. It was but fitting that the statues of these most famous representatives of the two distinct elements of the Canadian people should have been placed alongside of the national legislature. They are national sentinels to warn Canadian people of the dangers of racial or religious conflict, and to illustrate the advantages of those principles of compromise and justice on which both Cartier and Macdonald, as far as they could, raised the edifice of confederation.

XXVIII.

CANADA AS A NATION : MATERIAL AND INTEL-LECTUAL DEVELOPMENT—POLITICAL RIGHTS.

THE population of the whole Dominion—still chiefly confined to the St. Lawrence valley and the Atlantic provinces—does not yet exceed 5,000,000 souls, though it has increased nearly five times since 1837. Of this population, 1,300,000 are French Canadians; the majority are English, Scotch, and Irish. At least 2,000,000 profess the Roman Catholic religion. The immigration of late years has been very insignificant, and has been practically nullified by the constant movement of Canadians into the United States—a movement which has been somewhat decreasing since the opening up of the Northwest and the greater facilities offered by the Dominion to energy and enterprise. Under these conditions the natural-born population amounts to about 85 per cent. of the whole. The people of Canada have already won for themselves a large amount of wealth from the riches of the land, forest, and seas, and an aggregate of the imports and exports now reaches $255,000,000 a year, or an increase of $145,000,000 within half a century. The North-west already raises upward of 36,000,000 bushels of wheat, or an increase of 18,000,000 in five years. Nearly $360,000,000 are invested in manufactures, chiefly of cotton and woollen goods. Some fourteen lines of ocean steamers call at the port of Montreal, which has now a population of over 250,000 souls. Toronto comes next in population, about 190,000, whilst the other cities, like Quebec, Halifax, St. John, Ottawa, Hamilton, and London, range from 70,000 to 30,000. The total revenue of the Dominion, apart from the local and provincial revenues, is about $36,000,000 a year—against only $300,000 in 1837—raised mainly from customs and excise duties, which are high, owing to the " national " or protective policy, although lower than those on similar goods in the United States. The expenditures of Canada, very heavy of late years for a small population, have been mainly caused by the development of the Dominion, and by the necessity of providing rapid means of intercommunication for trade and population in a country extending between two oceans. Canals, lighthouses, the acquisition and opening of the Northwest railways, government buildings, have absorbed at least $240,000,000 since 1867, and it is not remarkable, under these circumstances, that a gross debt has been accumulated within half a century of about $315,000,000, against which must be set valuable assets in the shape of buildings and public works necessary to the progress of a new country. The public buildings, churches, and universities display within a quarter of a century a great improvement in architectural beauty, whilst the homes of the people show, both in the interior and exterior, decided evidences of comfort, convenience, and culture. Instead of the fourteen miles of railway which existed in 1837, there are about 15,000 miles in actual operation, affording facilities for trade and commerce not exceeded by any country in the world.

The mental outfit of the Dominion compares favourably even with that of older countries. The Universities of Canada—McGill in Montreal, Laval in Quebec, Queen's in Kingston, Dalhousie in Halifax, and Trinity and Toronto Universities in Toronto—stand deservedly high in the opinion of men of learning in the Old World and the United States, whilst the grammar and common school system, especially of Ontario, is creditable to the keen sagacity and public spirit of the people. We have already seen the low condition of education of fifty years ago, only one in fifteen at school; but now there are 1,000,000 pupils in the educational institutions of the country, or one in five, at a cost to the people of upwards of $12,000,000, contributed for the most part by the taxpayers of the different municipalities in connection with which the educational system is worked out. In Ontario the class of school-houses is exceptionally good, and the apparatus excellent, though there is an injurious tendency to burden pupils with too many subjects, and in that way encourage superficiality. In French Canada, to whose progress I devote a special

27

chapter in view of its exceptional character and influence in the confederation, there is an essentially literary activity. The intellectual work of the English-speaking people has been chiefly in the direction of scientific, constitutional, and historical literature, in which departments they have shown an amount of knowledge and research which has won for many of them laurels outside of their own country.

The working out of a system of government adapted to the necessities of countries with distinct interests and nationalities, has developed in Canada a class of statesmen and writers with broad national views and a large breadth of knowledge. On all occasions when men have risen beyond the passion and narrowness of party, the debates of the legislature have been distinguished by a keenness of argument and by a grace of oratory—especially in the case of some French Canadians—which would be creditable to the Senate of the United States in its palmy days. Any one who reviews the twelve volumes already published by the Royal Society of Canada, founded by the Marquis of Lorne, when governor-general, will see how much scholarship and ability the writers of Canada bring to the study of scientific, antiquarian, and historical subjects. The names of Todd, Kingsford, Scadding, Read, Pope, Stewart, Patterson, and Withrow will be recognised by Canadians as those of conscientious workers in history and constitutional learning. In science the names of Sir William Dawson, Dr. George M. Dawson, and of other native Canadians

on the list of the English and Canadian Royal
Societies are well known in the parent state and
wherever science has its votaries and followers.
The poets, William Kirby, Archbishop O'Brien, John
Reade, Charles Roberts, Bliss Carman, Frederick J.
Scott, Pauline Johnson, Ethelwyn Wetherald, Archibald Lampman, Duncan Campbell Scott, James
David Edgar, and Wilfred Campbell have won recognition even in a country like Canada, where still
is wanting the inspiration of a wide field of culture,
and of that generous encouragement which can
hardly be expected in a country of prosaic needs.
Miss Pauline Johnson is the child of an English
mother and a head-chief of the Mohawks at Brantford. The historical novels of Major Richardson,
William Kirby, and Gilbert Parker, show the rich
materials our past annals offer for romance. Mr.
Parker's enthusiasm for his theme is sustained by his
bright, attractive style. *Sam Slick's Sayings and
Doings* is still the only noteworthy evidence we have
of the existence of humour among a practical people,
and his " wise saws " and " sayings " were uttered
more than half a century ago. Yet, on the whole, if
great works are wanting nowadays, the intellectual
movement is in the right direction, and according as
the intellectual soil of Canada becomes enriched with
the progress of culture, we may eventually look for
a more generous fruition.

Canadian art has hitherto been imitative, rather
than creative, though of late years, as the Chicago
Exposition proved, Canadian artists have produced
several pictures which show an individuality of

expression, colour, feeling, and a knowledge of tech-
nique which illustrate the influence of study and
experience in the best European schools, especially
of Paris. The names of L. R. O'Brien, George
Reid, Bell-Smith, Robert Harris, J. W. L. Forster,
W. Brymner, and Miss Bell are among the most
notable names of English Canadian artists. The
Marquis of Lorne and the Princess Louise, during
their residence in Canada, did much to stimulate
a wider taste for art by the establishment of a
Canadian academy, and the holding of annual
exhibitions.

Self-government exists in the full sense of the
term.   At the base of the political structure lie
those municipal institutions which, for completeness, are not excelled in any other country.   It is in
the enterprising province of Ontario that the system
has attained its greatest development.   The machin-
ery of these municipalities is used in Ontario to raise
the taxes necessary for the support of public schools.
Free libraries can be provided in every municipality
whenever the majority of the taxpayers choose.
Then we go up higher to the provincial organisa-
tions governed by a lieutenant-governor, nominated
and removable by the government of the Dominion,
and advised by a council responsible to the people's
representatives, with a legislature composed, in only
two of the provinces, of two houses—a council appointed by the Crown, and an elective assembly; in
all the other provinces, there is simply an assembly
chosen by the people on a very liberal franchise,
manhood suffrage in the majority of cases.   The

PARLIAMENT BUILDING AT OTTAWA.

421

fundamental law, or the British North America Act
of 1867, gives jurisdiction to the provincial governments over administration of justice (except in criminal matters), municipal, and all purely local affairs.
In the Territories, not yet constituted into provinces,
there is a small elective body or house who select a
financial committee to assist the lieutenant-governor.
These Territories are also represented in the two
houses of the Dominion Parliament. The central or
general government of the Dominion is administered by a governor-general, with the assistance of a
ministry responsible to a Parliament, composed of a
Senate appointed by the Crown, and a House of
Commons elected under an electoral franchise, practically on the very threshold of universal suffrage.
This government has jurisdiction over trade and
commerce, post-office, militia and defence, navigation and shipping, fisheries, railways and public works
of a Dominion character, and all other matters of a
general or national import.   Education is under the
control of the provincial governments, but the rights
and privileges of a religious minority with respect to
separate or denominational schools are protected by
the constitution.   The common law of England
prevails in all the provinces except in French Canada, where the civil law still exists.   The criminal
law of England obtains throughout the Dominion.
The central government appoints all the judges, who
are irremovable except for cause.   Although the
constitution places in the central government the
residue of all powers, not expressly given to the
provincial authorities, conflicts of jurisdiction are

constantly arising between the general and local governments. Such questions, however, are being gradually settled by the decisions of the courts—the chief security of a written constitution—although at times the rivalry of parties and the antagonisms of distinct nationalities and creeds tend to give special importance to certain educational and other matters which arise in the operation of the constitution. All these are perils inseparable from a federal constitution governing two distinct races.

The appointment of the governor-general by the Crown, the power of disallowing bills which may interfere with imperial obligations, and the right which Canadians still enjoy of appealing to the judicial committee of the Queen's Privy Council from the subordinate courts of the provinces, including the Supreme Court of Canada; the obligation which rests upon England to assist the colony in the time of danger by all the power of her army and fleet, together with the fact that all treaties with foreign powers must be necessarily negotiated through the imperial authorities, will be considered as the most patent evidences of Canada being still a dependency of the Empire. Even the restraint imposed upon Canada with respect to any matters involving negotiations with foreign powers has been modified to a great degree, by the fact that England has acknowledged for over thirty years that Canada should be not only consulted in every particular, but actually represented in all negotiations that may be carried on with foreign powers affecting her commercial or territorial interests. A notable example of this new imperial policy was the Washington Convention of 1871, which settled the Alabama and other questions of difference between the United States and Canada. England recognised the direct interest of the Dominion in the subjects under discussion, by the selection of the able premier of the Liberal-Conservative government, Sir John Macdonald, as one of the commissioners. The most satisfactory result of this conference was the appointment of a commission which, after full deliberation, gave Canada and Newfoundland a compensation of five millions and a half of dollars for certain concessions that were made to the United States on the valuable fishing grounds of British North America. In the diplomatic discussions between England and the United States as a sequence of the seizure of Canadian vessels engaged in catching seals in the open waters of Bering Sea, the English Government was largely influenced by the opinions of the Canadian ministry in relation to a matter affecting Dominion interests.

One of the members of the court of arbitration, which assembled at Paris in 1892, and decided the question at issue in accordance with the principles of international law, fought for by the British and Canadian governments, was Sir John Thompson, an able lawyer of Nova Scotia, who became premier of the Dominion soon after the death of Sir John Macdonald, and was himself struck down only a few months after the settlement of the Bering Sea question, when summoned to Windsor Castle to take before the Queen the oath of a privy councillor of

England—a dramatic close to a short though exceptionally successful career.

It was an imperial man-of-war that brought the remains of Sir John Thompson to the city of Halifax, where representatives of all parts of Canada buried them with honours which few statesmen have ever received. This tribute of respect was due to a Canadian statesman whose appointment on the Paris arbitration was a direct acknowledgment of the importance of Canada in imperial councils. With the national development of Canada the conditions of the relations between England and Canada are such as to ensure unity of policy so long as each government considers the interests of England and of the dependency as identical, and keeps ever in view the obligations, welfare, and unity of the Empire at large.

XXIX.

FRENCH CANADA.

As this story commenced with a survey from the heights of Quebec of the Dominion of Canada from ocean to ocean, so now may it fitly close with a review of the condition of the French Canadian people who still inhabit the valley of the St. Lawrence, and whose history is contemporaneous with that of the ancient city whose picturesque walls and buildings recall the designs of French ambition on this continent.

Though the fortifications of Louisbourg and Ticonderoga, of Niagara, Frontenac, and other historic places of the French régime in America have been razed to the ground, and the French flag is never seen in the valley of the St. Lawrence, except on some holiday in company with other national colours, nevertheless on the continent where she once thought to reign supreme, France has been able to leave a permanent impress. But this impress is not in the valley of the Mississippi. It is true that a number of French still live on the banks of the great river, that many a little village where a French

QUEBEC IN 1896.

127

patois is spoken lies hidden in the sequestered bayous of the South, and that no part of the old city of New Orleans possesses so much interest for the European stranger as the French or Creole quarter, with its quaint balconied houses and luxuriant gardens; but despite all this, it is generally admitted that the time is not far distant when the French language will disappear from Louisiana, and few evidences will be found of the days of the French occupancy of that beautiful State of the Union. On the banks of the St. Lawrence, however, France has left behind her what seem likely to be more permanent memorials of her occupation. The picturesque banks of the St. Lawrence, from the Atlantic to the great lakes of the West, are the home of a large and rapidly increasing population whose language and customs are so many memorials of the old régime whose history has taken up so many pages of this story.

The tourist who travels through the province of Quebec sees on all sides the evidence that he is passing through a country of French origin. Here and there in Quebec and Montreal, or in some quiet village sequestered in a valley or elevated on the Laurentian Hills, he sees houses and churches which remind him of many a hamlet or town he has visited in Brittany or Normandy. The language is French from the Saguenay to the Ottawa, and in some remote communities even now English is never spoken, and is understood only by the curé or notary. Nor is the language so impure or degenerated as many persons may naturally suppose. On

STREET IN A FRENCH CANADIAN VILLAGE NEAR QUEBEC.

the contrary, it is spoken by the educated classes with a purity not excelled in France itself. The better class of French Canadians take pride in studying the language of the country of their ancestors, and are rarely guilty of Anglicisms, though these have necessarily crept into the common parlance of mixed communities, where people are forced to speak both French and English. In some rural districts, isolated from large towns, the people retain the language as it was spoken two centuries ago—though without the accent of the old provinces of their origin—and consequently many words and phrases which are rarely now heard in France, still exist among the peasantry of French Canada, just as we find in New England many expressions which are not pure Americanisms but really memorials of old English times. In French Canada the Anglicisms are such as occur under the natural condition of things. The native of old France has no words for " clearing " the forest, making maple sugar, " blazing " a way through the woods or over the ice and snow of the rivers and lakes, and consequently the vocabulary of the French Canadian has been considerably enlarged by local circumstances. In the summer resorts of the lower St. Lawrence the influence of the English visitors, now very numerous, is becoming more evident every year, and French habits are becoming modified and the young folks commence to speak English fairly well. Away from the St. Lawrence, however, and the path of the tourists, the French Canadians remain, relatively speaking, untouched by English customs.

Nos institutions, notre langue, et nos lois has been the key-note of French Canadian politics for over a century. At the present time the records and statutes of the Dominion are always given in the two languages, and the same is true of all motions put by the Speaker. Though the reports of the debates appear daily in French, English prevails in the House of Commons and in the Senate. The French Canadians are forced to speak the language of the majority, and it is some evidence of the culture of their leading public men, that many among them—notably Mr. Laurier, the eloquent leader of the Liberals, and first French Canadian premier since 1867—are able to express themselves in English with a freedom and elegance which no English-speaking member can pretend to equal in French. In the legislature of the province of Quebec, French has almost excluded English, though the records are given in the two languages. In the supreme court of the Dominion the arguments may be in French, and the two Quebec judges give their decisions in their own tongue.

The people of French Canada are very devout Roman Catholics. The numerous churches, colleges, and convents of the country attest the power and wealth of the Church, and the desire of the French Canadians to glorify and perpetuate it by every means in their power. The whole land is practically parcelled out among the saints, as far as the nomenclature of the settlements and villages is concerned. The favourite saint appears to be Ste. Anne, whose name appears constantly on the banks

of the St. Lawrence. We have Ste. Anne de la
Pérade, Ste. Anne de la Pocatière, and many others.
We all remember the verse of Moore's boat song :

> " Faintly as tolls the evening chime,
>   Our voices keep tune and our oars keep time,
> Soon as the woods on shore look dim,
>   We 'll sing at St. Anne's our parting hymn."

This village, situated at the confluence of the St.
Lawrence and Ottawa rivers, is generally known as
Ste. Anne de Bellevue, and still retains some of
the characteristics of a French Canadian village,
notwithstanding its close neighbourhood to the English-speaking settlements of Ontario.   Jesuits, Sulpicians, and Recollets have done much to mould the
thought and control the political destiny of the
people under their spiritual care.   The universities,
colleges, and schools are mainly directed by the
religious orders.   The priests, as this story has
shown, have been very active and conscientious
workers from the earliest days of Canadian history.

Canada, too, has her Notre Dame de Lourdes, to
whose shrine the faithful flock by thousands.   Some
twenty miles east of Quebec, on the banks of the
St. Lawrence, is the church of Ste. Anne de Beau-
pré, or, as the Saint is more particularly known, La
bonne Ste. Anne, who has won fame in Canada for
miraculous cures for two centuries at least.

This historic place rests under the shelter of a
lofty mountain of the Laurentides, on a little pla-
teau which has given it the name of the " beautiful
meadow."   The village itself consists of a strag-

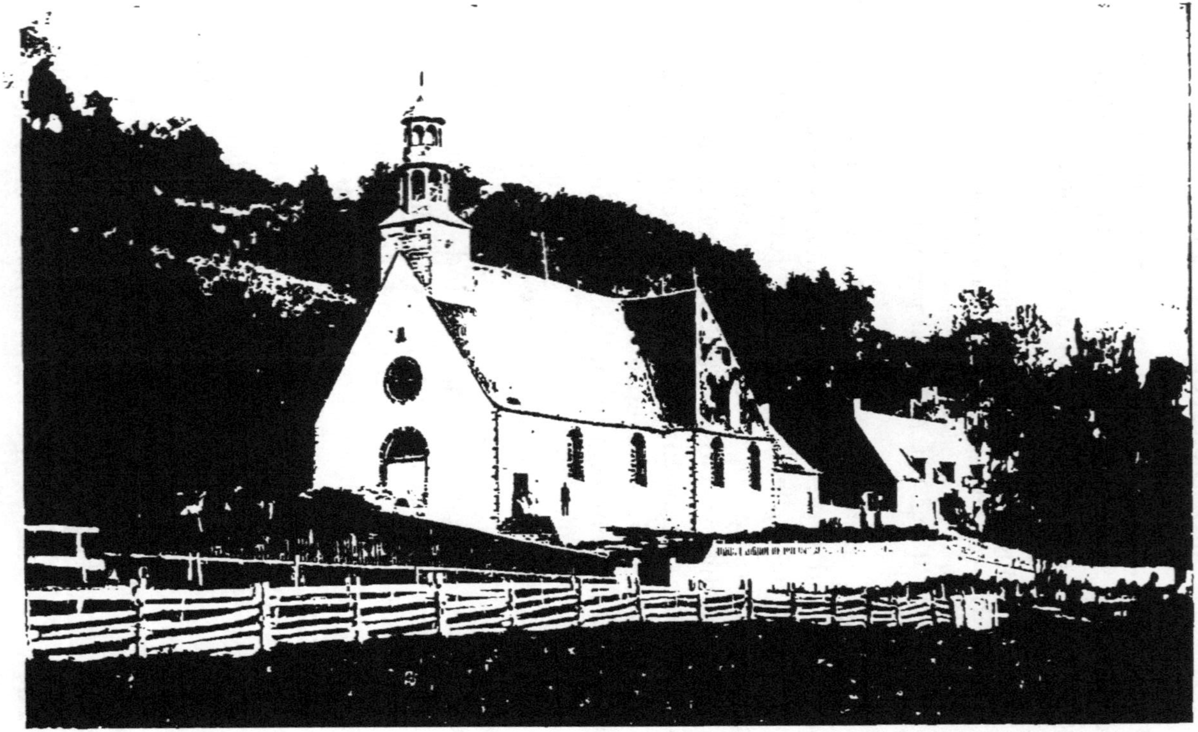

OLD CHURCH AT BONNE STE. ANNE, WHERE MIRACLES WERE PERFORMED.

gling street of wooden houses, with steep roofs and projecting eaves, nearly all devoted to the entertainment of the large assemblage that annually resorts to this Canadian Mecca, probably some sixty thousand in the course of the summer. Here you will see on the fête of Ste. Anne, and at other fixed times, a mass of people in every variety of costume, Micmacs, Hurons, and Iroquois—representatives of the old Indian tribes of Canada—French Canadians, men, women, and children, from the valleys of the Ottawa, and the St. Maurice, and all parts of Quebec, as well as tourists from the United States. The handsome grey stone church—now dignified as a " basilica "—which has been built of late years, attests the faith of many thousands who have offered their supplications at the shrine of La bonne Ste. Anne for centuries.* Piles of crutches of every description, of oak, of ash, of pine, are deposited in every available corner as so many votive offerings from the countless cripples that claim to have been cured or relieved. The relic through which all the wonderful cures are said to be effected, consists of a part of the finger bone of Ste. Anne, which was sent in 1668 by the Chapter of Carcassonne to Monseigneur de Laval. The church also possesses several pictures of merit, one of them by Le Brun, presented by the Viceroy Tracy in 1666.

The situation of many of the French Canadian

* The illustration represents the ancient church which was built in 1658, but was taken down a few years ago on account of its dangerous condition, and rebuilt on the old site near the basilica, in exactly the original form with the same materials.

villages is exceedingly picturesque, when they nestle in some quiet nook by the side of a river or bay, or overlook from some prominent hill a noble panorama of land and water. The spire of the stone church rises generally from the midst of the houses, and the priest's residence or presbytère is always the most comfortable in size and appearance. The houses are for the most part built of wood. The roofs are frequently curved, with projecting eaves, which afford a sort of verandah under which the family sit in summer evenings. Some of the most pretentious structures, especially the inns, have balconies running directly across the upper story. Many of the barns and outhouses have thatched roofs, which are never seen in any other part of Canada. The interiors are very plainly furnished, in many cases with chairs and tables of native manufacture. A high iron stove is the most important feature of every dwelling in a country where the cold of winter is so extreme. Whitewash is freely used inside and outside, and there is on the whole an air of cleanliness and comfort in the humblest cottage.

The loom is still kept busy in some villages, and a coarse, warm homespun is even yet made for every-day use. The *habitant* also wears in winter moccasins and a *tuque bleue*, or woollen cap, in which he is always depicted by the painter of Canadian scenes. But with the growth of towns and the development of the railway system a steady change is occurring year by year in the dress of the inhabitants, and it is only in the very remote settlements that we can find the homely stuffs of former times. Old dresses and old customs are gradually disappearing with the old-fashioned calèche, in which tourists once struggled to admire French Canadian scenes.   As a rule, however, the people live very economically, and extravagance in dress is rather the exception.   On gala days the young wear many ribbons and colours, though arranged with little of the taste characteristic of the French people.   Both old and young are very sociable in their habits, and love music and dancing.   The violin is constantly played in the smallest village, and the young people dance old-fashioned cotillons or *danses rondes*.   The priests, however, do not encourage reckless gaieties or extravagance in dress.   Now and then the bishop issues a Pastoral in which the waltz and other fast dances, and certain fashionable modes of dress, are expressly forbidden, and though his mandates are no doubt soon forgotten in the cities and towns, they are, on the whole, religiously observed in the rural communities.   The feasts of the Church are kept with great zeal, — especially the *fêtes d'obligation* — and consequently the French Canadian has holidays without number.

No class of the population of Canada is more orderly or less disposed to crime than the French Canadians.   The standard of the morality of the people is high.   Early marriages have been always encouraged by the priests, and large families—fifteen children being very common—are the rule in the villages.   The *habitant* is naturally litigious, and the amount in dispute is, in his opinion, trifling compared with the honour of having a case in court,

A CANADIAN CALÈCHE OF OLD TIMES.

437

which demands the attendance of the whole village. The temperate habits of the French Canadian make them necessarily valuable employés in mills and manufactories of all kinds. Indeed, they prefer this life to that of the farm, and until very recently there was a steady exodus of this class to the manufacturing towns of Lowell, Holyoke, and other places in New England. A large proportion of the men employed in the lumbering industry of Canada is drawn from the province of Quebec. As their forefathers were *coureurs de bois* in the days of the French régime, and hunted the beaver in the wilderness, even venturing into the illimitable Northwest region, so in these modern times the French Canadians seek the vast pine woods which, despite axe and fire, still stretch over a large area watered by the Ottawa and other rivers.

In commercial and financial enterprise, the French Canadians cannot compete with their fellow-citizens of British origin, who practically control the great commercial undertakings and banking institutions of Lower Canada, especially in Montreal. Generally speaking, the French Canadians cannot compare with the English population as agriculturists. Their province is less favoured than Ontario with respect to climate and soil. The French system of sub-dividing farms among the members of a family has tended to cut up the land unprofitably, and it is a curious sight to see the number of extremely narrow lots throughout the French settlements. It must be admitted, too, that the French population has less enterprise, and less disposition to adopt new machines and improved agricultural implements, than the people of the other provinces.

As a rule, the *habitant* lives contentedly on very little. Give him a pipe of native tobacco, a chance of discussing politics, a gossip with his fellows at the church door after service, a visit now and then to the county town, and he will be happy. It does not take much to amuse him, while he is quite satisfied that his spiritual safety is secured as long as he is within sound of the church bells, goes regularly to confession, and observes all the *fêtes d'obligation.* If he or one of his family can only get a little office in the municipality, or in the " government," then his happiness is nearly perfect. Indeed, if he were not a bureaucrat, he would very much belie his French origin. Take him all in all, however, Jean-Baptiste, as he is familiarly known, from the patron saint of French Canada, has many excellent qualities. He is naturally polite, steady in his habits, and conservative in his instincts. He is excitable and troublesome only when his political passions are thoroughly aroused, or his religious principles are at stake; and then it is impossible to say to what extreme he will go. Like the people from whom he is descended—many of whose characteristics he has never lost since his residence of centuries on the American continent—he is greatly influenced by matters of feeling and sentiment, and the skilful master of rhetoric has it constantly in his power to sway him to an extent which is not possible in the case of the stronger, less impulsive Saxon race, with whom reason and argument prevail to a large degree.

In the present, as in the past, the Church makes every effort to supervise with a zealous care the mental food that is offered for the nourishment of the people in the rural districts, where it exercises the greatest influence. Agnosticism is a word practically unknown in the vocabulary of the French Canadian *habitant*, who is quite ready to adhere without wavering to the old belief which his forefathers professed. Whilst the French Canadians doubtless lose little by refusing to listen to the teachings which would destroy all old-established and venerable institutions, and lead them into an unknown country of useless speculation, they do not, as a rule, allow their minds sufficient scope and expansion. It is true that a new generation is growing up with a larger desire for philosophic inquiry and speculation. But whilst the priests continue to control the public school system of the province, they have a powerful means of maintaining the current of popular thought in that conservative and too often narrow groove, in which they have always laboured to keep it since the days of Laval.

It is obvious, however, to a careful observer of the recent history of the country that there is more independence of thought and action showing itself in the large centres of population—even in the rural communities—and that the people are beginning to understand that they should be left free to exercise their political rights without direct or undue interference on the part of their spiritual advisers. English ideas in this respect seem certainly to be gaining ground.

LOUIS FRÉCHETTE.

In the days of the French régime there was necessarily no native literature, and little general culture except in small select circles at Quebec and
Montreal. But during the past half century, with
the increase of wealth, the dissemination of liberal
education, and the development of self-government,
the French Canadians have created for themselves
a literature which shows that they inherit much
of the spirituality and brilliancy of their race. Their
histories and poems have attracted much attention
in literary circles in France, and one poet, Mr. Louis
Fréchette, has won the highest prize of the French
Institute for the best poem of the year.   In history
we have the names of Garneau, Ferland, Sulte,
Tassé, Casgrain; in poetry, Crémazie, Chauveau,
Fréchette, Poisson, Lemay; in science, Hamel, La-
flamme, De Foville; besides many others famed as
savants and littérateurs.   In art some progress has
been made, and several young men go to the Paris
schools from time to time.   The only sculptor of
original merit that Canada has yet produced is
Hébert, a French Canadian, whose monuments of
eminent Canadians stand in several public places.
Science has not made so much progress as belles-
lettres and history, though Laval University—the
principal educational institution of the highest class
—has among its professors men who show some creditable work in mathematics, geology, and physics.
In romance, however, very little has been done.
    The French Canadians have a natural love for
poetry and music.   Indeed it is a French Canadian
by birth and early education—Madame Albani—who

has of late years won a high distinction on the operatic stage. No writer of this nationality, however, has yet produced an opera or a drama which has won fame for its author. The priesthood, indeed, has been a persistent enemy of the theatre, which consequently has never attained a successful foothold in French Canada. Sacred music, so essential a feature of a Roman Catholic service, has been always cultivated with success.

The *chansons populaires*, which have been so long in vogue among the people of all classes in the province of Quebec are the same in spirit, and very frequently in words, as those which their ancestors brought over with them from Brittany, Normandy, Saintonge, and Franche-Comté. Some have been adapted to Canadian scenery and associations, but most of them are essentially European in allusion and spirit. The Canadian lumberer among the pines of the Ottawa and its tributaries, the *Métis* or half-breeds of what was once the great Lone Land, still sing snatches of the songs which the *coureurs de bois*, who followed Duluth and other French explorers, were wont to sing as they paddled over the rivers of the West or camped beneath the pines and the maples of the great forests. It is impossible to set the words of all of them to the music of the drawing-room, where they seem tame and meaningless; but when they mingle with " the solemn sough of the forest," or with the roar of rushing waters, the air seems imbued with the spirit of the surroundings. It has been well observed by M. Gagnon, a French Canadian, that " many of them have no beauty except on the lips of the peasantry." There is "something sad and soft in the voices that imparts a peculiar charm to these monotonous airs, in which their whole existence seems to be reflected."

I give below the most popular and poetical of all the Canadian ballads, and at the same time a translation by a Canadian writer:*

À LA CLAIRE FONTAINE.   TRANSLATION.

À la claire fontaine   Down to the crystal streamlet
M'en allant promener,   I strayed at close of day ;
J'ai trouvé l'eau si belle   Into its limpid waters
Que je m'y suis baigné.   I plunged without delay.
Lui ya longtemps que je t'aime,   I 've loved thee long and dearly,
Jamais je ne t'oublierai.   I 'll love thee, sweet, for aye.

J'ai trouvé l'eau si belle   Into its limpid waters
Que je m'y suis baigné,   I plunged without delay ;
Et c'est au pied d'un chêne   Then 'mid the flowers springing
Que je m'suis reposé.   At the oak-tree's foot I lay.

Et c'est au pied d'un chêne   Then 'mid the flowers springing
Que je m'suis reposé ;   At the oak-tree's foot I lay ;
Sur la plus haute branche   Sweet the nightingale was singing
Le rossignol chantait.   High on the topmost spray.

Sur la plus haute branche   Sweet the nightingale was singing
Le rossignol chantait ;   High on the topmost spray ;
Chante, rossignol, chante,   Sweet bird ! keep ever singing
Toi qui as le cœur gai.   Thy song with heart so gay.

Chante, rossignol, chante,   Sweet bird ! keep ever singing
Toi qui as le cœur gai ;   Thy song with heart so gay ;
Tu as le cœur à rire,   Thy heart was made for laughter,
Moi je l'ai-t à pleurer.   My heart 's in tears to-day.

* *Songs of Old Canada.* Translated by W. McLennan.

Tu as le cœur à rire,
Moi je l'ai-t à pleurer ;
J'ai perdu ma maîtresse
Sans pouvoir la trouver.

Thy heart was made for laughter,
My heart 's in tears to-day ;
Tears for a fickle mistress,
Flown from its love away.

J'ai perdu ma maîtresse
Sans pouvoir la trouver ;
Pour un bouquet de roses
Que je lui refusai ;

Tears for a fickle mistress,
Flown from its love away,
All for these faded roses
Which I refused in play.

Pour un bouquet de roses
Que je lui refusai ;
Je voudrais que la rose
Fût encore au rosier.

All for these faded roses
Which I refused in play—
Would that each rose were
growing
Still on the rose-tree gay.

Je voudrais que la rose
Fût encore au rosier,
Et que le rosier même
Fût dans la mer jeté.
Lui ya longtemps que je t'aime,
Jamais je ne t'oublierai.

Would that each rose were
growing
Still on the rose-tree gay,
And that the fated rose-tree
Deep in the ocean lay.
I 've loved thee long and dearly,
I 'll love thee, sweet, for aye.

À la Claire Fontaine has been claimed for Franche-Comté, Brittany, and Normandy, but the best authorities have come to the conclusion, from a comparison of the different versions, that it is Norman. In *Malbrouck s'en va-t-en-guerre*, we have a song which was sung in the time of the *Grand Monarque*. Of its popularity with the French Canadians, we have an example in General Strange's reply to the 65th, a French Canadian regiment, during the second Northwest rebellion. One morning, after weeks of tedious and toilsome marching, just as the men were about to fall in, the General

overhead the remark—" Ah ! when will we get
home ? "   " Ah, mes garçons," laughed the
General—

> " Malbrouck s'en va-t-en guerre
>   Mais quand reviendra-t-il ? "

> " Malbrouck has gone a-fighting,
>   But when will he return ? "

and with their characteristic light-heartedness the
men caught up the famous old air and the march
was resumed without a murmur.

These *chansons populaires* of French Canada afford
some evidence of the tenacity with which the people
cling to the customs, traditions, and associations of
the land of their origin. Indeed, a love for Old
France lies still deep in the hearts of the people,
and both young and old study her best literature,
and find their greatest pride in her recognition of
their poets and writers. But while there exists
among the more influential and cultured class a
sentimental attachment to Old France, there is a
still deeper feeling, strengthened by the political
freedom and material progress of the past forty
years, that the connection with the British Empire
gives the best guaranty for the preservation of
their liberties and rights. This feeling has found
frequent expression in the forcible utterances of
Mr. Laurier, the present Premier of the Dominion.
No doubt the influence of the Roman Catholic
priesthood has had much to do with perpetuating
the connexion with England. They feel that it is

Wilfrid Laurier

447

not by a connexion with France or the United States that their religious and civil institutions can be best conserved.

All classes now agree as to the necessity of preserving the federal system in its entirety, since it ensures better than any other system of government the rights and interests of the French Canadian population in all those matters most deeply affecting a people speaking a language, professing a religion, and retaining certain institutions different from those of the majority of the people of the Dominion.

No French Canadian writer or politician of weight in the country now urges so impossible or suicidal a scheme as the foundation of an independent French nationality on the banks of the St. Lawrence. The history of the fifty years that have elapsed since the dark days of Canada, when Papineau wished to establish a " Nation Canadienne," goes to show that the governing classes of the English and French nationalities have ceased to feel towards each other that intense spirit of jealousy which was likely at one time to develop itself into a dangerous hatred. The spirit of conciliation and justice, which has happily influenced the action of leading English and French Canadian statesmen in the administration of public affairs, has been so far successful in repressing the spirit of passion and demagogism which has exhibited itself at certain political crises, and in bringing the two nationalities into harmony with each other. As long as the same wise counsels continue to prevail in Canada that have heretofore governed her, and carried her successfully through critical periods, the integrity of the confederation is assured, and the two races will ever work harmoniously together, united by the ties of a common interest,—always the strongest bond of union·—and a common allegiance to the Empire to whose fostering care they already owe so much.

INDEX.

www.ingramcontent.com/pod-product-compliance
Lightning Source LLC
Chambersburg PA
CBHW032009110726
47901CB00004B/1025